Praise for *Hidden In Plain Sight*

The schools of our nation are filled with students who desperately need to be reached with the hope of Jesus Christ. *Hidden in Plain Sight* is a unique resource that will inspire and equip you with practical tools to reach students on their turf.
—**Dr. Kermit Bridges,** *President, Southwestern A/G University*

Being involved in a ministry that reaches out to students on public school campuses, I can see firsthand the value of a book like *Hidden in Plain Sight*. To my knowledge, there are few resources like this available today. This book will encourage you, challenge you, and equip you as you work to reach this generation.
—**Rick Bowles,** *Executive Director, Dallas/Fort Worth Fellowship of Christian Athletes*

Can you imagine what would happen if we possessed the keys to each of the schools in our communities? In order to obtain these keys that unlock the doors to thousands of unreached students, one must have the right methods and relationships. *Hidden in Plain Sight* walks you through these methods, and will challenge you to build the relationships needed to win a city for Christ.
—**Rick Dubose,** *Superintendent, North Texas District of the Assemblies of God*

D1279494

For too long, the Church has struggled to hold the attention of the up-and-coming generation. Few great events, programs, or gimmicks are able to convince twenty-first century youth to fall in love with Jesus and remain committed to Him as they transition into adulthood. In *Hidden in Plain Sight*, Kyle Embry and a team of successful leaders offer insight and strategies that will effectively equip one to reach this generation of students. If you desire to set them ablaze with the message of the cross, this is the best training manual available today.
—**Steve Hill,** *Pastor & Evangelist, Dallas, Texas*

We live in a society that invests little time with our youth when it comes to spiritual matters. Many leaders are unsure of what they should do, and unaware that the public schools are accessible for them to influence. *Hidden in Plain Sight* fills this void by providing heart and vision, as well as practical steps, for reaching this generation of students.
—**Gerald Patterson,** *Senior Pastor, More2Life Church, Irving, Texas*

Do you long to reach your community with the hope of Jesus Christ, but have no idea where to start? If so, *Hidden in Plain Sight* is a must-read. This book will inspire, challenge, and equip you with practical tools to reach your community, beginning with the schools.
—**Chad Benson,** *Senior Pastor, Lifegate Church, Burleson, Texas*

I have seen, firsthand, the vision and passion that motivates Kyle Embry to reach the public schools in our communities. That passion exudes from the pages of *Hidden in Plain Sight*. Kyle and the team assembled to produce this book offer directives that do not come from the desk of academia, but from the trenches of everyday life. This is a practical, hands-on directive for reaching one of the most difficult, but most fertile mission fields in our nation today.

—**Curtis Tucker,** *Senior Pastor, Westwood Christian Fellowship, Weatherford, Texas*

A few years ago, I set out to make a difference at my school, but I had no idea what I was doing. I was unsure of how to begin a conversation with another student about Jesus, but I somehow managed. I wish that *Hidden in Plain Sight* had been available for me to read back then. It should be required reading for every Christian student who attends public school.

—**Josh Sizemore,** *Student, Lewisville, Texas*

Through the ministry of Youth Alive North Texas, I have entered into relationship with Jesus and have been able to make a difference in the lives of others through Him. When a Seven Project outreach was held at my junior high school three years ago, a seed was planted in my heart. I didn't cry or fall to my knees, but my life was in the process of being changed forever. It finally hit me later that night; I began to weep as I longed to know Jesus on a personal level. Since that time, I have been very involved in a local church and have formed friendships that will last a lifetime. I have been fueled with a passion to enter my high school and share the love I have received from Christ with others. I can't imagine living without it and I desire to help as many people as possible to experience what I have experienced.

—**Lauren Hightower,** *Student, Belton, Texas*

As parents of two students who lead Bible clubs on their school campuses, Youth Alive has been a huge resource to our family. They have partnered with us and with our church to equip our kids to be effective club leaders. A passion has been birthed in them to reach their schools, and they have been given the tools they need to lead successful clubs. Kyle and his team consistently provide them with support and encouragement every step of the way. They know that they are not alone as they work to reach their campus, and Youth Alive has played a key part in that. We are so excited for the release of *Hidden in Plain Sight* because we know that it will only further equip students to reach their schools for Christ.

—**Matt & Kari Payne,** *Parents, McKinney, Texas*

»HIDDEN IN PLAIN »SIGHT

America's Unreached Mission Field

Written by twenty leaders who are passionate about reaching students in public schools

Project Manager/Editor-in-Chief: Jared Stump

General Editor: Nancy Smith (authoritypressonline.com)

Cover and Interior Design: Christy McFerren (authorlaunch.com)

Published in Dallas, Texas, by Youth Alive North Texas.

This book is dedicated to every person who has given their life to reach students across the nation. What you do matters.

CONTENTS

CONTENTS

Students

Everyone

Foreword

In a day where many students have been turned off to the idea of "church" and over-sensitized to the message of modern-day culture, one must find an avenue to reach these students while maintaining the potency of the Gospel. This quandary has faced many a youth minister over the years. It has stood in the way of what I knew God wanted to do in my own church.

Several years ago, I was crying out to the Lord for answers on how to reach the masses of lost and hurting students, when He birthed a vision in my heart to reach the schools in my community. Where else do the vast majority of teens congregate each and every day? Where else would every parent want their children to be? Where else would the government provide transportation to and from? The schools are the answer!

This proved to be a turning point in my life and ministry. Now that I knew *where* to go to reach a generation of students, I needed a strategy in order to execute this vision. I was not aware of any books like this one at that point. It took years of trial and error for me to build an effective ministry that reached thousands of students in public schools across my city each week, literally meeting them where they were at.

You will find that this book is not written by "superstar" preachers that regularly hold spectacular gatherings to amaze the masses. Rather, it is written by ordinary men and women like yourself who utilize simple strategies to reach one student at a time, transforming them into disciples who reach out to others.

Just writing this foreword brings great excitement to my heart as I think of all of the leaders and students that will grab ahold of these powerful strategies and principles. The enemy of your soul hates when you wake up and begin to make a difference in your sphere of influence, and he will do anything possible to distract or hinder you from getting ahold of the principles in this book that God can use to transform your approach to student ministry.

Value the words on these pages. Ask the Holy Spirit to give you vision and direction. Meditate on what He speaks to you. Move forward in bold obedience as He reveals your plan of action. Seize the day, like Joshua, who loved to leave the camp early and catch the enemy by surprise. Rise up, men and women of God, as you watch Him do great things beyond your wildest dreams.

Joel Stockstill
Teaching Pastor
Bethany World Prayer Center
Baton Rouge, Louisiana

Introduction

As a regional Youth Alive director, it is my job to reach students in my district, which composes 114 counties across multiple geographic regions of Texas. This is accomplished by building relationships, one person at a time. While I do work with some students directly, much of my time is spent empowering youth pastors to reach students.

I am aware that I simply cannot connect with *every* student in my region personally. I can, however, empower youth pastors to reach schools and students. These youth pastors in turn train their leaders, and together they empower the students who already attend their churches, inspiring them and equipping them with the tools they need to reach their friends for Christ.

Once students begin to reach students, a movement—an out-of-control multiplication—begins. This movement will touch schools I will never step foot in and students I will never have the opportunity to speak to personally.

Last summer, I was on an airplane headed from Dallas to Florida for the annual Youth Alive directors' retreat. During that two-hour plane ride, I realized that there was a need for a book that detailed the process for reaching schools. Perhaps there have been some books written previously on this topic, but they are few and far between.

As I walked the concourse of the Fort Lauderdale airport, I called my friend Jared Stump. Jared had been working with Youth Alive for the past year and a half as our photographer, but I knew that he was also an aspiring writer. We talked for nearly an hour. Three months later, the first words hit the page. It has been a long journey since that initial conversation, but we believe that the end result will be greater than anything we can imagine.

This book was written with the help of eighteen leaders who have a history of reaching students. Throughout this book, you will hear many stories and specific examples of how each individual leader reached the schools in their community. They are the ordinary heroes who rarely make it into the spotlight.

You will also hear about Youth Alive's specific four-point strategy to reach students. We are not naive enough to believe that our ways are the only ways to reach students; we simply want to share the strategies that we have utilized, and start a conversation about what works and what doesn't. Every community is different, and different communities call for different strategies.

This book is divided into two primary sections. One is for leaders, the other for students. And it ends with a story. Why? Because no matter how long you have been in ministry, you must always remember that every person has a story, and that people and their stories matter to God. That being said, I would encourage students to read the leaders' section and leaders to read the students' section. Perhaps we can learn something from each other.

If you are a pastor, youth leader, intern, parent, grandparent, or student, this book is for you. If you are rich, poor, educated, uneducated, simple-minded, theologically advanced, experienced in ministry, inexperienced in ministry, dumb, smart, young, old, cool, dorky, attractive, unattractive; this book is for you. This book is for anyone who wants to reach his or her community, and we want to help you do that by inspiring you with a small snapshot of the past few years of ministry in our corner of the world. Thanks for reading.

Kyle Embry
Dallas, Texas
April 2013

Leaders and Parents

Chapter One

OUR STRATEGY

Kyle Embry

The stage was set. The crazy crowd games had been prepared and rehearsed. The giveaways were waiting to be strategically handed out to visitors. The worship team had picked two acoustic songs and practiced them in front of the mirror until they were *American Idol* quality. And the strong evangelistic sermon contained a powerful, unforgettable, larger-than-life illustration. The timeline for the event seemed flawless.

This was just another youth service for me, except it wasn't. On this particular Wednesday, we had decided to have service in the park to shake things up. The goal of the evening was to have a big crowd in the middle of the park, see our core students pushed out of their comfort zones, new teenagers connect with our church, and souls saved.

I had prepared a message about encountering Christ and Him taking us to new heights. To illustrate this, I had rented a Genie lift to preach from, and each time I hit a point about going to new heights, I would literally ascend into the air over the park full of students.

This night was going to be perfect. The only problem was, very few people showed up. It was our lowest attended Wednesday night service of the year. Even our core students failed to show for this strategic outreach. The large park showed little activity, except for a couple of people jogging around the perimeter. Sure, we had fun, gave away some stuff, and worshiped God under an open sky, but the whole night was by and large a failure. We completely missed the mark of what we had originally set out to accomplish.

As I drove home later that night, I asked myself where things had gone wrong. Was it the actual event—the timeline, set-up, giveaways, the speaker? Or did we fail weeks and months before in our preparation and promotion for what was intended to be the biggest night of the year?

Looking back, I see that myself and my youth leaders had a passion to reach students in our city, but we were under the impression that doing so must revolve around big events. These events can act as a net to draw in new students, but they cannot be the only method used to reach new students. The big event

"Failure is simply the opportunity to begin again more intelligently."
-Henry Ford

needed to be a part of a larger strategy. The problem was, we had no strategy. And the only "big picture" we had in mind was our one-night "big event." We foolishly thought that having one hot night would double our youth ministry and put smug grins on all of our faces. Ironically, the reverse occurred, and we had our worst night of the year. After this untimely failure, we returned to the drawing board, seeking the best strategy to grow our youth ministry in order to connect students to Christ.

I believe there are four consistent doors through which students enter our churches. The first of these doors is church families. More than likely, there are already students who attend your church with their parents on Sundays who are not involved in youth ministry. Target these unconnected students, as well as families who are new to the church, instead of just hanging out with your regulars week after week.

Another huge opportunity for growth is students inviting their unchurched friends. This is simple, but not always easy.

The key is for youth leaders to train and continually motivate students to be a witness for Christ outside of the four walls of the church.

The third opportunity to grow a youth ministry is the schools. Schools are an intimidating place for many. However, most schools are in desperate need of help, but will rarely ask for it from a church. We have to show up even if they never ask us to. Growth in youth ministry will steadily happen when we begin to view the school as our mission field.

Finally, contrary to my experience in the story you just read, big events can boost growth in a youth ministry when executed properly. It is good protocol to have diligent follow-up teams ready to engage new students into the life of your church and youth ministry, beginning the process of making disciples.

Let's face it: as youth pastors, we have a very easy job, and a lot more free time than we realize.

After several years of serving as a youth pastor, the Youth Alive strategy was thrown in front of my face. At first, it seemed like something else I did not have time for. Like most youth pastors, I thought that I was too busy. That was little more than an excuse to not get out there and do my best to reach students. Let's face it: as youth pastors, we have a very easy job, and a lot more free time than we realize. Too often, the greatest ideas and solutions to our biggest ministry problems are missed because we think we are too busy to listen and do our homework.

As I sat at my desk, I quickly dissected the components of Youth Alive—so that I wouldn't have to think about it ever again. But then I realized that the Youth Alive strategy was a Biblical model that every youth ministry should implement for growth, discipleship, and outreach. This strategy would become the framework for everything I did to reach students, as it involved prayer, student empowerment, networking, and outreach.

And he called his twelve disciples together and began
sending them out two by two, giving them authority to cast out evil
spirits. - Mark 6:7, NLT

Prayer is the beginning and end of our relationship with God. When we are in continual communication with Him, our needy lives are connected to His unlimited resources and power. Jesus knew that the disciples would not only need to pray, but would need Him to pray. He consistently modeled the necessity of pulling away from the cares of life to find strength, solace, and supernatural power.

Prayer is not something we do if we have time. Rather, it is the catalyst for the growth of our ministries and entry into the schools. If I am lacking passion, I pray. If I am lacking creativity, I pray. If I am losing focus, I pray. If I am easily distracted, I pray. Prayer has to be a core component of the life of a youth pastor and transferred to the students that they disciple.

I have heard many reports over the years of mothers who have prayer walked their kid's campuses where there were no Bible clubs or other spiritual activities taking place. After months of prayer, the walls began to break, and students felt called to start clubs on their campuses. One student in Southeast Texas creatively crafted a prayer book, and after obtaining permission, left it on a table by the front office. It wasn't long before the entire book was filled with names and prayer requests. The response shocked him and his friends, as they met before school on Friday mornings to pray over the needs and requests.

Prayer works, and it works for everyone; it should not rest solely on the shoulders of the leader. As pastors, we must equip those in our churches to pray for themselves, on their own time.

Prayer is not something we do if we have time. Rather, it is the catalyst for the growth of our ministries and entry into the schools.

The success and future growth of youth ministry hinges on prayer. Creativity, insight, favor, and open doors come when we spend time with God. The calling of God often comes when we spend time in prayer.

*And he called his twelve disciples together and began sending them out two by two, **giving them authority** to cast out evil spirits. - Mark 6:7, NLT*

Titles are nice, but they carry little weight in today's culture. What makes a difference is the authority on your life. Jesus understood this concept as well. The Pharisees and other religious leaders of His day loved their titles and honorable seats in the city,[1] yet they did not have the authority on their lives that Jesus' disciples did. Jesus prayed over His first twelve disciples and gave them power, not a title or position.

As youth pastors, we must constantly remember that what we do is not about having a title or position, but rather having authority and transferring that authority to our students. I believe that when a student begins to understand their God-given authority and anointing, they will bring the Kingdom of God to their school.

If you are going to step out onto the battlefield, it is important that you first receive the anointing. Jesus understood this.

Monopoly is a stressful and intense game that is played often around my house. In the beginning, we waffled around with all of the different rules that had been passed down to us by others. My wife and I read the rulebook cover to cover and kept it handy during the game. It became like our "gaming bible," which gave us an authority to play by the correct rules. You may have heard it said that you can play by your own rules when it comes to youth ministry, but I think we

When a student begins to understand their God-given authority and anointing, they will bring the Kingdom of God to their school.

should pay attention to the models and principles that Jesus taught His disciples.

We are called to help students grow into the image of Christ. We are called to transform our communities and schools. This will only happen when youth pastors catch the vision of sending students out in power, rather than asking them to come in and play games. This is what true discipleship looks like.

Across the nation, students are beginning to walk in the authority and anointing as the first century disciples, even without the title of youth pastor, class president, or most popular.

*And he called his twelve disciples together **and began sending them out two by two**, giving them authority to cast out evil spirits. - Mark 6:7, NLT*

I love the fact that Jesus sent His first disciples out in pairs. Why? Because we do not have to go out and try to reach our communities alone. We can work together. This is not a liability, but a privilege. God has blessed us with relationships with other believers so that we never have to take on a mountain alone. You will hear this concept repeated continuously throughout this book, because it is crucial. You may be able to reach the people in your church on your own, but you will never be able to reach an entire community on your own.

I think Jesus knew that we would all have bad days. I think He knew there would be times when we would think the wrong things, say the wrong things, and have poor attitudes. Covenant relationships with other believers can combat this problem. Whenever you are weak, your friend can be strong. Whenever you don't know what to say, your teammate can step in and save you. Sharing their faith is terrifying for most teenagers, but it is much easier when they have a friend by their side and a youth pastor cheering them on.

In the process of reaching out to your local schools, time must be spent building intentional relationships with youth pastors, teachers, coaches, principals, businesspeople, and others who have influence in the community. These people will be key when it comes to unlocking doors you cannot open on your own. But these are not just people to help you accomplish your mission. While the help they give you will be valuable in the moment, the relationships that you cultivate will last a lifetime.

As a youth pastor, there is more to do in your community than putting together a cute sermon and an entertaining, well-organized Wednesday night youth service. To win a school means to be in a school. A lack of finances is never a valid excuse for not reaching the schools. Just show up. Your presence is far more powerful than you realize.

In my travels across the region, I am often asked by youth pastors and students alike, "How do we reach our schools?" I always respond in a similar manner, telling them that there is no magic formula. The quickest route is to partner with those who are already doing it. Show up to school events, get to know people, be quick to respond to needs as you see them. Repeat this process over a period of time, and you will make an impact on your community. Reaching a school will not happen overnight or within a lone school year; It takes a dedicated, faithful youth pastor.

This mentality must also be transferred to your students. They are watching you, following your lead. If they see you networking and uniting with others, they will as well. Students should be using any resources they can get their hands on to reach a school. They should partner with different "types" of students and churches from a variety of denominations. When the students and the youth pastor are networking like this, the results will be immeasurable.

To win a school means to be in a school ... Just show up. Your presence is far more powerful than you realize.

Networking also includes prayer groups and Bible clubs. The thought of students from every denomination and background imaginable coming together as a team to influence and change their school is pretty mind-boggling. Encouraging your students to get involved in prayer groups and Bible clubs at their school—even if they don't know anyone in these groups—sets them up for success. The truth is, together we reach more!

I have heard reports of churches that supply student-led Bible clubs with donuts, advertising, training, and more. Students will win when they have youth pastors, leaders, and churches standing behind them. Students will lose when they are out their on their own, with no help from a youth pastor or a church. I have seen many students ignited with a passion to start a Bible club on their campus, only to burn out before the end of the semester because they had no support.

They went out and preached that men should repent. And they were casting out many demons and were anointing with oil many sick people and healing them. - Mark 6:12-13

Jesus called ordinary, common men from the villages, seashores, and marketplaces to become His first disciples. He then spent months and years showing them how to do ministry. He displayed the Kingdom of God to them by forgiving sins, performing miracles, healing those who were sick and oppressed by the devil, and even resurrecting people from the dead before their very eyes. Throughout this time of public ministry, He would pull those closest to Him aside for private times of refreshing, teaching, and instruction. He would speak in parables to the multitudes, then explain the principles laced within them to the disciples when they were secluded.

Finally, after three years of training, Jesus began to prepare the disciples for His departure. The time was coming when the disciples would do the things that Jesus had shown and taught them, when they would turn the world upside down. Before He left, Jesus promised that the Holy Spirit would be sent to remind them of everything He had taught them during this relatively short time.[2]

I started my two kids, Mallory and Tyson, out riding bikes at a young age. We began with training wheels, and I rode my bike in front of them, leading the way. Then the training wheels eventually came off and I came alongside them, giving them instruction and encouragement. Eventually, the time came for me to get behind them, and let them lead the way. Mallory may be riding a hundred yards ahead of me, but I am still behind her, cheering her on every step of the way.

When Jesus got behind the disciples, I believe it fulfilled the Scripture written long before by the Prophet Isaiah: *"Your ears will hear a word behind you, 'This is the way, walk in it,' whenever you turn to the right or to the left"* (Isaiah 30:21).

Though Jesus was behind them, He was not far from them. He was actually very close by as they were spreading His Kingdom throughout the earth. At this point, the process was two-fold, as the disciples were still learning as they went out and began doing. Discipleship is not found only in a classroom or church. It is functioning at its best when the classroom and the field collide for hands-on training.

Discipleship functions at its best when the classroom and field collide for hands-on training.

The disciples went to cities that Jesus never personally visited, and they saw tremendous success. They quickly discovered that the power He had shown them was now in them. In the same way, our culture is in need of a generation of students who are full of the Spirit and the power of God — students possess bold faith, are witnesses of Jesus Christ, and live radical lives of worship to Him.

For I will pour out water on the thirsty land and streams on the dry ground; I will pour out My Spirit on your offspring, and My blessing on your descendants. - Isaiah 44:3

In my early days as a youth pastor, I thought ministry was a walk in the park and all it took was one big moment to hit the jackpot, one big event to boost us to mega-church status. I now realize that this perspective isn't any different than playing some sort of spiritual lottery, and I have seen this "lottery mentality" at work in the lives of many pastors today.

Statistics prove that winning the lottery is nearly impossible. The actual odds of winning the Mega Millions lottery are 1 in 175,711,536.[3] But "with God all things are possible,"[4] right? Here's a better question: If you actually did win the lottery, would you be able to handle the success?

Billie Bob Harrell, Jr. played the Texas lottery one summer day in 1997 after clocking out of his mundane job at Home Depot, where he stocked the shelves for a living. Within 24 hours, Bill and his family were celebrating his winning the $31 million jackpot and his first $1.24 million annual payout. Finally, they had found happiness, purpose, and fulfillment! Or not.

What seemed like the light at the end of the tunnel would actually be the beginning of the end for the 47-year-old Texan. But it all began innocently enough. Billie Bob quit his job at Home Depot, took his family to Hawaii, donated tens of thousands of dollars to his church, bought cool houses and hot cars for his friends and family, and even donated 480 Thanksgiving turkeys to those in need.

Somewhere along the line, he made a bad deal with a company that gives lottery winners lump-sum payments in exchange for their annual checks. This deal left him with substantially less than what he had won.

I can't help but wonder how many youth pastors have made bad deals in an attempt to gain quicker results that have left them with less than what they had before.

Within a year, Billie Bob and his wife Barbara Jean had separated. On May 22, 1999, he was found dead inside his home due to a self-inflicted gunshot wound. His financial advisor later said that Billie Bob had told him, "Winning the lottery was the worst thing that ever happened to me," shortly before his apparent suicide.[5]

The problem with the lottery mentality is it banks on something great "just happening" without one putting in any effort. This stands in stark contrast to the character of God, who rewards faithfulness. As the Psalmist says, *To the faithful you show yourself faithful; to those with integrity you show integrity* (Psalm 18:25, NLT).

In a world that is constantly changing, we must model for this up-and-coming generation what faithfulness looks like. Students don't need to look for a magic formula or the seven secrets of success; they just need to show up every day and shine the light of Jesus to everyone around them.

I love hearing reports of students getting involved in prayer groups, school assembly outreaches, *See You at the Pole* rallies, mentoring programs, and community service projects. All of these are just as important as the Wednesday night youth service. If you want to reach out to your community, start with the schools.

Endnotes

1) Luke 11:43

2) John 14:26

3) Source: Google ... *(56 choose 5)*46*

4) Matthew 19:26

5) Source: Time Magazine Article, *The Tragic Stories of the Lottery's Unluckiest Winners*, Terri Pous, November 28, 2012

Chapter Two

IS ANYONE BEYOND REACHING?

Dave Roever

I finished the assembly and waited in the middle of the gym floor as several hundred students gathered around me, in typical fashion. Typical, because kids flock to me after an assembly, wanting to talk, hug, cry—anything to get some personal attention. I was enjoying this one-on-one time when the principal walked up to me with a young man in tow.

"This is Luke, Mr. Roever."

That introduction would profoundly affect my life.

In hushed tones the principle continued, "Luke was found under his house where his father kept him chained. He doesn't speak much, Mr. Roever, but I thought you might want to say something to him."

Luke wore old shoes with no strings, no socks, and blue jeans with holes that were earned the old-fashioned way. A faded army jacket partially covered a dingy gray T-shirt. He had a ball cap pulled down low to avoid eye contact and, I presume, to cover his bald head, shaved due to lice.

I'm a hugger. I believe in personal human contact. It stems from my childhood where I found my greatest security in my parents' arms.

I bent down to hug Luke.

I'd scarcely touched him when he jumped back and stiffened. I was shocked. What did I do?

"You can't hug Luke, Mr. Roever," the principal said; then he proceeded to tell me why.

No one could hug Luke because of his father. The only time the man unchained him was when he wanted to use Luke for his own deviant purposes. The degenerate savage had sodomized Luke for two years. He'd beaten him into such fear that the boy had lost all sense of reality.

A short time before our visit to the school, Luke had been released from the state hospital, with the hopes of him being mainstreamed back into society, but it was not working. He was ridiculed by peers and laughed at by classmates, and that was just the beginning.

This was the first time I could ever remember being told I couldn't hug a child. I didn't like it. I didn't like the fact that a man could do to a child what that beast had done to Luke.

I had a job to do. I refused to be denied communication with this boy. I put my hand under his chin, raised Luke's face and looked intently into his troubled eyes. Were they his father's eyes? I hoped not.

"Luke," I said, "I love you."

Did his ears hear me? Or were those the ears of his father — deaf to reality, deaf to love? Was Luke beyond reaching? Was there any ember of hope left in this child?

I said it again, "Luke, I love you."

No response.

I went on, "I'm not going to hurt you. I'm going to hug you."

"Luke, I'm going to put my arms around you. It will not hurt, and it is not dirty. Not all men are like your daddy."

"I want you to know that I accept you with my embrace, and I welcome you into my world. So get ready, Luke."

I carefully slipped my arms around the residue of an abused, traumatized shell of a human being. His eyes darted wildly around in search of an escape route, in case escape became necessary, but he didn't jerk away.

Have you ever hugged a telephone pole? My arms were wrapped around rigid sinews and muscle stretched over bone.

I told Luke five more times I loved him. Then I prayed for him.

No response. I ached inside, feeling that I had failed. As I turned to walk away, I heard a mumble.

I looked back over my shoulder to see a tear-soaked face on a broken little guy saying two words. "Thank you."

Have you ever seen four hundred kids cry in unison?

Have you ever seen a principal leap for joy even though it wasn't the last day of school?

Have you ever felt like you could laugh until the whole world laughs with you?

I have.

The story you have just read is true.[1] The names were changed to protect both the innocent and the guilty. Some names were left out. Left out like the young boy Luke. Left out of the loop of love. Left out of the loop of hope. Sadly, I can attest that in my personal experience, addressing more than seven million students over the last three decades, there are thousands of kids just like Luke who have been left out.

I have been conducting assembly programs in high schools across the country since 1976. Surely, I thought, when I turned sixty-five, no kid would want to listen to a stuffy old man and grandfather of four. I can't be that old! But they say that age is only a state of mind and if that is the truth, I am only nineteen. I still ride motorcycles and chase my wife around the house. I don't want to grow up. One of my biggest fears of aging was that I might become disconnected from a generation of young people and no longer be able to communicate in a school assembly. But regardless of my aging body, students still listen and hang onto every word that comes out of my mouth. Why do they still listen to me after all these years?

Last fall, I spoke to more than 54,000 teenagers at The Fieldhouse in Indianapolis. The facility was not large enough to accommodate the entire crowd at once, so I spoke to three groups of 18,000 students back-to-back-to-back. I honestly could not believe that in the booming, echoing facility that I would be able to communicate effectively, but I have never felt more connected with my audience. It was just the opposite of what I had expected.

When reviewing the video that they gave to me afterwards, I analyzed everything: my speech, my body language, my content ... everything. The content was very confrontational. I confronted the students on their sexual behavior and on a young man's treatment of a young lady. It was so personal that I even scolded them for texting and driving, not to mention wailing on them about drinking and driving. I addressed drug abuse, cheating, and other unacceptable behaviors. Time after time I received standing ovations. Why the standing ovations?

Regardless of my aging body, students still listen and hang onto every word that comes out of my mouth.

I have found that the older I get, the better the students receive my message. I find this amazing. Across the nation, Christian youth organizations often look beyond people of my age bracket for what they consider to be an up-and-coming star. It never fails. The young star will get through a presentation, and for the most part, the students are polite, but I find many times they endure rather than enjoy the presentation. The stars seem to be more interested in hairstyle, dress code, language, music, all the Disney do-dads, rather than substance and a serious approach to meet the needs of the youth.

What does this old man have that these young stars don't seem to have? The most basic ingredient. It is so basic, historically sound and traceable all the way to the Garden of Eden. There are simply no starlit, smoke-and-light sound effects that can replace what kids are crying out for—loving authority figures. You know, moms, dads, and if you really want to get old, grandparents.

When a person of authority (regardless of age) shows up at school and tells the students the truth based on a history founded in integrity, character, and morality, they can't get enough of it. It's like water to a dry potted plant. There are immediate results, returns that can be measured and calculated. After a presentation of truth, I have parents, teachers, administrators, and students themselves who respond with words that drive me to my knees, leaving me stunned, almost baffled. I hear the whispers of, "Thank you," and they walk away.

My biggest frustration is not when the kids give up; it's when the elders give up. People who know me are very much aware of my position on passion. If you don't have passion for something, if you're not driven by a vision, if you cannot speak in anticipation of the next move in your life, then please don't waste my time. It is not wise to say things like, "I wish God would show me something to do" when you are around me.

There are simply no starlit, smoke-and-light sound effects that can replace what kids are crying out for — loving authority figures.

The lust for entertainment that our society has is inconceivable to me — the wasted hours sitting in front of video games and the television. I'm not talking about the students alone. I'm talking about the youth leadership who actually watch a clock to see when their day is finished so they can go home. In my decades of ministry, I have never allowed a clock to decide when my day of connecting with America's youth has ended. My passion drives me. I sleep with it. I eat with it. I am consumed by it.

How can we shun such a great mission field as the school campus? While it is impossible for me to accept all the opportunities presented, I cannot imagine others with empty schedules who consider stepping foot on the campus to be too much effort. Some may consider themselves "not called" or unqualified to go into the schools. Some youth leaders say things like, "I tried, but they wouldn't let me." Why have you given up so easily? Where is your imagination? Where is your creativity? Are you seriously telling me that you cannot think of a solution?

The key to opening the door to a public school requires observance and human intelligence, not unlike "intelligence" in fighting a war on terror. It requires more than boots on the ground. Eyes and ears must be open. One cannot gather "intelligence" sitting in an office behind a desk, pretending you are busy. One must be in the field, behind "enemy lines," communicating with the students and with their educators. This is imperative.

My passion drives me. I sleep with it. I eat with it. I am consumed by it.

The first step to building a relationship between your church and a school lies in discovering the most pressing and important need of the school. Is it suicide? Drugs? Alcohol? Teenage pregnancies? Sexual misconduct? Cheating? Inter-school rivalries that have gone too far?

Whatever the problem, find it and then proceed to make yourself a master on that same point of conflict by cramming every bit of knowledge on the subject into your mind. Prepare yourself. You wouldn't take a knife to a gunfight, or a water pistol to a four-alarm fire. Load your mental weaponry with all the stats, the latest findings, and pour yourself into that subject as you pour that subject into yourself.

The next step is obvious. Someone said it and it is true. Nothing happens if you don't show up. Don't be sitting around waiting for opportunities to fall like manna from heaven and land themselves on your desk. Get out there and make yourself available to meet the needs of the school.

Never allow yourself to become discouraged by the voices that scream at you that you can't. I remember one time when a parent-teachers association worked with a local church and invited me to speak to every school within their entire district. However, the largest school in the district said that I would not be permitted to give my presentation to their student body.

I went on to give my presentation to every other school in the district. After each assembly, students went home talking about it. It wasn't long before parents with older children who attended the school that denied me began to get angry. They began to ask school officials why I was permitted in every school except one.

The local newspapers became involved. They approached the belligerent principal, who had been adamant in his refusal of my presentation. He found cameras in his face, as reporters asked why I had not been allowed to speak in his school. In this situation, I did not have to defend myself once. The students defended me. The parents defended me. The community defended me.

Nothing happens if you don't show up.

By the end of the week, the superintendent of schools fired the principal. You heard right. They sent him packing! So the following Saturday, I spoke in his school. Yes, on a Saturday. There was a follow-up rally for all the schools and we went with the largest venue in the community, which was the school where I had been denied to speak the week before.

Thousands of students showed up that day. I was invited to return to the community the following year. This time, I spoke at all the schools. The new administrator, eager to keep his job, extended a warm welcome to me as I gave my presentation to his students.

Finally, I get extremely tired of living down other speakers' stupidity. That doesn't sound very godly, does it? The truth is, I don't like paying for the sin committed by another person. Even God doesn't require that of me, but many school officials do. I have a long and sordid history of foul experiences that follow on the heels of some speaker who was invited to speak in a school, who swore he would not mix his personal faith and religious language into the daytime presentation, which would be a violation of perceived "separation of church and state."

I remember one speaker who crossed every line he could find. He broke every promise he had made to the school, and concluded what was supposed to be a "secular" message by giving an "invitation." I suppose he told himself that since he might never have a chance to do an assembly at that school ever again, he needed to bring it home for the Kingdom of God.

The truth is, he did all of this more for himself than the Kingdom. He did it for bragging rights. He did it to boast of the numbers of kids who "responded" to his message. And the final thing he did was slam the door shut in my face, as the administration assumed that I was in the same camp, and that I too would break my promises and cross the line.

Make no mistake, I want every student in the school to come to know Jesus, but I am also very aware that the school will not tolerate being used and thrown away like a dirty towel, having done little more than perpetrated my own personal agenda.

I have had to sign contracts, write exhaustive letters, and endure endless telephone conversations to reassure administrators that I would not follow in the wake of the misdirected programs that were conducted in their schools previously. That is the reason why I do night rallies. The school facilities can legally be rented for the purpose of conducting religious programs at night, after school hours have ended.

Students come to these night rallies voluntarily. Often times, their parents come in order to "check you out." And you have the chance of a lifetime to encourage a community and make a difference in the lives of thousands of teenagers and their parents. This proves that you can play by the rules and still achieve tremendous results.

There is a Luke out there who is waiting for somebody to break his chains. He is waiting for someone to love him. Pick any school and you will find a student like Luke who is experiencing the same or worse trauma. Without your intervention, those students may never be saved.

IN REVIEW:

1.   Do the human intel. Find the greatest need of the school and community. Prepare yourself through extensive research and seek out the stats to verify your understanding.

2.   Make yourself available to serve the needs of the school.

3.   Make personal contact with the principal. Superintendents have a far more political agenda and are less likely to make tough decisions. Principals will take a risk. Be his friend. Explain your qualifications and allow him to understand you are an off-campus community leader and in support of

his efforts. Let him know that you want to help him and his school.

4. Take what you can get, even if it is only a small classroom setting. You eat an elephant one bite at a time. If you don't get a full assembly with standing room only and a cheering crowd acknowledging your magnificence, get over it. Make your first impression so profound the administrators cannot wait to schedule you for the entire student body. And after the big bang of your up-front presentation, establish one-on-one contact with every student that you can. Hang around; talk with the students who approach you. Don't just disappear backstage.

5. For heaven's sake, follow the rules. If you can't keep the promise, don't make the promise. Respect the authority of that school.

6. Follow up. Continue to be a friend to the principal and let your church and/or youth group prove their undying support. Volunteer to paint classrooms. Do physical labor, such as outdoor cleanup. Build the relationship between your church and the school you are trying to reach.

Endnotes

1) Adapted from *Nobody's Ever Cried for Me*, Dave Roever, 1992.

Chapter Three

TRAINING FOR CAMPUS MINISTRY

Garland Owensby

The Stakes are Different: My girlfriend and I never fought. Then I proposed. That's when the fighting began.

In retrospect, I know why the engagement brought on such strong emotions. It was because, at that moment, the stakes had been raised. There was much more at risk. We had both decided that if we were to go through with marriage, divorce would not be an option. I realized that prior to the engagement the stakes were lower because either of us could walk away with minimal entanglement. It was like training to prepare for the greater challenge of marriage.

Training for youth ministry on the collegiate level is similar. The risk is lower because you are not going to get fired if you get a "C" in a class. Your job and livelihood are not at stake. The university provides a four-year, or perhaps longer, period of time in which the student can learn both inside and outside of the classroom how to engage with campus ministry and youth culture without the risk of making a mistake that could jeopardize the vocational ministry position.

I am a professor at a private Christian university. Each fall, the volunteer coordinator for the local school district speaks to the students in our Youth Evangelism class. Her presentation is succinct as she advises students of the process of volunteering on the campus. She also shares the ins and outs of serving on the campus, including the limitations of expressing faith. She is a Christian and is empathetic to those that desire to reach students, yet the current federal laws and school policies bind her.

Several years ago, I landed my first youth pastor job in North Carolina. The first time I walked on to the campus of the local high school was quite intimidating. I met with the vice principal, introduced myself and explained that I would like to eat lunch with my students on campus. She politely smiled and explained that that campus was closed to youth pastors during lunchtime because of the inappropriate behavior of one youth pastor who had begun to preach from atop a cafeteria table.

I went back to my office, prayed and thought about how I could gain access to the campus. The stakes were too high to just give up and walk away. Reaching the campus was a non-negotiable for me. As I was thinking through different ideas, I thought about how I had just returned from a one-year missions assignment in El Salvador and pondered if the school had a need for a bi-lingual volunteer.

The second meeting with the vice-principal was different. This time I asked if there was an area in which I could volunteer on the campus. She smiled widely as I explained that I was bi-lingual.

For the next year, I served alongside the Spanish teacher at the school, assisting her students in the morning. She even gave me the opportunity to share about my time in El Salvador. In the afternoons, I would assist the remedial English teacher with one-on-one tutoring in the classroom.

This lesson in persistence is one that I pass along to my students. I know there are youth pastors reading this that have had a similar experience of rejection in their pursuit of campus ministry. But instead of being persistent you settled into an office routine and remained absent from the campus. I wish you could have been in a university setting and had the opportunity to get on the public school campus as a class assignment. You would have had someone intentionally and decidedly insist that you reach the campus — or else! That low-risk experience, when only a grade was at stake, would have served the purpose of teaching you the process of getting on the public school campus, serving humbly, and persisting in your calling.

One day while volunteering at that North Carolina high school, the Spanish teacher approached me with a predicament. She carried double duty, teaching both Spanish and German. The school had agreed to host German foreign exchange students for three weeks, but had discovered they were short on host homes. She asked if I would be interested. After a quick check with my wife, I offered our home. The teacher emphasized that the German student was to have a typical American experience.

The stakes were too high to just give up and walk away. Reaching the campus was a non-negotiable for me.

A few days later, I was standing at the airport with the other hosts watching as the students from Germany exited their aircraft. Most were clean-cut and well dressed, until a young man with long hair and a jean vest festooned with death metal patches and pentagrams debarked the plane. In my head I laughed and whispered to the Lord, "He's mine, isn't he?"

Sure enough, this young man who loved death metal was to stay with this conservative pastor for three weeks. We asked him to attend youth service and Sunday morning service with us. My wife and I served the church as both children's and youth pastors, so he would go to kids' church with us each Sunday morning.

Many of our volunteers were high school students and they embraced him as part of their missional living. He spent his time in the United States traveling to beautiful locales and visiting our nation's capitals with its exquisite memorials and world-class museums.

At the end of his time with us, I asked what was his favorite experience of the three weeks had been. Without hesitation he responded, "Kids' church," because he had heard and participated in a presentation of the Gospel on a level that he could understand.

My students reached out to someone very different from them and were able to love him in the name of Jesus because of a volunteer opportunity on the public school campus that I had to persist in order to obtain. I had the same choice that many of you have. You can settle into your office routine, or you can use your education and opportunities to be persistent in reaching the campus. Who knows what could happen in your life and the lives of your students?

Once you are hired as a youth pastor, it is essential that you pursue campus ministry. In some cases, you will be welcomed with open arms, especially if your intention is to serve the administration and faculty. But on occasion you will be met with closed doors. Through prayer, determination, and creativity you can find a way in, but time after time I have witnessed youth pastors who heard "no" once or twice and then became so busy in the office that they gave up on campus ministry.

You can settle into your office routine, or you can be persistent in reaching the campus.

The stakes are too high to give up when it pertains to campus ministry. That is why the Apostle Paul tells us that we must not become weary in doing good. We can't afford to neglect reaching the largest gathering place for students in our communities. There is the eternal, spiritual nature of campus ministry as a youth pastor, but there is also the practical purpose of understanding and reaching youth culture. When the youth pastor is not involved on the public school campus, there is no benefit to the church.

A few years later, I became a youth pastor in a larger town in Central Florida. Getting on campus at the schools there was a bit more difficult than it was in North Carolina, though not impossible. I had to be persistent in carving out time for campus ministry and reaching out to the campus, especially as my church demanded more from me in regards to time and administration.

One way that I was able to build a bridge was through the use of our facilities. The church that I was at was blessed to have the largest auditorium in town. We offered the building for baccalaureate and as the back up in case graduation was rained out. Despite numerous obstacles and a myriad of things vying for my attention, campus ministry

> *Let us not lose heart in doing good, for in due time we will reap if we do not grow weary.*
> *- Galatians 6:9*

remained an important part of my ministry while I was a youth pastor in Florida.

Training Gives You an Edge: *Adolescents are so easy to understand. The teenage brain is not hard to comprehend. And youth ministry, theology, and communicating scriptural truth are simple.* I don't believe any of that for a second, but I am amazed at how often youth ministers will denigrate their own profession. Can you imagine a brain surgeon saying something like, "Well, I went to school for over a decade, but really, it's just brain surgery!"

I believe it is time for youth ministers to respect their calling and vocation more than they do. The call to reach and disciple students is challenging and worthy of more training than reading the latest hot book, listening to a podcast, or attending the next big conference. All of those are good, but there is the assumption of a strong base from which to build. Every day I receive email newsletters from companies that research adolescents for the purpose of using that research to market to students. They take seriously the call to sell temporary products to teenagers. They invest millions into hitting the ground, engaging with, listening to, and observing students. Can youth ministers take seriously the call to reach students by committing themselves to intentional vocational training coupled with practical ministry experience?

In the words of C.S. Lewis, *"In the Gospels, it would seem our Lord finds our desires not too strong, but too weak. We are half-hearted creatures. Fooling around with drink and sex and ambition when infinite joy is offered us. Like an arrogant child who wants to go on making mud pies in a slum because he cannot imagine what is meant by the offer of a holiday at sea. We are far too easily pleased."*[1]

I believe that some who say that education in ministry is not beneficial are satisfied to make mud pies because they cannot imagine the worlds opened by higher education. We are far too easily pleased with our own attempts.

There are those for which youth ministry seems to be a native language. They feel it. They are the intuitive youth pastors. Then there are those of us who benefit from the guided, intentional instruction and mentoring. There is a benefit of beginning a life-long search for deep thinking and discernment of culture, societal woes, and God's word. I often wonder if the intuitive could be so much better if he or she submitted himself to the discipline of training. I know of the benefit to those who are not as intuitive. I have seen it in my life and the lives of many students who have sat in the university classroom.

It is time for youth ministers to respect their calling and vocation more than they do.

On a daily basis, we put faith in those who are professionally trained to do their vocation. We rely on doctors, teachers, bankers, politicians, and our local police force. When they fail it is often because of laziness or the belief that they can fool those less educated. That should not be the case with ministry. Souls are eternal and more important than the temporal physical being, and yet most would never allow a physician with no training to operate on them. May there be a day when our youth ministers are not lazy with the exegesis and preaching of the Word or the practice of their mission.

The Assignments are Intentional and Non-Negotiable: For years, I have struggled with my weight. I have had periods where I have lost weight, only to gain it back. At one point, I lost sixty-five pounds, which was a tremendous accomplishment for me. I even ran a marathon.

The periods of time in which I have lost the most amount of weight had similar themes. They were group settings where I was accountable. I lost weight when I had someone holding me accountable for what I ate and how often I exercised. I gained weight or lost only a small amount when I had the attitude that I could do it on my own, or that I was disciplined enough to overcome my weaknesses alone.

The great lie many of us believe is that we can accomplish whatever we wish on our own. I have repeatedly heard an argument when it comes to training for youth ministry that goes something like this: *Why can't I just self-educate? I'll read some books and attend a few conferences, and I'll get all the information I need.*

I understand the logic of this, and while it can work for some, it requires a level of discipline and follow-through that most of us, if we are honest, do not have. How many unread books sit in your office right now? How many books have you intended to read but abandoned after the first chapter? How many times have you reviewed your notes and applied principles from a conference you attended?

Think about the last conference you attended. Was it inspirational or application oriented? Did you walk away with hundreds of pages of notes or merely a refreshed soul? Believe me, the latter is valuable and necessary, but it is not all that is needed to be successful in ministry.

Another side to the discussion is that we tend to be very selective in what we read and the voices we bring into our lives. When training for youth ministry, I believe it is important to not only know your position, but also to be exposed to those that see the world differently than you do. It's important to be exposed to voices with which you disagree. It's valuable to read books that you would not have picked up had the choice been left to you to make.

It's important to be exposed to voices with which you disagree because it challenges and stretches you.

When was the last time you read something you did not want to read? I can tell you of times when I was told to read books while in college that changed and shaped my worldview in a positive way. There have been times when I had to read a text and completely disagreed with the author, but it stretched me. It forced me, as iron sharpens iron, to learn and discern and hone my own beliefs. If you always order vanilla ice cream, you will never discover the possibility that you might enjoy mint chocolate chip.

The Mentoring is Intentional: I often hear people say, *We learn more by what is caught than by what is taught.* This would seem right on the surface and is a true statement for many things, but not everything. If this were an absolute truth we would stop preaching and having discipleship classes and instead, we would just hang out with one another.

Think of the academic and the practical as two lungs that are necessary for breathing. In the words of Kyriacos Markides, *"Christianity, a Catholic bishop in Maine once told me, has two lungs. One is Western, meaning rational and philosophical, and the other Eastern, meaning mystical and otherworldly. Both, he claimed, are needed for proper breathing. Both the mystical and the rational approaches to God were part of the early church. They were only set asunder by subsequent historical developments."*[2] One without the other is unhealthy. Wisdom without zeal and zeal without wisdom are both fatal.

I just want someone to mentor me. This is the number one complaint that I hear from young ministers. It was my complaint as a young minister. I thought my pastor would take me under his wing and ask me how my devotions were, how my prayer life was progressing and if my family was all right. That, however, did not happen. I thought my pastor would recommend a book or send me to a conference, but that also did not occur.

More than twenty years have passed, and I have not noticed a change. Young youth ministers desire to receive a mentor in their senior pastor, but instead receive an employer. They envision a Paul and Timothy relationship whereby *Wisdom without zeal and zeal without wisdom are both fatal.* the pastor communicates vision and affirmation. But it doesn't always work out that perfectly. They sometimes end up working for someone who requires them to supply their own vision and affirmation.

I often have former students who need someone to listen to them and coach them contact me in search of guidance. The investment in university training offers a lifetime supply of networking with other students and proven leaders.

Some will point out that Jesus merely walked with His disciples, but this idea neglects the historical context. First, none of us are as knowledgeable as Jesus. Second, the disciples were all Jewish men who in their childhood would have undergone systematic, intentional, and intense biblical schooling that would make our contemporary discipleship methods look silly. The disciples would have had a foundation of biblical training that far exceeded what high school graduates receive today. The leadership was intentional. His help was eternal. The apostolic network was established.

Life-Long Learners: I am a huge Disney fan. Go ahead; call me a Disney geek if you want. I can take it. Walt Disney World opened in Orlando in 1971. Within six months of the opening, my family drove our station wagon with faux wood paneling down I-95 from Pennsylvania to Florida. That trip to Disney World was the first of many. I would estimate that I have visited at least fifty times since 1971. A photo of myself from that initial visit, sitting next to Goofy on Main Street U.S.A., still holds a place of importance in my home.

In the mid-1980's, the Disney fanatic in me took hold. I was attending college near Orlando and was able to visit the Disney parks often. While the attention of my friends was primarily focused on the rides, my mind was captured by the attention to detail, tradition, and imagination that was on display. I realized that there was a world my friends were experiencing, and then there was another which I enjoyed.

I began to read books and subscribe to magazines, and with the advent of podcasting, listened to multiple programs about Disney. What amazes me is how often I will read an article or listen to an interview and realize how little I know about a particular topic. There were people who saw beyond the rides and could speak about the architecture. Experts who knew that Tower of Terror was a great ride, but also knew why items were placed in exact positions.

In recent years, Disney has offered a special program called "Lunch with an Imagineer." An *Imagineer* is a Disney dreamer. They can have an engineering background or a design background. An Imagineer's job is not just to dream, but to design, and give purpose to attractions at Disney. They create stories behind attractions. In fact, there are some attractions where the Imagineer knows the story, but it is not posted anywhere for the guests to read. Why? To design something worth returning to, the engineer must understand both how something works but also why something works and is worth doing.

Many youth ministers know how to do ministry, but do they really understand how adolescents work? The church is great at knowing *how* to do ministry, but not always at *why* we do ministry the way we do.

Albert Einstein once said, *"Education is the progressive realization of our ignorance."* I have found that to be very true in my own life. When I first began to teach youth ministry at the collegiate level I thought that I knew what I was doing. Until I began to research and discover there was a world of expertise about youth ministry of which I did not have an inkling.

It is possible to do youth ministry without a formal education, but education opens up a world that not everyone experiences. For instance, the church typically ignores the area of adolescent development. I don't know that I have ever heard a session on individuation and faith development at a seminar nor have I had a youth pastor excitedly tell me about the new book he read about adolescent egocentrism and its effect on worship. And yet I would argue that to not deeply understand the adolescent—body, mind, and spirit—is a disservice to the One who created them.

Most of us desire immediate results. But those of us who have been in youth ministry for more than a decade know what it is like to get lost in the routine of preaching about the same issues, hearing the same problems, doing the same outreaches and missions trips and fundraisers. In the depth of your soul, you may find yourself asking, "Is this it? Is this really all there is?"

Please do not give up on student ministry! What you need is to embrace the depth of the call to minister to students. When I plan a message for students I not only know biblically what I want to say, but I'm also thinking doctrinally and developmentally. There are powerful messages that speak to students because it is not only God's Word, but it addresses a developmental need in the adolescent. Take a class on adolescent development, psychology, sociology, or another area that will stretch you to think about ministry differently.

I have found so much value in taking classes outside of my fellowship as well. Other denominations are thinking about student ministry and Jesus in ways that will challenge the youth ministry veteran, but you have to put yourself in the position to be challenged without the ability to just shut the book and put it on the shelf.

I was speaking at a summer camp once, when a female student approached me during the altar time. She was visibly upset. My heart broke as she spoke of her traumatic life. Her boyfriend had proclaimed his love and stated his desire to marry her, but once they had sex, he dumped her. The scars were beyond emotional; they were also physically present on her arms. Self-injury had become a way to cope with the hurt.

I asked her to tell me about her father. She broke down in tears. She told me her father had molested her at a young age and was now in prison for the crime. The reason I asked about her father was based on my education in counseling and adolescent issues. The presence of the Spirit was amazing over the next few moments as I prayed with the young woman.

The Holy Spirit could have given me a word of knowledge, but He had already given me access to knowledge through academics. If God owns all truth, then as ministers we have access to that truth. One girl's life was impacted because of education and the Spirit working together. We should rely on the Spirit, but also use the truth and wisdom that God has made available to us.

This is what the Apostle Paul did when he traveled to the city of Athens, Greece, as detailed in Acts 17. He carefully walked around the city making observations and then engaged trained, intelligent philosophers with not just an understanding of the Scripture, but also an understanding of their influential texts.[3]

Can you imagine a moment when you are on the school campus and a student begins to share their life struggles, and you are able to ask specific questions that lead them to ask you spiritual questions? This is what can happen in a Seven Project school assembly. Though we cannot speak about Christ directly, we can ask questions, informed by academic truth and empowered by the Spirit, which can cause students to search their hearts and reach out to a Christian friend or leader who is present on the campus.

We should rely on the Spirit, but also use the truth and wisdom that God has made available to us.

Conclusion: The stakes for reaching students are high and the public school campus is a place of high impact. The campus needs skilled, trained, and disciplined leaders who will persist in serving and reaching the public school campus. This will necessitate investment of resources— physical, spiritual, and financial—but the return on the investment is well worth the sacrifice.

Endnotes

1) *The Weight of Glory and Other Addresses*, C.S. Lewis, 1965

2) *The Mountain of Silence*, Kyriacos Markides, 2001, Pages 235-236

3) Acts 17:28 - "For in Him we live and move and exist." (From *Cretica* by Cretan Poet Epimenides, 600 BC) "As even some of your own poets have said, 'For we also are His children.'" (From *Hymn to Zeus* by Cleanthes, 331 BC)

Chapter Four

SCARED TO STEP OUT?

Andrew Burr

As a youth pastor, I've got a pretty sweet set up. There is a 5A high school located less than a mile from my church, which I drive by several times a day. Every time I have been on campus, I have been welcomed with open arms. Those times, however, are few and far between.

I want to be on that campus. I need to be on that campus. I should be out making connections at that school. I know there are needs there that my church family could meet. I know exactly what I should be doing, but I am not doing it.

I hate this. I know that I should be doing something to reach out to that school. I know that if something doesn't change, I will have to answer to God one day for how I didn't.

I attended a small private school growing up. There were twelve students in my 8th grade class. I transferred to a 5A high school for my freshman year, where I was little more than a fish out of water. I'm naturally a rather shy individual. During my first two years of high school, I hung out with people I didn't like because it gave me someone to sit with at lunch. Outside of riding the bench on the secondary freshman basketball team, extracurricular activities held no appeal to me because I knew it would involve more social interactions.

Today, I love seeing our entire community come out on Friday nights to support our local football team, but I didn't back when I was in high school. In four years, I only attended one game, and I refused to sit in the student section.

If your high school experience was anything like mine, you can probably relate to the feelings of anxiety I go through every time I even think about stepping foot on campus. For many of us, high school was a difficult time in our lives, and that should motivate us as youth pastors to be more active in reaching out to students.

Why is it that I still deal with emotional baggage from high school more than ten years after graduation? I'm an adult; I should be over it by now, right?

I have found that there are two primary things keeping me away from the school: my insecurity and my fear. Which means there is really only one thing keeping me off campus: me.

Can a youth pastor admit that? This one just did.

Over the years, I've come up with some great excuses in an attempt to justify not being on campus. The one I default to the most is, *I should be raising up volunteer leaders to do that.* Which is true. I should be raising up volunteers to be in the schools. Basic math will tell you that the presence of multiple leaders is more effective than just one. The problem is, I can't tell my volunteer leaders to get involved in the local schools and expect them to get excited about it and jump in headlong. I have to show them what this looks like. I have to model it for them. This is quite difficult when I'm not doing it myself.

Another excuse I will use is, *I don't know how to get on the campus.* This can be a legitimate excuse, especially for a youth pastor who is new to the ministry. But this excuse becomes illegitimate when you have been using it week after week, month after month, year after year.

A third excuse I will use is the classic: *I don't have time.* Leading a student ministry is a huge responsibility. There is lots of stuff that needs to be done. Not to mention that part of my job description that says, "And other duties deemed necessary."

I tend to take that part of my job quite literally. I fill my schedule with things that need to be done, so that I won't have time to get out of the office and go to the school. The problem is not *what* I am doing, but *how* I prioritize my calendar. I don't just sit in my office and tweet all day. The things I fill my schedule with are real things that must be done at some point. The problem is, because I place a greater priority on these tasks than being at the school; when my schedule fills up, going to the school is the first thing to drop off.

For many of us, high school was a difficult time in our lives, and that should motivate us as youth pastors to be more active in reaching out to students.

As with any job, there are not enough hours in the day to get everything done. There will be things that will have to wait. There will be things that simply never happen. But I must take an honest look at my schedule and decide what is most important. If I had to choose between going to the schools or checking another item off my to-do list, which would I choose? Which is more important? Which do I value more? These are both things that are important, but if I can only choose *one*; I need to choose the schools each and every time. But it doesn't exactly play out that way.

I have found that the reason why I don't prioritize being at the school is because it pulls me out of my element and makes me uncomfortable. I do what I want and what is more comfortable for me over what may have the potential to make a greater impact in the lives of students.

This has got to change. But how do I overcome this? How do I get past my fears and insecurities? How do I get past *myself*?

I think it ultimately comes down to this: Do I care more about the lives and souls of students than I do my own personal fears and insecurities? Is my heart so in tune with God's heart that I posses not just my love, but God's love for the students, teachers, and faculty of the schools in my community?

Most of us would quickly answer a resounding "yes" to those questions, but I would encourage you to take some time to *really* think about it. Be honest with yourself. Talk it out with your spouse or a close friend if you need to. Just don't ignore it. This is a question we must ask ourselves. This is a question we must have the courage to be honest with ourselves about.

Take an honest look at your schedule and decide what is most important.

I have reached a point in my life where I am no longer satisfied with my cheap excuses. I now call them what they are, shields for cowardice.

While I have to admit that "drive-by" prayers are powerful, I know that they are not enough. As a youth pastor in this community, God is calling me to do more. I must step out in order to reach those that He has called me to reach.

When I read the Scriptures, I see that most of the people who did great exploits for God were scared out of their minds. But they took their eyes off of themselves and their lack of ability and looked to the greatness of God and His ability. As the Psalmist writes, *"I lift up my eyes to the mountains – where does my help come from? My help comes from the LORD, the Maker of heaven and earth"* (Psalm 121:1-2, NIV).

When God called Moses to go and deliver the children of Israel, Moses was terrified and full of excuses (Exodus 3), but he was finally able to step out in faith and God used him to do a great work.

I guess Joshua was pretty freaked out about taking over for him, because God appeared to him early on and told him to be strong and courageous (Joshua 1:6-9).

Gideon claimed that he was the weakest and the least, so God told him that He would be with him (Judges 6:14-16), and Gideon brought deliverance to his people.

David was able to go up against Goliath (1 Samuel 17) because he knew that God was with him, and we have been inspired by him ever since.

Do you possess not just your love, but God's love for the students and teachers of the schools in your community?

Do you see the trend here? All throughout the Old Testament, God called His people to do great exploits. They were almost always afraid at first, so God told them not to fear, because He would be with them.

God has not changed. He is still with us in whatever we face, and there is no need for us to be afraid when He is on our side. If He has called you to be a youth pastor, won't He help you reach students? Won't He be with you even when you get pushed outside of your comfort zone? Won't He empower you to accomplish a great work that will leave a mark on your community forever?

If fear were not trying to hold you back from stepping foot on the school campus, you would charge ahead with a false confidence in your own strength. You can't do it on your own — and you don't have to. God will be with you. God will go before you. God will give you grace in the areas where you feel weak and insecure.

But he said to me, "My grace is sufficient for you, for my power is made perfect in weakness." Therefore I will boast all the more gladly about my weaknesses, so that Christ's power may rest on me. That is why, for Christ's sake, I delight in weaknesses, in insults, in hardships, in persecutions, in difficulties. For when I am weak, then I am strong. - 2 Corinthians 12:9-10, NIV

Moving forward is intimidating to most people. But rather than scare us, this should excite us to the possibilities that are available to us because we have access to the power and resources of a great and powerful God. Miracles happen when

Be strong and courageous! Do not tremble or be dismayed, for the Lord your God is with you wherever you go. - Joshua 1:9

we place ourselves in positions where God can show off. When we rely on our own strength, we fail to give God the opportunity to accomplish what we could never accomplish on our own. Sometimes all we have to do is step out and show up, and He takes care of the rest.

I shudder to think of the opportunities I have already missed, but with God's help, I won't let any more slip away.

As I conclude this chapter, I am reaching into my pocket for my car keys, so that I can drive a mile down the road to the high school. God has entrusted me with the task of reaching students who attend this school, but really He is the one who reaches them. I just have to show up and do whatever He leads me to do. I can't wait to see what happens. After all, God is on my side.

Chapter Five

MAKING A STRATEGIC ENTRANCE INTO THE SCHOOL

Steven Reed

When I was in junior high, my youth pastor approached me and asked me to run sound for our service. I told him that I had no training or experience, and asked him how he expected me to do that. His response? "Just make it happen."

I wasn't sure if he had a lot of confidence in me, or if he was just out of options. Either way, this phrase would become the driving force behind everything I wanted to achieve in life. It's fairly easy to not take "no" for an answer, but persisting and not giving up when things get difficult is much more difficult.

I ended up running sound that night for our youth service, and things didn't turn out nearly as bad as I had thought they would. I didn't have a clue what I was doing, but I made it happen.

When God led me to pastor students in a suburb on the south side of Fort Worth four years ago, I had no idea that plans had been made to build a junior high school across the street. For many, this was nothing more than an ordinary building project. But for me, I knew that God had strategically positioned me to reach out to this campus.

As construction began on the school, I began to think of ways that I could get involved. I could volunteer to grade papers or assist the coaches, or even sweep the hallways. I was willing to do whatever they wanted me to do; I just wanted to be present on the campus.

As the school neared completion, I began to seek out teachers and coaches utilizing the district website and Facebook. I messaged them and offered to help them in any way they needed. I did not receive a single response. I'm sure they were thinking to themselves, "Who does that? What's his angle? What does he want in return?"

I knew that God had placed me here at this point in time to reach out to this campus.

I was sitting in my office one day, feeling defeated, even though I understood why they had ignored me. I could feel that God was trying to get my attention.

I leaned back in my chair and began to whisper to the Lord. I told Him that if He wanted me to reach the school, I would keep trying.

I sat there in the quiet, awaiting His response.

And then that magical phrase popped into my head.

"Don't just try, make it happen."

At that point I knew there was only one thing for me to do. I had to keep persisting. I had to make it happen.

Things were still difficult for some time. I made several phone calls and sent countless emails offering any type of assistance. I still received zero responses. It reminded of my high school years and that awkward dating scene that was so memorable. But there I was out of high school, and I still had trouble talking to people and building relationships with them. I was a grown man, married, and still experiencing rejection as if I were in high school all over again.

I recall those dating years, not so long ago, when the most courageous thing I did in life was talk to a girl that I liked. As I would approach her from across the hallway, the rejections I had experienced in the past would work their way into my mind, and most of the time I would turn and walk away. But then there were the other times where the possibility of a girl liking me in return and perhaps wanting to hang out with me sometime would win out over my fears of rejection. I would somehow manage to work up the courage to talk to a girl and ask her out.

That was high school; but are the rest of our lives really any different? How often do we, in ministry and in life, give up when we experience a little rejection? And how does that rejection, and other experiences, keep us from trying again?

After I would pass the talking phase and move into the dating phase, I had to shift gears. It was now about building a relationship and not just talking. But let's be honest, my perspective of "building a relationship" at the time *I had to keep persisting. I had to make it happen.* meant doing whatever I had to do to get her to make out with me. So after many failed "relationships," I had to admit that my plan was not the best plan for finding my soul mate.

I began to seek God and His direction for my life, and how my future wife would play a role in all of that. And then in college, I met Elizabeth. I was afraid to talk to her at first, but there came a point where that was no longer the case. At that point, I was well on my way to building a relationship with her. We were married on June 23, 2007, a year before I accepted the youth pastor position that I am in presently.

I don't think the process of building relationships, whether romantic or professional, ever really changes. It seems that it is the same in our adult lives as it was in high school. We're more mature, of course, but we're still afraid of rejection.

During my search for an inlet into the school, I was still in that phase of building the relationship that was the most difficult. One day, I discovered that there was a need for parents or teachers to fill the roles that were open on the executive board of the Parent-Teacher Association. I was neither a parent nor teacher, but I decided to contact them anyway and ask if I could serve on the board. They replied with the date and time of the first meeting.

You know that feeling that you get when you are shocked that the girl you asked out didn't say "no?"

I had finally found a way into the school. Sort of. They had not yet said yes, but they had said I could come to the meeting.

My wife and I went to the meeting, which was held in the library of the new junior high school. As we were mingling with the other parents and teachers before the meeting began, one question kept popping up.

"Who are *your* kids? You two look awfully young to have middle schoolers."

We silenced our fears of rejection and calmly told each person who asked us that although we did not have kids who would attend the school, we were youth pastors at the church across the street, and we wanted to help out the school in any way we could.

You could sense their skepticism and discomfort with our answer. I thought to myself, "Great! Now we're the weirdos who want to be around teenagers, even though we have no kids of our own. Maybe we can quietly leave right now before any harm is done."

Suddenly, the meeting began and we were trapped on the far side of the room opposite the exit. As I looked around, I realized that the vice principal and I were the only men in the entire room. I was grateful my wife was with me; otherwise it would have just been straight up awkward.

(On a side note, would it benefit our schools if we have more adult males involved in the behind-the-scenes stuff? Just wondering.)

During the meeting, they passed around sheets of paper that listed all of the open positions that needed to be filled. There were no specifications that said you *had* to be a teacher or parent, so I saw this as my place to work my way in. As I looked over the list, I began to contemplate, because I knew that I had little spare time available, and I had no idea how much of a time commitment the open positions on the PTA would require. As I was scanning the list, I came across a role that I didn't think would require much of my time, but would still give me some level of influence. When it came time to volunteer for that position, I simply raised my hand and said, "I wouldn't mind doing that." Before I knew it, I was officially elected onto the board, and I didn't have a clue what I was getting myself into.

My new position gave me the opportunity to meet dozens of teachers and faculty, as well as parents from the community. Everyone I encountered was amazed that I was willing to serve on the campus even though I did not have any kids who attended the school. I felt acceptance from them, and was excited about being a part of something important. I thought to myself that this must be what it feels like when people volunteer at my church, and that was when I realized that the principal of a school is a lot like the senior pastor of a church, and they need volunteers just like we do.

I was finally passed the "talking phase" in my relationship with the school. I began to encourage the students in my youth ministry to make a list of ideas of ways we could serve the school in that first school year. At some point, I had the opportunity to chat with the vice principal, who offered me a tour of the school.

As we were walking and talking, I casually asked if it would be all right for me to serve the faculty lunch on the administrative day before school was officially to start. He

Everyone I encountered was amazed that I was willing to serve on the campus even though I did not have any kids who attended the school.

responded positively and connected me with a representative at the school that I would coordinate the details of the lunch with. And so I called Chick-fil-A and ordered a bunch of chicken sandwiches. I also ordered tote bags in the school colors, with text on the side stating that my church supported our local junior high school.

After we had fed everyone, we passed out the bags, and I stepped to the front of the room to share a few words of encouragement. I let the teachers and faculty know that my church was there for them; I told them that they could ask us for anything, and we would help in any way that we could.

Following the lunch, the vice principal approached me and proclaimed, "Whatever you need, you got it!"

I was startled at first, and didn't know exactly what he was referring to. I clarified that we didn't desire anything in return for our efforts, that we were just doing it because we wanted to show our love and appreciation for the school.

He went on to say, "We have this brand-new facility with a state-of-the-art gymnasium and auditorium, and if you ever want to use it for anything, it's yours." He continued to tell me how grateful he was and how much he appreciated what our church was doing to serve his school.

We had done it. We had gotten our feet in the door and made our mark on the school. And it wasn't even open for business yet. Our heart was simply to bless the faculty. In doing so, they gave us an open door to bless the school in even greater ways.

As I walked across the street to my church later that afternoon, hundreds of ideas began pouring into my head of ways my church could utilize the facilities of a brand-new $42 million dollar junior high school.

Later on in the school year, I had a conversation with the vice principal at a PTA meeting. He mentioned that a lot of teachers haven't had any time off, and he proposed a "teacher night out," where someone would watch the kids at the school so that the teachers could go out with their spouses for the evening. He asked if I would be interested and available to host this event, and I quickly told him that I would be glad to do it. I had no idea what the event would look like, who was going to help me, or how I would pay for it, but I knew that this was another opportunity that I would be foolish to say "no" to. The vice principal was ecstatic. Once again, he connected me with people at the school who I could plan the event with.

That was the moment when I settled in my heart that no matter what the school asked me to do, I would say "yes" immediately, and figure out how I would make it happen later. I knew that if I ever told the school "no," it would give them a reason to doubt the purity of our intentions.

The teacher's night out event ended up being a huge success. We rented a bounce house and set it up on one side of the gym. On the other side, there were rounds of basketball, volleyball, and jump rope taking place. There was also a movie playing in the cafeteria.

Little did I know when I said "yes" to putting on this event, that it would fall on the same night as the final game of the World Series. But as the parents began arriving later in the evening to pick up their kids, I saw how grateful they were to have a night off, and that made it totally worth it. And then they began asking me where our "tip jar" was located. We didn't have one, so they just began handing us money.

At the end of the night, we counted the "tips," and discovered that there was enough money to cover all of the expense that we had put into the event. When you set out to serve others, God has a way of making sure that you are taken care of as well.

When you decide that you are going to influence and reach your local school, the word "no" cannot be in your vocabulary. The minute you say "no" to something, it causes someone to pre-filter you out the next time they have a need.

I wanted to make sure that the school could always count on us. I was determined to do whatever was necessary, regardless of the amount of time and energy it would require from me, to make sure the school knew that they could count on my church.

Over the next several months, God gave us many more opportunities to serve the school and truly *be* the Church. We served as chaperones on field trips, judges for spelling bees, and even provided Starbucks coffee for all of the teachers one morning before school began. We also sponsored their 5K fundraiser and gave them gifts for Christmas.

Through all of this, I was connected to the volleyball coach, who asked me to help start a Christian club on the campus that would meet each Thursday during the fall semester. In November of that year, we were able to bring in Kyle and the Youth Alive team to do a school assembly for the entire school.

When you decide that you are going to influence and reach your local school, the word "no" cannot be in your vocabulary.

The biggest opportunity for influence came about when the principal asked me to be on the Site Based Committee Team because she viewed me as a community leader. This committee is given the opportunity to look over the school's budget and determine how and where any excess grants or funds should be spent. Talk about a huge opportunity for influence!

One of the experiences that brought me the greatest joy was when the principal brought a parent to me and told me that I could be a better help to them than she could. Each time we said "yes," it would increase our credibility with the school, which resulted in them asking us to do more.

Whenever you develop a "yes" attitude, you will build influence, and I believe that the greatest way to influence and impact a community is through the local schools. As you begin to serve your local school and meet their needs, you will gain greater insight into the needs of your community, and you will have a greater influence over the people in your community as well.

Join the PTA, chaperone the school dance, be a judge at the spelling bee. Do whatever it takes to show the school that you are there for them and not just to further your own agenda. This will change their perception of you from merely a youth pastor looking to preach to a class, to a community leader who desires to make the community as a whole a better place for everyone. In turn, this will expand your influence outside of the church world and into the hearts and lives of the people in your community.

Give, and it will be given to you. They will pour into your lap a good measure — pressed down, shaken together, and running over. For by your standard of measure it will be measured to you in return. - Luke 6:38

We typically use this verse to refer to financial giving, but I believe that it applies to giving in all capacities. Just like God blesses us for giving financially to the local church, when we give to the school, He does the same thing.

I remember one occasion when the junior high cheerleaders needed to sell baked goods to raise money for uniforms. They contacted me and asked if we would allow them to come to the church on a Sunday and sell their baked goods in the foyer before and after our services. When I presented this idea to my pastor, he didn't see the value in it at first. I told him that this would be a great opportunity to bring people in the community to us and allow us to connect with them, and he quickly changed his mind.

The cheerleaders came one Sunday and even did a cheer during the services. With them came their parents and siblings. Not only did we expose the cheerleaders and their families to the amazing love of Jesus Christ, who could meet their spiritual needs, but we also helped them raise the money to buy the uniforms, meeting their physical needs.

But where does the whole "it will be given to you" part fit in? Well, two of the families—who would have probably never have come to church had it not been for the fundraiser—now attend our church regularly, and their teenagers are involved in our youth ministry. This "outreach" of sorts, which cost us nothing in terms of finances or energy, proved to be a win for my church, a win for our youth ministry,

"Until the Church becomes a change agent in society outside its four walls, it's just a spiritual country club."
-Mark Jobe

and a win for the Kingdom of God. Stop saying "no" and start saying "yes."

As you begin to pour out your time, talents and treasure into your local schools, people will take notice. As you humble yourself, serving and waiting for God to exalt you to a place of influence, He will begin to work in the hearts of the people you serve. He will work His love into their hearts long before you get the chance to speak His love into their ears.

Let your light shine before men in such a way that they may see your good works, and glorify your Father who is in heaven.
- Matthew 5:16

Chapter Six

GO AND MAKE DISCIPLES, NOT JUST CHURCH ATTENDERS

Adam Herod

I first became a youth pastor nine and a half years ago, at a church in Central Texas. Back then, I didn't think the job entailed much. Just keep it relevant, have a few "big nights," change the world, and you're golden. If only it were that easy.

I remember my first Wednesday night in my new position. It was actually the first sermon I had ever preached. I'll admit I was scared, but at the same time it felt very right. I felt as if I had found what I was born to do.

I quickly began making plans and setting goals to build my new youth ministry. I asked all the right questions, attended several conferences, and sat down for coffee with other youth pastors that I considered to be successful. I even dropped in on a few of their youth services and began imitating them at my own church. (You've never done that before, right?)

My primary focus quickly became Wednesday nights. We did all the "right" things; we even ran busses to pick up kids who would not have been able to get to church otherwise. I made sure all of my core students had Matthew 28:19 memorized. My youth ministry began to grow. Things looked great, at least on the outside. I felt successful. A few years passed. And then, things begin to change.

You know those special moments that you have with God that define your life? I have had a few of those, and I will never forget any of them. In this particular case, I felt challenged to reach out to the schools in my community. But I had no idea where to start. So I used all the typical excuses. I told myself that schools are not very welcoming to youth pastors. I told myself they would never let me in the door. This went on for some time.

Finally, I decided to stop by the local middle school one day. I walked into the office, told them I was a youth pastor, and asked if there was anything I could do to help them out. You know how they responded? *We will get back to you.* That wasn't exactly the answer I was expecting, but I only have myself to blame for that. I had gone in completely unprepared. I hadn't stop to think about what I could do for them *specifically.*

The next day, I went back with an entirely different angle. I told them that my church wanted to provide lunch for all of the teachers and staff. I respectfully asked if we would be allowed to do this, and if so, what would be the best day and time to do so. My approach was completely different, and so was their response.

The following week, I served lunch to the staff of the middle school (all one hundred and fifty of them) that I thought I would never get into. They were totally shocked. Several people told me that they had never had a minister come and offer to simply serve them, with no strings attached.

This simple act of kindness flung the doors wide open. I now had access to the middle school that was basically unobstructed. I showed up week after week. And then, my next God-moment happened.

My basic routine was to go to as many schools as possible and sit with my students. I would engage in conversation with them and their friends and simply ask if they attended church anywhere on Wednesday nights. If they didn't, I would invite them to come hang out with us. I felt as though I was being an example to my students by inviting unchurched kids to our youth group in front of them. I was hoping to model what I wanted them to be doing every single school day. And it worked for a while. We gained many students utilizing that method.

I was at home one night when I had my God-moment. While watching *Veggie Tales* (no, I'm not kidding). It was the episode with the bunny — the one with Mr. Nezzer and Rack, Shack, and Benny. It told a familiar story from the Old Testament, when King Nebuchadnezzar attempted to make Shadrach, Meshach, and Abednego bow down and worship his idols. He was essentially trying to build and solidify his own kingdom.

I felt challenged to reach out to the schools in my community. But I had no idea where to start.

It started messing with my spirit. Here I was going around to schools, inviting students to my youth group and setting an example for my students. How wrong could that be? But God began to speak to me and I began to ask myself what was motivating me. Was it a desire to build God's Kingdom, or my own personal empire?

Things changed from that point on. I realized that I was not setting the right example for my students. I was never called to go to schools and merely ask students to attend church. That is not the full extent of the Christian life. That is not the full extent of following Jesus. If coming to church is the highlight of my life in Christ, I have greatly missed the point.

Matthew 28:19 talks about going and making disciples, not just church attendees. It would be much easier if Jesus had said, "Go unto all the world and make church attenders," but that is not what He said.

I was teaching my students to invite their friends to attend church so that the church could make disciples. We are robbing this generation of the opportunity to play a part in God's process of transforming lives if we continue to do that. What happens when they graduate and go off to college? What is their role in the process at that point in their lives?

The local church provides a weekly gathering place where we can come together to worship God, receive solid Biblical teaching, and build relationships, but what about the rest of the week? True discipleship does not occur when one attends a church service. It happens in community. It happens in real life. And it happens in the context of relationships.

This is the same way that Jesus instructed His disciples. He took them on the road. He gathered with them around the dinner table. He shared life with them. And the instructions that He gave them were given within those contexts. Jesus gave more practical instruction to His disciples in everyday life than He did in the "big moments." When He told them to go to Jerusalem and wait until they received the Holy Spirit, He did it while He was sharing a meal with them.[1]

The early disciples didn't need to go to a conference and take a bunch of notes; they just needed to hang out at Dairy Queen or Waffle House and talk with Jesus for a couple of hours. It's not wrong to go to a conference. In fact, it can be quite beneficial. But there are some things that can only be learned through relationships and interaction with other Christ followers.

I now realize that I must take the bulk of my attention off of Wednesday night's youth service, and evenly distribute it to the rest of the week. I must focus on the complete cycle of life that my students find themselves in. I need them living for Jesus every day, not just on Sunday morning and Wednesday night.

I now tell my students *not* to invite their friends to our youth group until they have first told them about Jesus themselves. I also tell them not to share Jesus with their friends until they have first been a friend to them and shown them unconditional love. People can always tell when you have an agenda, and they are likely to shut down if they think you are only being nice to them because you want them to come to your church.

Some may disagree with this, but I feel as though I am teaching my students to become Christians for life, and to encourage those that they reach to do the same. I don't want my students to have a relationship with Jesus that only lasts while they are in school and attending my youth group.

In 2007, LifeWay research conducted a study, which showed that seventy percent of teens stop attending church for at least one year between the ages of eighteen and twenty-two, and many of them don't return to church until after they turn thirty.

Many students build their faith on their parent's faith. They grow up in church and attend youth services. They believe God is real, but they never have their *own* relationship with Him. They never understand what it means to walk with Him daily. Because their faith is more of an idea than something they have actually experienced, it tends to erode when the storms of life hit. This happens

True discipleship happens in community, in real life, in the context of relationships.

especially as students graduate high school and move on to college. For the first time in their lives, they are away from their parents. This is typically when they begin to think about what they truly believe, and what they only believed because someone told them to.

We are called to make disciples. Unfortunately, many of us view discipleship as simply giving students a list of the "ten rules every good Christian should follow." But it is more than that. It is about having a relationship with Jesus. It is about having a foundation of personal experience, rather than someone else's experience. It is about growing in one's knowledge of and obedience to Christ as we encounter His presence and seek to be more like Him in the way we live our lives. This happens through setting aside time to spend with Him on a regular basis, as well as involving Him in the daily aspects of our lives. It does not happen simply through memorizing a list of rules. It is easy to act like a "good Christian," but will you cling to Jesus when life gets tough?

There is one story in particular that I will always remember. I was sitting with Joe, one of my students, at lunch. I happened to notice a young man eating alone across the room. He looked a lot different than everyone else in the cafeteria. He was dressed in all black, including black eyeliner and nail polish. I asked Joe what his name was. He just shrugged.

"Let's go." I said, as I picked up my lunch. Joe and I walked over and sat down at the table with the young man, whom I would later find out was named Jonathan.

"What do *you* want?" Those were the first words to come out of his mouth as Joe and I sat down.

"Nothing. We just saw you over here by yourself and wanted to come eat lunch with you."

No response. He sat there in silence, saying absolutely nothing for the entire lunch period. Before leaving to head back to my church office, I told Joe that we were not going to give up. For the next month, Joe and I sat with Jonathan at lunch every chance we got, and he never once joined in our conversation. But he did overhear many conversations about church and upcoming events.

On one particular Thursday, Joe and I were sitting with Jonathan discussing our service from the previous night. We were talking about the altar time and exchanging stories of the students who had responded to Jesus. That is when Jonathan finally spoke up.

"You know I'm an atheist, right?"

I hesitated for a moment, knowing that he was trying to get us to react so that it would be easier to push us away. "Well, I am a Christian, but I would still like to be your friend. Is it alright if we continue to sit with you?"

We sat with Jonathan at countless lunches after that tense exchange. Over time, he began to join in on our conversation. He slowly opened up to us and began to let down his walls. He began to look for us in the cafeteria and make a point of sitting with us.

One day, it was clear that Jonathan was having a rough day. Joe and I asked him what was wrong and he began to tell us his story for the very first time. He talked a lot about his home life and really opened up to us. At the end of lunch, I asked if we could pray with him, and he said "yes." Several months later, Jonathan asked Jesus to come into his heart, right there in the lunchroom. He began attending a church near his house, and as the school year progressed, we saw God do an amazing work in his life.

He asked Jesus to come into his heart, right there in the lunchroom.

Reaching Jonathan took time. It did not happen overnight, and it probably would not have happened at all if we had tried to force Jesus on him in the beginning. We simply loved him and did not judge him for being different. And then He met Jesus, the only one capable of changing his heart. He never ended up in my church or youth group, but he did end up in the Kingdom, and that was worth the time it took to invest in his life. Would you put the same effort into reaching out to students if you knew they would never end up in your *youth* group? How we answer this question will determine which kingdom we are more interested in building, and it is much more important to contribute to God's Kingdom than it is our own.

As time went on, I realized that I did not want to just pastor a youth group; I wanted to pastor schools. That's when I discovered the schools in my community had a Fellowship of Christian Athletes (FCA) group that was already going strong. If the school already has a solid Christian club, join it and help make it even better. This can be far more effective than doing your own thing and potentially ending up in competition.

I teamed up with FCA at several schools in my city. At first, I simply showed up and did whatever I could do to help out. I would set up the sound system, pass our donuts, even sweep the gym floor after our meetings. Over time, the group grew to about 200 students attending the weekly meeting, which was 25% of the school. It was an amazing movement to be apart of.

I have found that there are many FCA leaders out there who are searching for help. They need people to help on the ground level as they reach out to students. After I had been serving for a while, a teacher told me that she had been leading the group for over a decade; I was the first youth pastor who had come in with no agenda, who was truly there to serve. I didn't ask to pass out fliers advertising my youth group or speak every week. In fact, most of the time I did little more than hold open doors as students entered the gym, or help clean up after they left. But people noticed — teachers, other staff members, even the principal.

I was on my way out one day after an FCA meeting, when I decided to stop by the office to say hello to the staff. The principal happened to see me and approached to ask me a question. She went on to tell me that she was going to get a cup of coffee and it would take her at least ten minutes, but there were two boys waiting in her office that were in trouble for fighting. She then asked if I would go in and talk to them while she was getting her coffee. Leaning forward slightly, she added in a hushed tone, "There are things I can't say, but you can."

Talk about God opening a door! When we honor Him by honoring those around us, He will work behind the scenes to open doors for us that we cannot open ourselves. Over the years, I have found that the best way to make an impact in the local schools is to simply be faithful. Start by serving, no matter what capacity you are asked to serve in, and be open and willing to do whatever God wants to do.

Ministry is made to happen everywhere, not just in our church buildings. The journey is more about fulfilling God's call on our lives than it is advancing in ministry. We should be as transparent in our failures and struggles as we are in our victories, and encourage others to do the same. We lead more by our actions than we do with our mouths. We've told students that the schools are their greatest mission field. The truth is, they are ours as well.

Endnotes

1) Acts 1:4-5

Chapter Seven

UNITED TO REACH A COMMUNITY

Jim Coursey

Shape Charge: A few years ago I was challenged by a thought that would change the way I view my community, other churches, and the vision of my ministry. This thought not only changed the way I did ministry, it changed my point of view. This change of vision was birthed in tragedy.

My youth group had just gotten back from attending our annual summer camp. The Holy Spirit had really moved among us during that time. The students were still buzzing from the experience. But two weeks later, two of my students came forward and confessed to our leadership that they had been raped. This change of vision was birthed in tragedy.

I am the husband of a beautiful wife. I am the father to three wonderful girls. To say that I took this hard is an understatement. I was devastated, searching for answers. But it was in this time of trying to make sense of things that a great truth was staring me in the face.

Every week we do our best to provide a safe environment for our students for the time that we have with them. For those few hours, they can come in and are able to be in a place where they are loved. For those few hours they can be honest. For a few hours they can step out of the "world" and into a safe environment. The truth is, they aren't always safe out there. The truth is, we live in a dangerous world where poor decisions can result in tragic circumstances.

I know this. You know this.

But how does this change and shape our vision?

Unexpected, sometimes painful circumstances happen all the time. They're a part of life. These adversities have the power to shape us, good or bad. I believe that God often uses these circumstances to shape us and build our character.

The Apostle Paul says it like this: *"Not only so, but we also glory in our sufferings, because we know that suffering produces perseverance; perseverance, character; and character, hope. And hope does not put us to shame, because God's love has been poured out into our hearts through the Holy Spirit, who has been given to us"* (Romans 5:3-5, NIV).

Nearly twenty years have passed since I pledged to serve our nation as a United States Marine. It was during this time that I had the opportunity to go to a school on demolitions, i.e. training with explosives. It was at this school that I first heard the term "shape charge." A shape charge is explosive material that is shaped to deliver a greater explosion. This is done simply by shaping or molding the explosive material into a different shape.

Most people are familiar with C4. For those who aren't, C4 is a clay-like substance that explodes when charged. If one were to explode an unshaped block of C4, it would make a huge explosion. However, if one were to take a small piece of that same C4, shape it and mold it, it would produce an even greater explosion. All of this is accomplished within the world of physics and math.

Hope does not put us to shame, because God's love has been poured out into our hearts. - Romans 5:5

But how does all of this talk of explosives apply to us?

If we want our faith to "explode," for it to become greater than where it is at present, then we must allow God to "shape" our lives. Great people and great ministries are shaped over time, often through adversity. It takes kneading, pulling, tearing, and stretching.

In my case, it wasn't until a couple of my students were sexually abused that my vision began to be shaped from ordinary to great. My vision grew from reaching the students in my group to reaching my entire community, and I knew that I could not do this alone.

Over the years, I have observed that few youth pastors rarely take the time and effort to build relationships with other churches, community leaders, and schools. Ministry in just your own church can feel as though it consumes every minute we have. But the truth is that if we want to reach our community, we are going to have to reach outside of our circle and get to know the leaders at the church down the street.

And so it was after this tragic event that I began to make the effort to get to know every pastor, youth pastor, and community leader in my city. I knew that if we all came together, we could positively influence one another towards our common goal. And we all shared the same goal, to "go and make disciples" of every person in our community. Yes, we all had different styles and ideas as to how to accomplish this. Yes, we differed in our theological backgrounds. Nevertheless, our core mission was the same across the board.

A good perspective of this scenario is found in reading the books of Nehemiah and Ezra. Nehemiah had a vision to rebuild the walls of Jerusalem. Ezra had a vision to restore the temple. Two very different visions, yet the mission was the same: the restoration of Israel. Is this not the same with the other churches in your city? God has given the pastors of each individual church in your city a vision, just as He has given you a vision. The accomplishment of each of these visions works toward the whole of the mission to reach your community.

The tricky part begins once you decide you want to work with the other churches in your community. That is when the questions begin, namely *How do we develop a culture of teamwork among all of the churches in our community? What does this look like? How does it work?*

Big Begins Small: I started meeting with nearly all of the youth pastors in my community on a monthly basis. We would meet at each other's churches, usually over lunch. Occasionally, we would discuss leadership principles or things that were taking place in our churches, but most of the time, we just hung out. We talked about our families, our struggles, our fears — the stuff below the surface-level.

> *God has given the pastors of each individual church in your city a vision, just as He has given you a vision.*

Honesty and transparency are the foundation of healthy relationships. They breed mutual trust and credibility. It's important to note that one must first build genuine relationships with the leaders in a community before the group can begin to develop a vision for their community.

How much time will this take? Honestly, it's a never-ending process. These days, there is a high turnover rate among pastors, particularly youth pastors. Four years at the same church was all it took for me to become the longest tenured youth pastor in town.

My goal in networking with other leaders in my community is to do my best to share my experiences and knowledge with them in order to help them grow their ministry. This can be quite the balancing act. How do I grow my ministry and help someone else grow his or hers at the same time? I don't try to do all the math; I just do as much as I can, as I am able. And it goes both ways. Most of the time, I am learning from the leaders who are learning from me.

Working together is honestly not that difficult. But it is time consuming. And it does require you to give up your pride and desire to be right all the time. Sometimes you even have to compromise for the sake of unity. For instance, one of the churches in my community doesn't believe in the usage of instruments in worship. While I could make what I feel is a solid Biblical case against this theology, what purpose would doing so serve? Is it really worth it? And are the people in that church really any less saved simply because they don't utilize instruments in worship or listen to instrumental music?

The leaders in my community have resolved to create certain events over the course of the year that intentionally do not incorporate instrumental music. This way we can include this church and partner with them for these events. When you start to include (rather than excluding) other churches in the work that God is doing in your community, you will be amazed at the increase in the amount of people that you are able to reach.

Honesty and transparency are the foundation of healthy relationships.

God honors us when we make the commitment to put our own opinions and desires away and unite together for one common cause. As the Psalmist says, *"Behold, how good and how pleasant it is for brothers to dwell together in unity! ... For there the LORD has commanded the blessing — life forevermore"* (Psalm 133:1,3b). It's remarkable to think that the entire chapter of Psalm 133 is dedicated to instructing us to live in unity.

Over the years, I have observed a "supernatural" unity amongst the leaders in my community. We have several musically talented youth pastors from a variety of denominations and theological backgrounds that will meet up and worship together. Trust me, when guys from four or five different denominations can agree on a set list, God is at work.

I believe that when we make the commitment to unite ourselves together, God comes and empowers us to actually pull it off.

Most of the time I am learning from the leaders who are learning from me.

As a wise coach once said, *"It's easy to get good players. Getting them to play together; that's the hard part."*

Domino Effect: Once we began creating and customizing events that would fit the needs of all of our churches, everything else just kind of fell into place. We would join together as a community — not just individual churches — and see hundreds of students worship together. This citywide ministry eventually grew to become more of an area-wide ministry, as our network grew to include youth pastors from four neighboring towns.

At one point, I personally put together a training event at my church that featured breakout sessions with different speakers. But rather than doing all of the sessions myself, I gave them to other local youth pastors. This would allow them to increase their influence to a new group of students, and it showed our students and churches that we are not in competition with one another.

Have you ever thought that perhaps God has placed you around the other churches in your community so that they can help fulfill the vision that He has birthed in you? Have you ever thought that perhaps you can also help fulfill the vision that God has given them? If you want to reach your community, it is crucial that you unite with other churches instead of being in competition with them. The "Us vs. Them" attitude is extremely toxic to the health of a local church as well as the Church as a whole.

Our unified efforts eventually led up to a community outreach to the schools in our city. But it did not happen overnight.

I first met with the youth pastors in the network and pitched the vision for a "outreach day," with a school assembly during the day and evangelistic service at night. They were on board, but we collectively decided that it would not be wise to introduce ourselves to the new superintendent of our school district by asking him to host a large event.

We met with the superintendent one morning and each took turns sharing our heart to serve the school in whatever way would be most beneficial to them.

Over the course of a year, we served the school through a number of small but important projects. This built up our credibility and trust with the administrators, to the point where they would email us with prayer requests on a regular basis.

Our network met again to discuss where we were at with hosting a school assembly at the end of the year, and I was asked to be the spokesperson to spearhead the event. Everyone was united, and we were anxious to move forward. But it took another year before the details of the event began to fall into place.

It is crucial that you unite with other churches instead of being in competition with them.

I was pretty busy over the course of that year. I don't think I could add up the number of phone calls, emails, and meetings I attended if I wanted to. If you think it's hard to get your own church on board for an event, try planning an event with eleven churches and two schools.

By the time the date for the event was set, the school that probably would not have said yes to this event had we approached them without building a relationship first was fully behind us. They trusted our leadership and credibility, and I'm sure they were surprised to see so many churches coming together to do *anything*, let alone an event this big.

The event went off as planned. Every financial need was filled, everything fell into place, and lives were changed. The event even made the front page of two local newspapers. This was due in large part to relational connections with the editors through our network of youth pastors.

Most of the big breaks that people get in life come through relationships. That is why unity is crucial — especially for the Church. Definitely for the Church.

I won't go into the logistics of the day, but I can tell you that the whole day was phenomenal. I heard about a student named Shelby who was really impacted by the anti-bullying message that was presented. She had been bullied by several students in the school, for no apparent reason other than the fact that she wore thick glasses. It's kind of ridiculous if you take into consideration that most everyone wears glasses or contacts these days, but this is the state of our culture, particularly in our schools. Bullying is a huge problem.

There were other stories from the day as well, and I'm sure the ones that made their way back to me were just the tip of the iceberg, but sometimes you have to stop and think about the one. Jesus spoke to large crowds on several occasions, but He spent just as much time and focused energy when He was alone with people who desperately needed His help.

We need to be willing to pour into "the one" even when the spotlight is turned off and everyone has gone home.

We need to be willing to pour into "the one" even when the spotlight is turned off and everyone has gone home.

That night, we rented out the high school auditorium for the night service, where a simple yet powerful presentation of the Gospel was given. Over two hundred students responded to the altar call, and the youth pastors (and volunteers from the churches) got the opportunity to pray for them at the front of the auditorium, where they were spread from one end of the room to the other.

We debriefed an hour or so later, and I heard a story of three girls who came up to one of our leaders in tears at the end of the night. They told him that they had been praying for their friend for three months, and she had accepted Christ that night. Those were the only words they could get out, as they broke down weeping under the weight of God answering their countless prayers in one moment. Moments like that make it all worth it.

"There is no limit to what a man can do or where he can go if he doesn't mind who gets the credit."
-Ronald Reagan

I heard another story later on of a woman from one of the churches. She was older than me, if I recall correctly, and though she had spent much of her life in church, she had never led anyone to Christ. That night, at the front of the high school auditorium, she prayed with four students to receive Christ.

None of this was easy. None of this was overnight. The "moment" was cool and powerful, but it took three years of hard work—three years of back-and-forth phone calls, emails and conversations—to lay the groundwork and relational foundations that made the moment possible.

You Can't Do It Alone: If you truly want to leave a lasting impression on your community, the first step is realizing that you cannot do it alone. Every church in your city may not want to get on board and help you, but find the ones that are willing and keep reaching out to those who are not willing at first. It's amazing how people change their minds when you love them even after they refuse to do what you want them to do. And if you truly desire unity, you're going to have to be willing to throw some of your own ideas on the ground and brainstorm with your team, coming up with ideas together as one.

I think that our greatest enemy is not so much Satan or demonic forces, but ourselves. The spiritual realm certainly comes into play, but most often our biggest enemies are our own pride and laziness. We have to get off the couch and be willing to work with others.

Most of the big breaks that people get in life come through relationships. That is why unity is crucial.

In Genesis 1, God blessed Adam and gave him the charge to fill the earth and subdue it.[1] According to Webster, "subdue" means to overcome or to bring under control, possibly by force. We are to subdue the earth. We are to overcome the earth. We are to bring the earth under control. We are to conquer it. It will be a fight. It will not be easy. Success will not come overnight. The Kingdom of God will be built with blistered hands and a sweaty back.

There will be times when you get discouraged. There will be days when you want to quit. In fact, you'll probably be met with what appears to be nothing but failure before you realize the progress. You have to make up your mind to keep moving forward no matter how difficult it gets, no matter how impossible it seems.

Today, I challenge you to begin thinking of other leaders in your community that you can partner with. Put the ones you don't get along with at the top of your list. Then, begin looking for ways to build relationships with them. Take them to lunch. Meet for coffee. Discuss their heart and vision for the community, and figure out how it fits

The Kingdom of God will be built with blistered hands and a sweaty back.

with yours. It's not about who has the better vision, it's about figuring out how all of the different visions fit together into one big vision that will leave an impression on your community for all of eternity.

Endnotes

1) Genesis 1:28

Chapter Eight

THE SMALL CHURCH THAT MAKES A BIG DIFFERENCE

Ricky Franklin

Six years ago, my family and I began the adventure of planting a church in a suburb of Fort Worth. Over the years, we saw it all: the ups and downs, the struggles and victories. In the summer of 2009, I was tired. I was about to turn forty, and my family was counting down the days to our Florida vacation. We were looking forward to some downtime in Orlando before the school year began.

A few weeks before our vacation, I received word from my volunteer youth pastor that he would not be able to take our students to youth camp. Knowing that our students—and my own kids—had been looking forward to it all year, I knew that I could not cancel. So I loaded up the van and drove my three teenage sons and a few other students an hour and a half to the campgrounds.

When we arrived, I noticed that the theme for the summer was *Dream Big*. I thought this was a bit cliché at first, but after a long week of services and activities under the blazing Texas sun, God spoke to me.

It was Thursday night, the final worship service of the week. Hundreds of teenagers filled the front of the room, worshipping Jesus in total abandonment, crying out to God to touch their generation. That's when it happened.

I was standing off towards the side, praying for our students, our church, and my survival through the final night of pranks, when a loud whisper exploded in my chest.

At the time, my church was renting a local middle school to meet in on Sunday mornings. An expansive new high school was nearing completion across the street—a $96 million dollar project that, when completed, would become the largest physical high school in the nation. It was set to open towards the end of August—right after my family's impending vacation—to freshmen and sophomores. On that first day of school, 800 students would enter the untouched halls, two of them being my own sons.

On that Thursday night at camp, I believe that the Lord spoke to me and told me that in forty days, our church would play an instrumental role in *"God sometimes speaks to us most intimately when He catches us off guard." -C.S. Lewis* establishing the atmosphere for this new mega-school. I quickly pulled my phone out of my pocket and counted down the days from that point to the first day of school. It was exactly forty days away. Just a coincidence? I don't think so.

The questions and doubts began to come the moment my feet hit the floor Friday morning, most of them revolving around how exactly we would go about setting the atmosphere for the new school. We were not the largest church in the community, and up to that point we had done very little to reach out to the schools. My oldest son had met with the principal a couple of times, but they were not on a first name basis or anything. I had only recently met Kyle Embry, who at that time was still fairly new to his position as Youth Alive director in our region. I had no clue that Youth Alive hosted an annual event specifically to train students to effectively reach out to their schools.[1]

We were largely unqualified, but God has a way of qualifying people to do things they are not qualified for if they are willing to move when He says to move.

On the drive home, my wife called and informed me that one of our neighbors had stopped my while I was gone, and she just happened to be the new president of the Parent-Teacher-Student Association (PTSA) at the new school. She knew that I was a pastor at a nearby church and wanted to invite me to join the PTSA board as the Spiritual/Character Chairman, where I would lead the way in creating character education programs for the school.

To be honest, I had no idea that such a position even existed. Before God spoke to me that Thursday night at camp, He was already setting things in motion.

I took the news to my congregation and we began to mobilize people to fast and pray for the principal, staff, and students who would be attending the new school in a few short weeks.

"If God has called you, you're qualified. The issue is never, 'Are you qualified?' The issue is always, 'Are you called?'"
-Mark Batterson

One Sunday morning in August, two days before the first day of school, my family and I were on the way home from Florida when we received word that our congregation had left the service and marched around the outside of the school. The walls of the school didn't fall down, but a wall of God's presence went up! Since that time, our church (as well as others in the community) have seen God do amazing things in the lives of students who attend that school.

Over the years, I have had the privilege of coordinating two character-building assemblies, as well as two Seven Project events, at the school. These events have brought hope to the student body — both Christians and non-Christians alike. Out of these large events, smaller opportunities to interact with students in their classrooms have sprung up. We created a weeklong *Character Week* right before Easter that ended up turning into a yearlong emphasis on the importance of good moral character in the lives of students.

Since then, we have rented out the school auditorium on three occasions for a night rally, where we saw a combined total of 150 students commit their lives to Christ. We also sponsor the student-led Youth Alive club at the high school, which has grown to include both feeder middle schools. During one week in particular, we saw more than twenty-five students commit their lives to Christ through all of the Youth Alive clubs across the board. The students who lead these clubs have developed small Bible studies that meet every day during lunch to disciple these students, as many of them are new to the Christian faith.

As a result of all of these outreaches, a network that involves pastors and youth pastors from several local churches has formed. This network is able to come together and do things far greater than any one church could pull off on their own.

All of these incredible things that have happened over the past three years can be traced back to that Thursday night at camp. I wonder what would have happened if things had worked out so that my volunteer youth pastor had been there with the students instead? I guess God knew that I needed to be in that place at that particular time.

It is important to note that the involvement I have had in reaching out to the school has not come without a cost. It has been full of ups and downs, including an attempted cancellation of one of the Seven Project events by a local atheist group. I was even featured on the front page of their newsletter last year. They used my Twitter profile picture and dubbed me "the most powerful man in the school district." I think they intended this to be an insult, but it actually came across as more of a compliment than anything else.

Ironically, none of the people in this atheist group have any connection to the school or any children who attend a school within the district. Isn't it interesting how people who are doing nothing to reach out to the next generation try to put a stop to those who are actually doing something?

God knew that I needed to be in that place at that particular time.

In my time of planting a church and reaching out to our local schools, I have come to realize how essential it is to cultivate a lifestyle of faith-filled prayer. Whenever I think of a person who lived a powerful, prayer-filled life, I think of the Old Testament warrior, Joshua.

Inside the Tent of Meeting, the Lord would speak to Moses face to face, as one speaks to a friend. Afterward Moses would return to the camp, but the young man who assisted him, Joshua son of Nun, would remain behind in the Tent of Meeting. - Exodus 33:11, NLT

Joshua was familiar with the presence of God before the day of battle ever came. Before he was ever launched into the role of primary leader of God's people, God had him remain in the Tent of Meeting for extended periods of time. In those days, this was the place where God's presence would manifest and where He would speak to His people. Today, we don't have to go to a specific Tent of Meeting, but God does want to meet with us if we will take the time to meet with Him. Before we are launched into the limelight, we need to take time to connect and communicate with God so that He will fill us with all that He is and give us courage, boldness, and the right words to speak at the right time.

When we fast-forward a bit in the Old Testament account of Joshua's life, we find that he was still seeking the Lord in the days immediately preceding the walls of Jericho falling. The walls would not have fallen had the people not fallen on their knees before God in prayer and been obedient to the instructions He gave them.

To me, the most intriguing story about Joshua is not about the fall of Jericho, but rather the battle of the tiny town of Ai. It seems that after the great victory at Jericho, Joshua and his leaders underestimated their need of the Lord's help in defeating this small city.

As a pastor, I have taught numerous times from Joshua 7 about the effects of sin by using the example of Ai. However, I see another lesson that we can learn from this story, and that is the day that Joshua chose not to inquire of the Lord, which was also the day that he lost the battle at Ai.

I cannot find a single reference in Joshua 7 where Joshua inquired of the Lord concerning the battle plan before he went to battle. Joshua's leaders convinced him to only send three thousand men rather than the entire army, due to how small Ai was. This resulted in the warriors that were sent meeting a sound defeat. The men of Ai chased them as they retreated, taking the lives of thirty-six fathers, brothers, and friends.

The text tells us that Joshua *then* went to the Lord, *after* all of this had taken place. I can't help but wonder if the lives of those thirty-six men would have been spared had Joshua sought the Lord before going into battle? Had they prayed first, Joshua and his leaders may not have ever realized the difference their prayers made; but the outcome would still have been different, in a positive sense. Perhaps they would have won the battle and lost none of their men in the process.

We need to take time to connect with God so that He will fill us with all that He is.

It is crucial that leaders get in the habit of inquiring of the Lord, taking anything and everything to Him before moving forward, no matter how confident they are of the outcome.

I am glad that we were intentional to spend more time in prayer as we did more outreaches to the high school near our church. I believe that because we put God first, He prepared us to gracefully move through challenges and obstacles we never would have planned on.

In closing, here are some takeaways that have helped us throughout the past three years of community outreaches. I pray that they will help you as you begin or continue your adventure of ministry and local outreach.

1.   Develop a strategic list of prayer points involving the schools for students and parents.
2.   Encourage prayer for local schools during personal and corporate prayer times. The local schools are still America's greatest mission field, especially for the local church.
3.   Mobilize your group to go out and do prayer walks.
4.   Senior pastors should include school campuses when they are preaching on local outreach.
5.   Empower youth pastors to have students praying for their schools on a regular basis during youth services.

The people within your ministry will value whatever you value as their leader. Let prayer be the forefront of whatever efforts you lead as you go forth to "conquer the land" that God is giving you.

"Prayer helps us see and seize the God-ordained opportunities that are around us all the time." -Mark Batterson

Endnotes

1) For more information on Together Training, visit www.youthalivetx.com

Chapter Nine

CARRIERS OF HOPE

Al Roever

For eight years, I had the pleasure of working with one of the premier school assembly speakers in the United States—Dave Roever. Dave is my brother, so I certainly have no illusions about his humanity. However, I am continually amazed at how God could use such a human vessel for His purposes. It is God's purpose to reach this younger generation, and He can use you to do so!

When they led Him away, they seized a man, Simon of Cyrene, coming in from the country, and placed on him the cross to carry behind Jesus. And following Him was a large crowd of the people, and of women who were mourning and lamenting Him. But Jesus turning to them said, "Daughters of Jerusalem, stop weeping for Me, but weep for yourselves and for your children." - Luke 23:26-28

One of my more enjoyable assignments was to speak to groups of pastors about Dave's program and the reasons why he is so committed to reaching students through school assemblies. Of course, Dave wants to tell young people that they can make it through whatever circumstances they are experiencing in their lives.

I remember one young man, about fifteen years of age, who once asked me if Dave's story was true. Having lived through it with him, it was easy for me to tell this young man that it was absolutely true.[1] He had approached me with his head down, shuffling his feet, but left with his head up and confidence in his steps. I could almost read his mind, *"If Dave can make it, so can I."*

That being said, to offer hope without offering the Giver of hope would be most frustrating. As I explained to those pastors, Dave isn't just interested in offering hope to students; He wants to introduce them to the Hope-giver, Jesus. As believers, we are all called to be carriers of hope to a broken and hurting world.

By far, most school administrators we encountered were more than happy to accommodate our request to utilize their gymnasium or auditorium for a night rally wherein we would present the Gospel. It was always an incredible experience seeing students — and often their parents — responding to the Gospel.

After a few years of doing assemblies and night rallies, we learned that students do not lose their freedom of speech when they step foot onto their public school campus.

It can hardly be argued that either students or teachers shed their constitutional rights of freedom of speech or expression at the school house gate. - U.S. Supreme Court; Tinker 383 US 506 (1969)

One of the most powerful ways to make a school assembly more effective is to have students fully prepared to share their faith with any students who might have questions following the assembly. We would typically begin a month in advance meeting with youth leaders in the area where Dave would be doing assemblies and teaching them how to approach answering the most common questions they might be asked. Some school administrators would even allow Dave to introduce local youth pastors in attendance at the assembly and refer students to them if they had any questions. While we could not mention Christ during the assembly, we could answer questions asked by students who approached us after.

But in your hearts revere Christ as Lord. Always be prepared to give an answer to everyone who asks you to give the reason for the hope that you have. But do this with gentleness and respect.
- 1 Peter 3:15, NIV

Perhaps one of the most pressing needs is for these assemblies to have some sort of follow-up discipleship. A pastor once posed the question, "Where will the new believers attend church?" If only it were possible to make sure each one landed in a church prepared to disciple them. As much as it grieves me to admit, some newborn Christians end up in dysfunctional church families.

We are all called to be carriers of hope to a broken and hurting world.

In actuality, the new believers will most likely attend the church that their friends attend. This fact highlights the power of relationships. Several years ago, I read a statistic that said each person has an inner circle of about sixteen people who they relate to in some way. Most of these people will attend church with their friend at least once. Of those who visit, somewhere around four will accept Christ.

It would be nearly impossible for me to overstate the need for Bible clubs on school campuses. However, the leaders of these clubs desperately need to be properly trained. It is here that the problems of dysfunctional church families can be resolved. Imagine healthy Christian young people bringing their friends to a healthy Bible club meeting and teaching them the things of God. Those friends would be a natural influence wherever they decided to attend church.

Many educators have informed me that the greatest problem young people face is a lack of self-esteem. Sometimes the solutions they implement to correct this perceived problem are actually worse than the problem itself. Structuring games and sporting events in such a way that there are no winners and losers does more to create narcissistic monsters than it does to build self-esteem.

In actuality, the problem is not so much a lack of self-esteem as it is a feeling of total insignificance, a perceived lack of self-worth. I believe that the required teaching of evolution in some way contributes to this perception. After all, three billion years of purposeless, meaningless, random mutations plus natural selection could hardly produce anything of objective value.

On the other hand, the knowledge that we are "fearfully and wonderfully made"[2] by the Creator of the universe—that there is a divine purpose for our existence—elevates our sense of significance immensely. Compound this with the Gospel message that God loved each one of us to the point that He sent His Son to die for us in order to establish an eternal relationship with us,[3] and our sense of worth and value sky-rockets immensely. If we are going to be carriers of hope to this generation, we must communicate to them that their lives have value because God created them and redeemed them to Himself through the death of His Son.

I recall often hearing Dave say to girls in attendance at the assemblies, "Honey, you're worth more than another notch on the belt of that boy who wants to get in your pants." The girls would always go ballistic when they heard this.

Your life has value because God created you and redeemed you through the death of His Son.

One of my responsibilities while working for my brother was to read through the letters written to him by students. One of those letters broke my heart. A fifteen-year-old girl wrote that if she had heard Dave speak two weeks earlier, she would still be a virgin.

One of our purposes for speaking to students on high school campuses is to give those fifteen-year-old girls reasons for respecting themselves, honoring themselves, and keeping themselves, because they have a glorious future ahead of them. And of course, it is equally important that we present the same message to all of the high school boys as well. This is part of the message of hope that we carry.

If I may, allow me to indulge myself for a moment. I believe that if we want to change our country, the best place to start is with the younger generation. There is no higher calling than that of youth ministry, for it is not merely a stepping-stone to something more important; it is absolutely imperative for the health and growth of the church.

Five days a week, young people gather together in one place, though certainly not in one accord. There, we can touch the lives of every kind of culture within our communities. And if we fail, our local churches will fail.

"Look, I am sending you out as sheep among wolves. So be as shrewd as snakes and harmless as doves." –Jesus[4]

As we seek to reach this younger generation, we are truly like sheep in the midst of wolves. That is why we must be wise and strategic, but at the same time gentle and harmless. We must know how to respond with love and grace when we are asked difficult questions, and point as many students as possible towards the hope that is found in Jesus Christ.

Endnotes

1) Read Dave's story at
   www.roeverfoundation.org/meet_dave_roever.php
2) Psalm 139:14
3) John 3:16
4) Matthew 10:16, NLT

Chapter Ten

PLANTING CAMPUS CLUBS

Landon Huie

Clubs Change Schools: A few years ago, I was serving as a youth pastor at a church in a small, but quickly growing town just outside of Dallas. We had just launched a Campus Club in the local junior high school. Here we were at week four, having to move into the library because it was the largest room that the school had available for us to meet in. I vividly remember students flooding into the room until there was not a seat left open in the entire room. There were well over two hundred students present, and a sense of excitement filled the air.

Each week, we brought in a projector and small sound system so that we could project the name of the club on the wall and play high-energy music as the students entered the library for the club. This was helpful since the club met at 7:30 in the morning, before school began.

On this particular morning, we saw over fifty students raise their hands to invite Jesus into their hearts. My interns and I were completely blown away. God was using our students to literally change the face of this school. As the weeks went on, we stood in awe at the high number of salvations that happened through this one Campus Club alone.

In this chapter, I will share several of my experiences in planting Campus Clubs at schools across the country. My hope is that through reading it, God will place a burden and an urgency in your heart to reach the schools in your community.

Every Place Where You Set Your Foot: I had just graduated from Christ for the Nations when I got my first youth pastor job at my dad's church. I had been there less than a year when I took our students to North Texas Youth Camp in Maypearl for the first time. I remember the guest speaker that week was a pastor named Jason Spears. After service one night, I approached him and asked him to pray with me about something. He nodded politely and asked what I wanted him to pray with me about. I told him that I wanted us to pray that God would open doors for me to plant a Campus Club at every public school campus in my community.

I don't remember everything that Jason prayed that night, but I do remember him quoting a verse that said, *"I will give you every place where you set your foot, as I promised Moses"* (Joshua 1:3, NIV).

After that encounter, I simply believed that God would give me every single campus that I stepped foot on. God gave me a promise that coupled itself with the passion I already had inside of me to reach schools. And then the next phase of the journey came, the part none of us enjoy, as God began to teach me the importance of patience. It wasn't unlike the process that Joseph had to walk through after God gave him a dream before he could fulfill that dream.

"Because we carry the Kingdom of God with us, we can change the atmosphere of every place we enter."
-Beth Helton

After we returned home from camp, I began to talk to my students about reaching their schools. I would preach it on Wednesday nights and push it in our small groups throughout the week, but my students just didn't seem to get it. We did not plant a single club during the fall semester. During this time, I felt the Lord telling me to focus on raising up the "laborers."

He said to his disciples, "The harvest is great, but the workers are few. So pray to the Lord who is in charge of the harvest; ask him to send more workers into his fields." -Matthew 9:37-38, NLT

As youth pastors, we are literally surrounded by the harvest. There are schools *everywhere*, and *every* school has students in it who don't have a relationship with Jesus. At first, I thought I had missed God when He told me that "now" was the time to reach the schools, and that we would be successful if we simply showed up. But what I didn't realize was that my students were not spiritually ready for such a mission. Although what God had said to me *was* accurate, I didn't have the timing quite right, and God was not *There will always be a harvest; it is our job to raise up laborers to bring in the harvest.* going to let me send my students to "war" without first sending them through "boot camp," so to speak. There will always be a harvest; it is our job to raise up laborers to bring in the harvest.

For the next few months, I focused on equipping my students, making sure they were spiritually healthy and had the knowledge and tools that they needed. It is not solely the job of the youth pastor to lead everyone to Christ. We must teach our students that they have a role to play, and encourage them to take responsibility for leading their friends to Christ. Our job is to show them how. I realized that I couldn't expect my students to disciple others if they weren't first discipled themselves, and I have learned that you cannot assume that every student is discipled, even if they love Jesus and attend church faithfully. And besides, there is always more for *all* of us to learn.

God began to encounter my students in a powerful way during the altar time at the end of our youth services. During this time, He placed a passion inside of them for the lost. We as youth pastors can preach "reach the lost" until we are blue in the face, but only God can ignite passion in the hearts of our students.

During the following spring semester, we started four Campus Clubs. In the same way that senior pastors plant church campuses, we as youth pastors plant Bible clubs on school campuses. Our students

Our students don't need to journey overseas to be a missionary; all they need to do is put on a backpack and go to school.

don't need to journey overseas to be a missionary; all they need to do is put on a backpack and go to school. They are surrounded by lost, hurting, and broken students that need a Savior. And they need *your* help as their youth pastor if they are going to launch successful clubs. Never leave them to handle the sometimes-challenging process entirely on their own.

Shifting My Perspective: I have been a full-time youth pastor for seven years. I used to think that success in youth ministry was the number of students I ran on Wednesday night. I got caught in the trap of comparing my youth ministry to others, and I was solely focused on raw numbers.

All of that changed when I met Joel Stockstill, a youth pastor from Bethany World Prayer Center in Baton Rouge, Louisiana. I saw the impact that his ministry was making on their city. He is currently in nearly three dozen schools, reaching over 3,000 students weekly. He sends out students from his ministry and interns enrolled in Bethany's ministry school to impact nearly every school in Baton Rouge.

The way I measure success in youth ministry has changed dramatically since I met Joel. Success is not just about what happens on Wednesday night, but what happens throughout the week. It's about raising up students in your youth group to minister to other students outside of the church setting. After all, Jesus did most of His ministry outside of the four walls of a church; should it be any different for us? It's great to have a place where we can all come together, but at some point, we must step outside of our churches and offices. We must physically go to the places in our community that we typically talk about reaching — from the comfort and safety of our offices.

I view Campus Clubs as where most of our ministry takes place. The schools are where the harvest is! We use Wednesday nights as a celebration night to recap what has happened throughout the week. I allow students that are leading clubs to share stories of salvations and healings, and showcase their club to our youth ministry. I feel that doing this highlights the mission that our ministry exists for. It also exhorts students who are reaching their schools, while encouraging and motivating other students to start a club on their campus.

Campus Clubs are where most of our ministry takes place.

True success is not just me leading ten students to Christ; It's when my students lead ten students to Christ. If I can duplicate myself by raising up students who have a passion for God and want to be used to reach their campus, our youth ministry will change from simply "addition" to "multiplication." This is why Jesus spent time with twelve disciples. He poured into them on a daily basis and then sent them to reach the world.

Youth ministry cannot revolve around a youth pastor, but around a passion for Jesus. We are all in different seasons. Some of us pastor youth groups for two years, some for six years, and others for twenty years. The point is, sooner or later your season will shift and change. God will eventually move you or call you to something or someplace different.

As a youth pastor, if I leave a youth ministry without raising up disciples to continue reaching the schools in the community, I have failed. I have to focus on developing and duplicating disciples and laborers at each church where I serve as youth pastor. I cannot put this off, because I never know when my season will change and I'll be moved someplace else.

Seeing What Others Cannot See: As a youth pastor, I love helping students discover their hidden potential. Part of discipling students is bringing them out of their box and pushing them past their comfort zone. The ability to see hidden potential inside of students is crucial.

I remember one junior high girl in my youth ministry who was very shy and introverted. I encouraged her to start a Campus Club at her school. She went home and prayed about it before coming back to me with a "yes." During the course of that school year, her club grew from the ground up to a total of forty students. She had posters for her club all over the school and her principal was even announcing it to the entire student body over the intercom. She is now a freshman and has started another club at her high school. But before leaving, she raised up some younger students to take over the club she had started in junior high school.

All of this happened because I saw something in her that she did not see in herself. I love how throughout the Scriptures, God used people that everyone else overlooked. Gideon was from the smallest tribe of Israel and David was the youngest of all his brothers. Even Jesus chose men who had ordinary jobs to be His disciples. Everyone has gold inside of them; sometimes you just have to dig through the dirt in order to find it.

Since I've been in youth ministry, my students have started nearly two dozen Campus Clubs. Most of those students would never have done it had they not had someone who pushed and encouraged them along the way. They needed me to believe in them, encourage them, and love them, regardless of whether they succeeded or failed.

You may have heard the old saying, *"People won't care how much you know until they know how much you care."* I believe this to be true. Let your students know how much you care for them, and it will open up the door for them to accomplish great things that they never imagined they could accomplish.

I was at Chick-fil-A recently with my wife and our two-year-old daughter, Avery. Avery really wanted to go play inside the play-place but was afraid to go by herself. So she looked up at me with her big, blue eyes and asked, "You go with me?"

As a dad, that melted my heart. "Of course I'll go with you," I replied.

We entered the play-place together, went up the stairs, through the tunnels, and down the slide. We did it over and over again. Avery had the courage to do something that she would never have done on her own had I not been with her. Last week, we returned to Chick-fil-A. This time, Avery had the courage to run and play all by herself, while I stood and watched.

I know this is a silly story, but it draws a lot of parallels to youth ministry. You see, many times students—regardless of how old they may be—are too afraid to start a club on their own. Honestly, it's scary enough for them to talk to their peers about Jesus in today's culture, and leading a club takes things to a whole new level. But if the student knows they are not doing this alone, that you will be there to help them, it is amazing how willing they will be to start a club at their school.

> *"Grace is the ability to see what someone can still become even though they've counted themselves out."*
> -Matthew Barnett

Over time, the students you might need to help in the beginning will develop the courage to lead the club on their own. They will join together with other students and take ownership of it. Of course, it is still healthy for you or other adults (such as parents) to be involved, but the club will eventually reach that point where the students are initiating more than the adults. That is how it should be, but it may not be like that in the beginning. They will need you to guide them through the early stages before they have the courage to take control of things themselves.

My desire is that you would be able to see your students the way that God sees them. Past the immaturities, flaws, and shortcomings; see through the eyes of the Apostle Paul, who wrote, *"I can do all things through Him who strengthens me"* (Philippians 4:13). The students in your youth ministry are world changers; they just don't know it yet! But if you can see it, they can achieve it.

Dreaming vs. Doing: During one season of my life, I served as a youth pastor in Arkansas. The town was small and the poverty level was high. The only thing for students to do on Friday nights was hang out at Wal-Mart. It was not uncommon for me to receive texts from students saying something to the extent of, "Want to hang out? I'm in the toy aisle at Wal-Mart."

In one meeting with our youth sponsors, I told them that if our competition for getting students in the doors was Wal-Mart, we had no excuse not to reach every student in town. We only had twenty students at the time, but I knew that God could—and wanted to—do huge things through them. So, I started talking to my twenty students about Campus Clubs. Within six weeks, they had planted six clubs. One of those clubs had over seventy students in attendance after only two weeks.

It's so easy as youth pastors to just sit back and dream, without ever actually doing anything. Don't get me wrong, dreaming is great, but how many of our dreams stay in our minds forever? How many of our dreams do we never actually attempt because we let fear or a limited view of God hold us back?

Sometimes it is necessary to wait on God before going after a dream, but I think that He is often the one waiting on us. Through prayer, He will make the timing obvious. But if you're afraid, it's probably a sign that you need to get your team and go after that dream.

"Figure out what you're most afraid of today, then ask God for the courage to decide that you aren't afraid anymore." -Bob Goff

As youth pastors, we need to constantly be throwing out the dream of starting a Campus Club to our students. I tell my students on a regular basis that they do not have to wait until after they have graduated Bible college to begin their ministry. They don't have to have read the entire Bible, memorized a certain number of verses, or mastered the art of communication. Once they have asked Jesus into their heart, there is no waiting period before God can use them to reach someone else.

Once students catch the vision that they are already qualified to do big things for God, it ignites something on the inside of them to go after it. Remind your students that God does not just call those who are able, but He takes those who are willing and makes them able.

 ⋘ ⋙

Let's Get Practical: Now that I have given you the heart and soul for Campus Clubs, I want to leave you with a few practical steps so that you can go out and actually do it. When I have a student come to me wanting to start a club, these are the action steps I give them:

1)   Find a teacher who will let you use their classroom to meet in.

2)   Set up a meeting with your principal and ask their permission to start a club. Do your homework before doing this; i.e. "I want to start a club that will meet at *this* time in *this* classroom, and *this* is what we will talk about." This lets the principal know that you are serious and not just goofing off.

3)   Find another student at your school who you can partner with. Don't try to do it alone!

I always tell my students that I will clear my schedule to attend a meeting with them and their principal so they don't have to go into their office alone. This is key! You cannot tell your students to start a club on Wednesday night and then be unavailable to help on Thursday morning.

Plan Ahead: Campus Clubs generally meet weekly. They can meet more frequently or plan events outside of school, of course, but a weekly meeting is a good place to start. When a new semester starts, I like to plan the meetings in advance for at least the first month. All the clubs that my students lead generally follow the same schedule during this time so that we are all on the same page.

Week 1: We kick off the month by playing an *I Am Second* video at each of our clubs. It is the same video at each club, and there are small group discussion questions afterwards. I have found that this is a great tool to get the students attention and open a dialogue. I Am Second is a ministry that films videos of people (usually well-known) sharing their stories of how Jesus changed their life. The videos can be viewed at no charge on their website.

Week 2: The second week of the month is usually when I go around and speak at each of the clubs. That way they know who I am (as the local youth pastor), and I have a chance to invite them to my youth ministry on Wednesday night. If I am bringing in a guest speaker, I will usually have them come speak to the club before they speak at my church on Wednesday night. I have found that this usually draws more students to my youth ministry and connects them to the church.

Week 3: The third week of the month is when the leader of the club will speak. I help him or her pre-write a message and go over how to present it so they are set up for success. One of the biggest roadblocks in the minds of students when it comes to starting a club is fear of public speaking. With our schedule, the student leading the club only has to speak once a month and they receive help with their communication skills. This gives them peace of mind, knowing that they will not be expected to speak every week.

Week 4: The fourth week of the month, I encourage each club to find a special project or way to serve the school. For instance, during the winter months we usually do a coat drive. One week, we collected fruit to give to a teacher in the school. There are countless ways that you can serve your school. This is key because it lets the school know that your club is for them and there to serve them.

I try to attend as many club meetings as possible, but I have found that I cannot be at every single one. That is why I recommend putting together a team of young adults to help with the clubs. I try to designate at least one young adult per club to be there to help and support the student leaders in any way that they can. If the students know that someone is there to help them, it gives them a new level of confidence.

I also encourage every student that leads a club to take attendance of their meetings. I believe that youth ministry size consists of how many people are being impacted on a weekly basis, not just a nightly basis. I have students in my youth ministry that have never attended a

Take a few minutes to watch some of the videos at IAmSecond.com

Wednesday night service—because our youth ministry is bigger than just a Wednesday night service.

Give it Time: There was a junior high student named Tyler who started a club at his school. I attended his club and brought doughnuts every week for an entire year. For the first three months, very few people attended. It was just myself, Tyler, and two of his friends. It was honestly getting quite discouraging. I even remember talking with my dad about the idea of shutting down the club, because it seemed to be making zero progress. My dad countered by telling me to just be faithful and see what God would do.

It was literally only a matter of weeks before Tyler's club grew from four students to fifty. The classroom that they met in became so full that it could barely contain all of the students who wanted to attend.

When one of your students starts a Campus Club, make sure they know (and you know) that it may take some time before they see the growth and results. I have seen clubs explode to over two hundred in weeks, while others stayed at three or four for months. I don't know why this happens, but I do know that God will take care of the growth if we simply stay faithful.

I planted, Apollos watered, but God was causing the growth. So then neither the one who plants nor the one who waters is anything, but God who causes the growth. Now he who plants and he who waters are one; but each will receive his own reward according to his own labor. - 1 Corinthians 3:6-8

I love this passage of Scripture because it states that while we all have different tasks, God is the one who produces the harvest. It is our job to plant the clubs, or to "water" existing clubs, but God is the one who will take care of the growth.

Though it was originally released in 1989, I believe the message in the movie *Field of Dreams* that says, *"If you build it, they will come"* is relevant for ministry today. I don't know if they intended for pastors to draw spiritual principles from the movie when they made it, but they are there regardless. I believe that if we love students, they will come. If we create a safe place where they can learn about God, ask questions, and be loved unconditionally, they will come.

Campus Clubs grow when you love God and love students. Even the Bible illustrates this. At one point during His ministry, the Pharisees approached Jesus and asked Him to name the greatest commandment in all of Scripture.

Jesus responded and told them that they should love God with all of their hearts, souls, and minds. At that point, I'm sure they thought they had it all together, but then He went on to say that there was a second equally important commandment that could not be separated from the first; He told them that they had to love their neighbors and treat them the same way they treated themselves.[1]

God will take care of the growth if we simply stay faithful.

I know, right? But Jesus didn't stop there. He went on to say that the entire Bible is essentially summed up in loving God and loving people. This is who we are called to be.

Endnotes

1) Matthew 22:34-39

Chapter Eleven

BASICS OF SCHOOL ASSEMBLIES

Jaroy Carpenter

As a student growing up in a small West Texas town, I always had great admiration for school assembly speakers. The way they would capture our attention and motivate us to come together was inspiring. I remember one speaker in particular who was great at expressing himself both verbally and physically. Listening to him speak made me want to motivate students as he did one day.

As I grew older, God placed a desire in my heart to become an athletic trainer, teaching physical education, health, and sports medicine in public schools. After high school, I attended East Texas State University, now Texas A&M University—Commerce. During that time, I worked at numerous youth camps. Upon graduating, I became the athletic trainer at a high school in a nearby city. I then worked the same job at another school in North Dallas, before serving as a youth pastor for ten years at a church in Irving.

During my time as a youth pastor, I began to desire putting together school assembly presentations once again. By this point, I had worked with the North Texas District of the Assemblies of God for many years, providing activities, recreation, and programming for youth camps. These years of working camps helped me refine my skills in communicating to large crowds of teenagers, and my background in teaching and youth ministry helped prepare me to go back into public schools to give presentations on choices, decisions, responsibilities, and relationships. My teaching background specifically enabled me to effectively communicate values and principles without directly mentioning God, and school administrators were also more trusting because my background was in education as well as ministry.

In preparation for my first school assembly, I asked three of my friends who had been presenting school assemblies for years to give me their advice. The first of these friends suggested that I first gather as much information as possible. In preparing for his presentation, he had studied a stack of books and carefully crafted his message. When speaking, he wouldn't waver one word from what he had planned to say. His presentation was extremely effective and I wanted to follow after him in this area.

The second friend I talked to told me to watch out for interruptions. He said that as an assembly speaker, you must know where the crowd is and how to work with them. The use of emotional, evocative, or humorous stories can help you connect with your audience and hold their attention. You must also have an alternative plan in case the

"We must dream, because we were made in the image of Him who sees things that are not and wills them to be." -D.L. Moody

presentation doesn't unfold the way you want it to. You have to have something to fall back on if it becomes apparent that your audience is bored and disconnected. This friend also told me about what he called the "float and sting principle." This is where the speaker "floats" on a topic, adding color and understanding to the point, and then "stings," moving on to the next point quickly enough that the audience won't lose focus.

The third of my friends gave me a much more flexible mode. He told me that each of his assemblies always concluded with the same result, but he never traveled the same path to get there.

Taking what I learned from my three friends, I formed a model school assembly presentation. I then began to travel with Dawson McAllister, presenting assemblies in schools across the country. This stage of my life enabled me to further develop and refine my communication skills.

It can be embarrassing now to go back and watch some of the video footage of myself speaking from those early days, but I have been able to learn from it. I often tell people that I have made enough mistakes in my life that I have learned how to do stuff right. Because I haven't been afraid to fail, I've been able to learn how to succeed.

In recent years, I have developed a school assembly presentation called the Gameday Challenge. It utilizes camp games which can be played in competition form among the different classes. After about twenty minutes of games, the students will gather and I will talk to them about living a life of integrity. I often enlist the help of student athletes from a local Christian university to help out with these activities. They will run the games and talk with the students about their experiences growing up, and explain how they learned to live lives of integrity.

This method has been successful as a unique way of reaching students by holding a "play day." This grabs their attention and acts as a backdrop to communicate the character of God without directly mentioning His name. Often, I will see students brought to tears as we speak. They feel the anointing and see that there is something different about us. On multiple occasions, a student has come up to me after an assembly and told me that they were seriously considering and even making plans to commit suicide, but the message of hope and perseverance caused them to change their mind. It is truly amazing to see the impact that a simple message can have on these students' lives.

Administrators may be reluctant to invite someone to do a school assembly, because they don't understand how one presenter can connect with a crowd of more than a thousand students when their teachers have trouble communicating with a group of thirty. I have found that it is the empowerment of the Holy Spirit, working through the speaker, that allows him or her to do this. You have to be confident that God has given you a message that will impact the hearts and lives of the students in a unique way.

Because I haven't been afraid to fail, I've been able to learn how to succeed.

Speaking at schools is one of the most challenging, but also one of the most rewarding things I have ever done. They only happen when you put in a lot of hard work, but it is well worth it. Effectively communicating to large groups of teenagers requires careful planning and execution. In order to hold their attention, what you are saying must be more important to them than what they want to whisper to each other.

The first step when you are coordinating a school assembly outreach is to network with other leaders in the community. Involve as many leaders as possible in the process. While one can simply go into a school, give a presentation, and then leave, I have found it is much more effective when the assembly is part of a strategic community outreach.

Once you have dropped the bug in several ears regarding a community outreach involving the schools, schedule a meeting with all of the leaders to discuss the vision and logistics. It is important that you define the goal and purpose of the outreach. This will come as you seek God's guidance and direction through prayer.

The second step is to create a list of schools in the community that you are looking to reach. Once this list is compiled, you can begin contacting the school administrators and present the possibility of doing a school assembly. I have found that the best way to do this is to personally visit the school and give an information packet to a specific person. It is helpful if you already have a relationship of some sort with the school. Once you have approached the school administrators, it is crucial that you keep in touch with them. Don't be afraid to follow up!

You will also want to be talking with the person you want to speak at the school assembly during this process. Have one or two back-up speakers available if your first choice cannot do the assembly on a date that the school requires. Also, remember that well-known (and even not-so-well-known) speakers usually book their events *months* in advance.

The third step is to make a "presentation agreement" with the school. This agreement is a contract with the school and provides a tangible expression of the school's commitment to sponsor the assembly and a commitment on your part to provide a speaker on the determined date. Once it is filled out, the contract should be sent to the speaker to make sure everyone is on the same page.

Assemblies are more effective when they are part of a strategic community outreach.

After the presentation agreement is signed, the fourth step is raising funds for the assembly. Primary expenses will include speaker fees and equipment costs, as well as travel, lodging, and food for the speaker and your team.

There are a number of ways in which funds can be secured for an assembly. You can talk to the owners and managers of local businesses to see if they would be interested in providing support. Contact the school's Parent-Teacher Association to see if they can contribute monetarily. Do not be afraid to ask the school itself to participate in raising funds. Most schools have anti-drug and alcohol funds which can go towards the cost of the assembly.

You can even apply for state grants through the Department of Education or Human Services. Coordinating the assembly with an anti-substance abuse initiative will provide a greater chance of obtaining grants. This process can take several months, so if you are going to apply for a grant, make sure to do so well in advance.

After a school assembly, holding a "comeback rally" on the night of the event can be a very helpful ministry tool. An important part of organizing a comeback rally is getting students to come to it. The most basic tools to draw back students are free food and giveaways. If you are going to do this, you will need to be sure to factor in the extra expense into the budget for the assembly.

In many cases, local businesses will be willing to sponsor these events by providing giveaways. Some of the most popular options are trendy tech items such as an iPod or iPad. Insurance policies can also be purchased to cover big-ticket items such as a large sum of money or a car that can be won by an "all-or-nothing" challenge such as attempting to make a half-court basketball shot.

If you really want to go all-out, creating a carnival-like atmosphere with food, games, and fun will draw in even larger crowds. Inflatables and portable zip lines are very popular. Contests are a big draw. Think dance contest, car pulling contest, or a battle of the bands. Another creative way to bring students in is to attempt some sort of Guinness world record.

The more elements you have at your comeback rally, the more you can "hype" it up during the daytime school assembly. Be sure to check with school administrators to make sure it is okay to mention the night event during the daytime event. Not all schools will allow this, which is why you want to partner with leaders in the community. Youth pastors can encourage their students who attend the school to spread the word amongst their classmates. Many well-attended comeback rallies are the results of these grassroots efforts.

The location of the rally can be an important factor in the effectiveness of the event. Most schools will allow you to rent their parking lots, gymnasiums or auditoriums, or you can find another neutral location. Regardless of where you hold the comeback rally, be sure to get multiple churches and youth ministries involved.

Youth groups can play a role in the preparation process and advertising for the comeback rally. If students do not get involved in promoting the rally, it will most likely not be a success. Utilize T-shirts, handouts, and flyers to help students promote the event. The goal is to create excitement and buzz in the community. This is especially easy if the schools you are reaching are located in a small community.

Well-attended comeback rallies are the results of grassroots efforts.

Start promoting the rally well in advance. Once the date is confirmed with the school, begin promoting! This should give you six to eight weeks for youth pastors to cast the vision to their students and get them the tools they need to promote the rally. Remember that the rally is a community *event*, not just another sermon.

Once the day of the assembly arrives, the order of service for a comeback rally is very important. You might start with thirty minutes to an hour of games, food, and fun. After this, the service will begin. It is nice to have a slideshow of pictures from the day's activities running while the students come in. This is an extra element that creates a personal touch, but it is not crucial. This is also a good place to include your "thank you's" to your corporate sponsors.

Begin the service by playing a video (Just pick something!), and then have the emcee kick things off with a game. This game could be a competition between the sections in the auditorium with the winners receiving coupons to a local restaurant. Follow this with an individual game or a drawing for the larger prizes.

If students do not get involved in promoting the rally, it will most likely not be a success.

Some have found that it is better to have the drawing for the big-ticket items after the altar call, but this is totally up to you. It is important to note that doing this can make the rally appear to be a bait-and-switch to some. If you choose to give away the larger items before the actual sermon, it is usually better for the overall mood and flow of events. There will probably be some students that leave after the drawing, and you will have to be okay with this. Remember, Jesus never forced anyone to follow Him. It has to be *their* choice.

After the giveaways, you can move right into the service, or you can set the mood by having a band play. They can kick things off with a popular cover song, and then perhaps move into a worship set with one or two songs. It should be noted that in communities outside of the Bible belt, it might be a good idea to just stick to cover songs and not do a worship set at all. Or another possibility would be to move the worship set to the end during and after the altar call.

The service should feature the same speaker from the daytime assemblies speaking at the night rally. If you are allowed to announce the night rally during the day, you can encourage students to come back to hear as the speaker shares more of his or her story.

The speaker cannot talk about God or faith during the daytime events, but they can at the night rally, even if you are still meeting in the school, because school is out of session and you are renting the facility. The students who are present have come to this event by their own choice, versus the daytime assemblies that are attended by the entire student body. It is important that these boundaries be respected in order to maintain a good relationship with school administrators.

The speaker's sermon should be around twenty-five minutes in length and should be evangelistic in nature. Personal stories and simplicity are key elements. Don't confuse students with a theological monologue of the entire New Testament. This will happen later as they grow in their relationship with Christ.

The altar call is the climax of the evening. Preparations should be made so that the altar call *Jesus never forced* can affect lasting change and not just *anyone to follow Him.* momentary emotional decisions. Having response cards, Bibles, and discipleship material to distribute, trained altar workers, and a follow-up plan are all important elements.

After the rally concludes, you should have a debriefing meeting with all of the leaders who were involved. This is the time to evaluate the ways in which the rally was effective, as well as the areas that can be improved upon in the future.

I recall one occasion where I was asked to speak at a school assembly outreach in a small Montana town. Mormons and Jehovah's Witnesses had a strong influence in the region, and the town itself seemed to have a cloud of depression hanging over it. Many students had recently committed suicide.

As I was leaving Texas, I was informed that there was a great controversy surrounding my coming to the town. The Mormons and Jehovah's Witnesses did not want someone who happened to be a Christian to hold assemblies in the local schools.

One member of the school board had even taken a quote from my website in which I described my desire to see students won to Christ and used it to suggest I would be preaching about Christianity in the assemblies. This was not true, as I have always done deity-free presentations when speaking in public schools.

Respect boundaries in order to maintain a good relationship with the school.

The man on the school board got the district attorney involved, and I was told that if the school allowed me to speak, members of the American Civil Liberties Union (ACLU) would get the school shut down. On top of that, a local newspaper began to defame me, further adding to the problem.

However, the Ministerial Alliance was able to secure a theater and local park where I could do my presentation. During that time, I called to mind the words of the Apostle Paul, who said, *"If God is for us, who is against us?"* (Romans 8:31).

After my presentation to the high school students, a local priest approached me and informed me that one hundred years prior, a circuit preacher had been tarred and feathered in that town; ever since it had been extremely difficult for Christian groups to deliver presentations of any kind.

During a night rally, we packed out an auditorium and many gave their hearts to Christ— including a Mormon missionary. But the battle was not over. We ended up bringing a lawsuit against the school board in order to protect the first amendment rights of people who happened to be Christians to speak in the schools. Though the school was granted summary judgment in an appeals court, the case helped to prevent the further restriction of the right to free speech.

As a result of the incident, all of the school board members were either lifted off the board or resigned. On top of that, the

"If you are not ready to face opposition for your obedience to God, you're not ready to be used by God." -Craig Groeschel

district attorney lost the next election to an inexperienced rookie lawyer in a huge upset. I was amazed to see that God had done a great work in spite of the opposition, and we just had to press on through it. Because we took a stand, this Montana community has not been the same ever since.

As I watch this generation, I see a generation that is crying out for help. My life motto in response to this has been the following: *I want to give this generation answers they can trust, a Jesus they can see, and a legacy they can leave.*

I will pour out My Spirit on all mankind; and your sons and daughters will prophesy, your old men will dream dreams, your young men will see visions. - Joel 2:28

I have based much of my ministry over the years upon Joel 2:28. I truly believe that God will pour out his Spirit on this generation, and I believe that school assemblies are a vehicle that God can and is using to accomplish this. I truly believe that school assemblies are a way to go into the "devil's territory" and throw him a curveball.

You can legally go into schools and discuss Kingdom principles without using the name of Jesus, giving students practical instruction on how to live a life of character and integrity through making positive choices and embracing responsibility. This prepares students for success in life and healthy relationships in their futures.

Look among the nations! Observe! Be astonished! Wonder!
Because I am doing something in your days — you would not believe
if you were told. - Habakkuk 1:5

Editor's Note: *There are numerous speakers across the nation*
who have experience and are available to speak at school assemblies.
With a little homework, you should be able to find one that you can
trust. There are also many different approaches to school assemblies.
For example, most assemblies have one speaker, but here in North
Texas we typically do an assembly with three speakers who take
turns speaking in short bursts of no more than ten minutes each. We
do this because we have found that it works best for us. We are not
looking for people to replicate our model unless it works for them.
That being said, there are some churches/youth pastors who will
never do a school assembly. That is okay! We are not so concerned
about how you reach out to students; we just want to encourage you
to reach out to students. Your methods must remain flexible and
should be tweaked or discarded if they are not producing the end
result of students coming to Christ and getting connected with a
local church.

Chapter Twelve

DISCIPLING A COMMUNITY

Steven McKnight

My wife Racheal and I live just outside of Dallas, where I serve as a youth pastor at a thriving church. My city is a mid-sized, lower socio-economic community of 15,000 where the church has the opportunity to serve its surrounding residents. My church happens to be right in the center of it all. The junior high school is only a few blocks from my church and the senior high is a couple of miles away. It's the perfect setting for ministry to happen.

The city is a meeting ground of old and progressive ideas, strong history, and emerging changes. The economic and social challenges the city faces are unique to any I've ever experienced. The opportunity for ministry has been extremely ripe, and it has been an excellent place for "rolling up the sleeves" and immersing ourselves in ministering to young people.

We moved here nearly ten years ago, and have utilized a number of strategies to reach out to the community over the years including block parties, fifth quarters, food programs, hosting kids' day-camps, and going door-to-door to invite people to church.

Three years ago, I began to talk with Kyle Embry about having a Seven Project in my city. He had just started out with Youth Alive at the time and was gearing up to do his very first Seven Project in another city much like mine.

It took nearly a year of meeting with other youth pastors and leaders in my city, taking them out for breakfast and lunch, before we were finally able to get Seven Project scheduled for the fall. We picked October, because it lies between the start of school and everyone getting busy around Thanksgiving and Christmas. Aside from early spring, it's really the only time you can pull off a successful outreach that involves students and the schools.

I was able to get thirteen churches besides my own involved for the outreach, but quickly found out that as the front man, I would have to take the initiative to make the event happen. It was a lot different than the city where I was youth pastor before, where my church and several other churches in town (of varying denominations) would gather together on a regular basis.

The Wednesday in October finally came, and the Youth Alive team descended on my city for the Seven Project. We had character-building assemblies at both the junior and senior high schools, speaking to over 2,000 students at both schools, before heading back to my church to rest before the service that night. We had rented out the performing arts center at the high school and planned a block party in the parking lot for two hours before the service. There was a mechanical bull, several inflatables, free food, and other activities for the kids who came back at night.

That night, over 800 students came back by choice to the openly evangelistic service, which we partnered with FCA to host. I had the privilege of delivering the altar call that night, and we received more than 150 salvation response cards from the students.

Follow-up is the key to any outreach. That is when the ministry *really* happens. Praying with people at the altar is great, but then you have to get to work and get involved in their everyday lives. That is where the local church comes in.

At the altar during Seven Project, we had the students who accepted Christ fill out response cards that were afterwards split up amongst the thirteen churches involved. My church spent the next week following up with the response cards we received through emails and text messages sent to the students, inviting them to a follow-up event in the park the following week.

At this event (which we called 'Seven in the Park'), I teamed up with about half of the youth pastors who had been involved with the initial Seven Project event to host the event in the park. It was more of a "fun day," centered around sports where new converts could build relationships with other Christian students. We served food and had about eighty students attend.

In the wake of Seven Project, we had dozens of kids that began coming to our youth group for the first time, with our weekly attendance jumping from 150 to around 180. But there was a bit of a challenge. The students would come straight from school, meaning there would typically be several dozen junior high students showing up in our church parking at 4:00 on Wednesday afternoons.

"Some evangelism today is obsessed with getting people to make a decision; the apostles were obsessed with making disciples." -Scot McKnight

What do you do when you have dozens of students showing up three hours before service? Some youth pastors would hand them a basketball, or tell them to come back in a couple hours, but we knew we could not waste this opportunity. It would be foolish for us to turn away the people we are trying to reach when *they* are the ones coming to us!

We started out by separating the guys from the girls and utilized the time for small groups. We would take no more than thirty minutes and teach them about Christ, and then feed them before the other students began showing up. Some students wouldn't arrive quite so early, but still well before the service began. We would take those students aside in another even smaller group in order to teach them about Christ as well. In a way, it was like we had a service before the service. Instead of running from 6:00-9:00, our Wednesday nights would run from 4:00-9:00 each week.

Early on, we had the new students fill out questionnaires so we could learn more about them. We wanted to know where every student was before we began discipling them. When the questionnaires came back, we were shocked to discover that almost every one of them reported that they lived with their mom and their dad was either in prison, dead, or they had no idea who he was. I gathered all my leaders together and shared my findings. "This is where these kids are," I said. "We've got to figure out a way to build a bridge to them."

It's nearly impossible to tell others about Jesus if you do not know Him yourself.

We then began to think towards discipleship for these new students. I knew that we could not expect them to go out and reach their schools until they had first been discipled, because it's nearly impossible to tell others about Jesus if you do not know Him yourself. We quickly discovered that many of them did not even know basic things about Jesus and the Christian faith, and we knew they needed at least the basics. I remember at one point asking the students how we are saved. A dead silence filled the room.

Our small groups eventually became known as "Foundation Classes," where we would take eight weeks and talk about what it means to be a Christian and serve the Lord. At the end of the first eight-week cycle, we handed out certificates to the students during our Sunday morning church service, which I had the honor of preaching and presiding over.

After church, each student was invited to bring their families to a free lunch in order to continue the celebration. This was a wonderful opportunity because most of the students who attended the classes had parents who did not attend church, but they came to church on this particular Sunday

There is no "one-size-fits-all" method for discipleship.

because their student was being honored; a few of these parents began attending our church regularly as a result.

A few weeks later, we hosted a baptism day for the students who had completed the classes and wished to be baptized. Then, we began another eight-week cycle of small groups for new believers. Our Foundation Classes were not just a one-time thing, they became a regular part of our Wednesday-night ministry to students from unchurched backgrounds.

There is no "one-size-fits-all" method for discipleship. You must correctly define your culture and understand your environment. You need to know the backgrounds of the kids in your city. Then, you can teach them who Jesus is and connect them to Him.

Rap music is very popular in our community, so one of the discipleship methods I used was to play a Lecrae music video that carried a positive, gospel-centered message and then simply ask them what Lecrae talked about in the song. I would then break it down using Scripture, and discuss how it can apply to our lives. This sounds very simple, but it worked. While I am all for teaching deep theological truths (that some would consider "reserved" for adults) to students, I also realize the power of simplicity. Sometimes all it takes is a simple music video to get the students engaged and the conversation started.

Building a solid foundation in the lives of your students is vital to the health of your youth ministry. If you have students showing up early, take advantage of that time to teach them more about their faith and Savior. It's not wrong to let them play basketball and have fun, and there should always be time for that, but don't be afraid to sit a group of students down for thirty minutes and talk to them about Jesus.

I found that another advantage of the Seven Project was that it empowered active Christian students as well as bringing in from the fringes students who had been observing the gospel message for a while without engaging. My son, Tristan, seems to have a natural spiritual gifting for evangelism. For the past few years, he has befriended several kids at his school and led them to Christ.

I remember one of these students in particular, a young man named Devondre. Tristan brought him over to spend the night a year and a half ago, and one of the first things they did was watch *The Passion of the Christ*.

As I was driving Devondre home the next day, I casually asked what he thought of the movie, and he told me that he had never known that Jesus rose from the dead. His response shocked me. How could a kid raised in the Bible Belt not know that Jesus rose from the dead? Don't even atheists and skeptics know that much?

How could a kid raised in the Bible Belt not know that Jesus rose from the dead?

It wasn't long before Devondre began following Jesus. Within the next year, as freshmen, he, Tristan and two other boys started a Youth Alive Bible club at their senior high school. They would meet on Friday mornings at 7:30 before school.

But getting the club started wasn't easy. The school has cycled through five principals in the last eight years, and this one made the boys jump through a lot of hoops. We prayed, and Tristan gained favor with a teacher who agreed to sponsor the club. It took multiple meetings with the principal, but five months later, the boys received permission to launch their club.

The school is located on the far north side of town, and Devondre lives on the far south side of town. Every Friday, he would wake up extra early in order to ride his bike to school to help co-lead the Bible club. Now that's commitment!

When I found out about this, our youth ministry bought him a new bike, which we presented to him in front of the youth group. Unfortunately, it was stolen a few weeks later, but the police were able to recover it. This is just one example of the countless small miracles that have rippled across our community since we hosted the Seven Project. This outreach was not the sole secret of our success, but it gave us a momentum that we carried over into the months and years that followed.

Since none of the boys who led the Bible club were very good speakers, my wife would write a script for them each week until they got to a place where they could lead the club on their own. This club has not only provided the students with a place to pray and dream over their school, it has helped developed these once shy boys into more confident public speakers. Who would have thought that a teenager who didn't know that Jesus rose from the dead would end up helping lead a Bible club at his school? And it all happened because someone reached out to him.

One of the things I loved most about this club was the diversity of it. This diversity was reflected even in the leadership. Tristan is Caucasian/Hispanic, one of the boys is fully Hispanic, one African-American, and the other is African-American/Caucasian. This is the perfect picture of the diversity of our community, the diversity of the school, and the diversity of the Kingdom of God.

Today, Tristan and his friends still lead the Bible club on Friday mornings at their school. They have not yet met the requirements for a Texas driver's license, but have led many friends to Christ and changed the courses of their lives. Ministries like Youth Alive and events like Seven Project empower students like these to reach their friends for Christ, and can be a momentous force behind their spiritual development.

Chapter Thirteen

WHATEVER IT TAKES

Josh Poage

As I get out of bed each morning, I typically ask myself, "Am I doing everything that I can possibly do to fulfill the call of Jesus, to reach people for Him?" Jesus gave us a perfect example of what we should be doing in our ministries: reaching people. I would even go as far to say that if you are not continuously reaching students, your youth ministry is not a ministry, but a social club for students to hang out in a positive environment. But if we spend any time in the Gospels, studying the teachings of Jesus, we will see that He was all about reaching unbelieving individuals.

There is a great story in the Gospel of Luke, where Jesus was eating dinner at the house of one of the religious leaders of His day. As He was sitting around the table, He began to tell a story, and He talked about a man who invited many people to a banquet.

When the day of the banquet arrived, this man sent his servant out to call all who had been invited, and they all declined with some pretty lame excuses. One of them said he had just purchased a field, and he needed to go look at it. Another said he had just purchased some oxen, and he needed to examine them. Still another said he would rather spend time with his wife. So the servant went back and reported these things to the man, who was not happy. He turned to his servant and said, "Hit the streets, and bring in every poor, crippled, blind, and lame person you can find. I want them to come to my banquet, since those who I first invited refused."

And so the servant did as the man requested, but there was still room at the banquet for many more. The servant reported these things to his master, and his master told him to go stand alongside the highway and compel as many who would come, so that the house might be full.[1]

If this story were told today and related to youth ministry, the man might have told his servant to go to the schools and compel as many as possible to come to the banquet. That is why, as youth pastors, we must teach our students how to "be Jesus" to their school, while at the same time identifying and reaching the students that no one else wants to reach.

Identify and reach the students that no one else wants to reach.

I once heard of a youth pastor whose ministry strategy was to reach the popular kids, because if you get them to come to church, they will bring their friends and followers. While this may work, it should never be our chief strategy. All this does is excuse the youth pastor from having to do the work necessary to reach students. And it excludes the students that need someone to reach out to them the most.

If you, as a youth pastor, are not involved in some way with the schools in your community, you need to get involved — no matter what the cost. This is crucial. The schools are the "front lines" for your students, so to speak, and they need you there with them to encourage and support them as they work to reach their friends for Christ.

I have found that the youth pastor's presence or absence from the schools will make or break a youth ministry.

I have found that the youth pastor's presence or absence from the schools will make or break a youth ministry.

Seven years ago, I started my first youth pastor job at a church in East Texas. While there, I was involved with four schools in the community. Getting in was not always easy, but I persisted, knowing that nothing is impossible with God.[2]

My presence in the schools helped encourage my students, stirring them towards becoming "missionaries" to their schools. Over time, my youth ministry experienced consistent and sustained growth, which I believe was due to our presence in the schools.

There was one girl in particular who got involved with my youth group because she was interested in our Fine Arts program, and she wanted to watch her friends perform. Somewhere along the line, she gave her life to Jesus and was sparked with a passion to reach her school. I told her that if she would do the groundwork, I would assist her in any way that I could.

It wasn't long before she started a Bible club in her school, which met each Friday at 7:00 am. I would bring in a sound system and some items to use as giveaways, and we would have a brief time of worship, a message, and prayer. After only three months of meeting, the club had between 100-150 students attending regularly, from all sorts of denominational backgrounds, as well as those who were unchurched. God was moving in the school and it was a beautiful thing to be involved with.

As students in the schools were beginning to commit their lives to Jesus, I began to disciple them, or at least get them plugged into a church where they could grow in their relationship with Him. I realized that if I was going to convince my students to be like Jesus at their schools, I had to be right there with them setting an example with my actions that backed up my words.

I began asking myself, "What would Jesus do at the school campus?" All of my thoughts pointed back to one thing: He would serve. He would help people in any and every way that He could.

I began my "service experiment" in the cafeteria. For one month, I helped the cafeteria workers by wiping down tables, taking out the trash, and helping clean up when lunch was finished. This absolutely shocked them, and gave me the opportunity to minister to them and other school staff as well. By serving others, I was able to give them a true picture of what Jesus is like, while at the same time setting an example for my students.

By serving others, I was able to give them a true picture of what Jesus is like.

After a month of serving in the cafeteria, I began asking some of my students to help me. I then challenged them to begin serving in other ways, such as after-school tutoring or helping the janitor clean up. I urged them to begin serving as a lifestyle, and I told them that if they were ever lacking in something to do, they could always ask their teachers or principal to point them in the direction of needs on campus.

As a few more months passed, I began to challenge my students in a number of other ways, such as holding Bible studies with their friends during lunch or carrying their Bibles with them *everywhere* for one month, especially to school. Contrary to popular belief, it's completely legal for a student to bring their Bible with them to school, and this is not the same thing as forcing the Gospel on anyone. It's important for youth pastors to make sure students know their rights when it comes to expressing their faith.

It's completely legal for a student to bring their Bible with them to school.

Over time, I began to see a change in the lives of the students I was challenging. They were moving outside of their comfort zones and ministering to those around them at school whenever they got the chance. I would see students serving each other in countless ways. They would even go out of their way to sit with those who were eating lunch alone, and invite these "loners" into their circle of friends.

I think the key to success for me was modeling service to my students, rather than just telling them to serve. This is the same concept Jesus used with the disciples. He "did life" with them, and would show them how to serve and minister, rather than just tell them how to do it and then walk away. You can talk about serving all day long, but if your students see you prefer to be served rather than serve others, they'll just dismiss your words as hypocritical.

For even the Son of Man did not come to be served, but to serve, and to give His life a ransom for many. - Mark 10:45

After five years of being a youth pastor at the church in East Texas, my wife and I decided it was time to move a few hours north, in order to utilize all that we had learned to help a struggling youth ministry rebuild from the ground up.

We arrived in our new city, located on the Texas/Arkansas border, to find a good-sized, predominately Caucasian church, which happened to be located in a predominately African-American neighborhood.

My first action step was to get involved in the schools. After the first week, two of the smaller schools opened their doors to me and another two shut me down. I worked with one of the larger junior high schools that was near my church for two weeks, going back and forth on paperwork before they finally said I could come and eat lunch with my students. And they were serious about me only eating with my students. I was told that I would have to sit alone with just my students at a table outside of the cafeteria.

I thought this was a little ridiculous, but agreed to comply with the school's rules. After two visits, I knew that it was not going to be possible for me to model servanthood to my students if we were not allowed to be anywhere near any of the other students outside of our group.

I met with the principal again, and politely asked if he would allow me access to the cafeteria.

"No," he replied firmly. "The only adults allowed inside the cafeteria are staff members."

I walked out of the school thinking about what he had said. *The only adults allowed inside the cafeteria are staff members.* I realized that, at that point, the only logical thing for me to do was to become a staff member. I had experience in driving buses, so I put in an application and within days, I was hired by the school district as a bus driver.

Becoming a bus driver for the school district was the best thing I have ever done in ministry. I told my pastor that I would use my salary as a youth budget since the church did not provide me with any type of budget and he agreed that this was a good idea. So here I was, driving a bus so that I could eat lunch with my students in the cafeteria at their school, while at the same time raising money to support my youth group.

Getting into the schools and teaching my students how to serve others caused the youth group to grow at an unbelievably fast pace. We were not exactly ready to handle the challenges that came with growing so quickly, let alone the kinds of kids we were bringing into the church.

Becoming a bus driver for the school district was the best thing I have ever done in ministry.

It wasn't long before we purchased a bus and began bussing kids from the neighborhood to church on Wednesday nights. After six months of running the bus route, we were bringing in about seventy kids and an additional seventy teens each week.

I thought that this was great, but I was shocked at how some people in my church responded. As I mentioned before, we were a predominately Caucasian church in a predominately African-American neighborhood. And because the students I was bussing in were mostly from the neighborhood, this meant that our church suddenly became very racially diverse.

Week in and week out, I would hear complaints from a few of the church members about the students I was bringing in to their church. It got to the point where the teachers of the younger students began to openly complain about "Josh's kids." They told me that they did not want me to bus them to church any longer if it meant they would be taking part in their classes. In an attempt to maintain unity within the church, my wife and I started a separate ministry for "Josh's kids" on Thursday nights, with the help of a few of our older students. So we would bus in teenagers on Wednesdays, and younger kids on Thursdays. This meant a huge increase in work, but I knew it was what I had to do. I could not turn away the kids who needed me to reach out to them the most.

Through our efforts of bussing students to church and the ministry that was happening at the schools, our youth ministry grew from seventeen preppy white students to a multi-cultural blend of 160 teens and 150 kids within a span of a year and a half. This was all because I made myself available to my students and showed up at their schools. They began to love and serve the students around them, and God did the rest.

I once heard Matthew Barnett (pastor of Angelus Temple and the Dream Center in Los Angeles) tell a story that stuck with me. He was standing in Echo Park, looking out over his mission field. It was full of drunks, prostitutes, dope heads, and homeless people. As he looked around, he asked God how he was supposed to build a church there, and God told him that if he would reach the people no one wanted, then He would give him the ones that everyone wanted.

When I look at the ministry of Jesus, I see that this was his philosophy as well. He took time to reach the people that no one else wanted to reach. He hung out with tax collectors, lepers, those who were possessed by demons, and even prostitutes.

He (Jesus) also went on to say to the one who had invited Him, "When you give a luncheon or a dinner, do not invite your friends or your brothers or your relatives or rich neighbors, otherwise they may also invite you in return and that will be your repayment. But when you give a reception, invite the poor, the crippled, the lame, the blind, and you will be blessed, since they do not have the means to repay you; for you will be repaid at the resurrection of the righteous." - Luke 14:12-14

I think that too often in youth ministry we bring people in and take them under our wing only when we have a specific purpose for them or think they can help improve our ministry. As you can see from the above passage of Scripture, we should not be looking to minister to people with the mindset of, "How can they help my ministry?" but instead the mindset of, "How can I help *them?*" When this is our mindset, we may not have a huge youth group or a lot of praise from people, but God will reward us. However, when we are ministering to people for selfish reasons, Jesus says that we will actually be the lowest in the Kingdom of Heaven.

I could not turn away the kids who needed me to reach out to them the most.

If you are not intentionally reaching out to the students that no one wants to reach, I would urge you to check your heart and motives. These are the people that Jesus reached. These are the people that we should reach. These are the people that need love the most.

God has not called us to minister in a comfortable environment with only the students we feel comfortable ministering to. If you are not reaching out to the students who have absolutely nothing to offer you in return—emo kids, alternative kids, poor kids, druggies—then I would dare to say that your ministry is more about you than it is about Jesus.

"Leaders move toward what other people run away from." -Darrin Patrick

I believe that if we will step outside of our comfort zones and have those awkward conversations with the students that no one else wants to reach, God will honor us and bless our ministries.

I am a senior pastor now, at a church in a town further south of the town where I was first youth pastor. It's a small town of little more than a thousand people, on the shores of a large lake.

As I look back over the seven years that I was a youth pastor, I can't help but notice that the students who really sell out to God and live passionately for Him are the students who don't have much other than Him, in terms of material possessions. Because God took their nothing and turned it into something, they are able to freely offer the little that they have to Him without reservations.

After my wife and I moved down here, one of the first things I did was try to get involved with the local school. I was quickly informed that only parents or legal guardians of students could enter the school, and I did not qualify. So I went home and made plans to move my brother-in-law (who lived in another town) in with us and I am now his legal guardian.

Even when it seems impossible, there is always a way. You've just got to get creative and find it. And in the mean time, do things that cause the school officials to want to let you in. Show them that you are there to serve them, and that you will be more of a help than a hindrance. And once you gain access to the schools, teach your students to become friends with the students they least desire to become friends with. Those are the students who need to experience the love and hope that Jesus offers the most.

"I try not to look at people as problems to fix or as resources to use, but as eternal souls with dignity."
-Eugene Peterson

Endnotes

1) This story is found in Luke 14

2) Luke 1:37

Chapter Fourteen

A TEACHER'S PERSPECTIVE

Stacey Hendrix

I became a teacher because I wanted to work with young people and make a difference in their lives. I wanted to invest in the future by investing in the next generation.

The classroom content, methodologies, and assessments are all necessary in order to develop students into well-rounded, productive members of society. However, there is another element to teaching that is invaluable: the connections that I make with students and the relationships that I build with them. I have found that when I foster an environment of honesty, trust, integrity, and accountability, my students not only learn information, but they become aware that I care about them personally and their success, which causes them to walk away from my classroom with a growing sense of acceptance. I believe this is one of the best ways to educate young people, whether in a school classroom on Wednesday morning, or a youth room on Wednesday night.

As a teacher and coach at a public high school, I am grateful for youth pastors who take the time to show up on campus and be involved in the lives of students outside of church. While I am able to influence students on a regular basis, encouraging them and speaking into their lives, youth pastors are able to have conversations with students that teachers cannot due to legal restrictions.

I have much more time with the students than a youth pastor does each week at church, and while I am able to speak into their lives to some extent, it is essential to have others on campus to "multiply" the number of adults speaking a positive message into the lives of students. This is where youth pastors and parents come in.

I was walking across the floor of the darkened gym one day after basketball practice, when I began to think about specific ways that youth pastors can come alongside teachers and make a positive impact in the lives of students. Showing up is good, but it is even better if they show up prepared. Presence alone does not make near as much of an impact as an intentional presence.

As you read below, you will hear a few of the ideas I jotted down in my phone of how youth pastors can help teachers reach students.

Idea #1: Build Trust with the Principal and Office Staff

Get all the advice and instruction you can, so you will be wise the rest of your life. - Proverbs 19:20, NLT

If a youth pastor (or any other leader) is going to be on the campus long term, it is essential that they build trust with the principal and the staff in the front office. Some principals are more trusting than others, but if the secretary doesn't like you, good luck getting in to see the principal!

Be intentional to ask about the campus rules and adhere to them. Every school is different. Some schools will require those who want to serve on the campus to fill out a lot of paperwork and be very specific about what they will do on the campus, while others are more laid back. This is why it is important to have an action plan, rather than just showing up.

One of the best ways to get "in the door" of a school is to be connected to a Bible club that meets on campus. Do some research and find out if there is an existing Bible club on campus. You can talk with students in your youth group to find this out. If there is, get your students involved. If not, help them start one. I believe that a previous chapter of this book walks you through that process, so I won't go into detail.

Idea #2: Network with Other Youth Pastors

Plans fail for lack of counsel, but with many advisers they succeed. - Proverbs 15:22, NIV

You can only do so much on your own. But if you network with other youth pastors and leaders in your community, you can accomplish things that are bigger than one person. If you know of someone who is already active and involved on a school campus, consider teaming up with them. That way, if a principal is reluctant to let you on campus, you can bypass a lot of red tape on the grounds that you are serving with an existing group. This group has likely already been checked out, so they should let you through with just a routine background check.

Meet with other leaders on and off campus. Take them to lunch. Get coffee with them. Brainstorm together. Pray together. Work together to reach the school.

Most people prefer to just do their own thing so that they can remain in control. Anytime you work with other people, you will encounter difficulties. You will have disagreements. You will not always get your way. What is important is that you remain committed to one another and work together towards the common goal of reaching a generation of students.

Idea #3: Maintain a Team Concept Between Denominations

I planted the seed in your hearts, and Apollos watered it, but it was God who made it grow. - 1 Corinthians 3:6, NLT

We all have different ideas and approaches when it comes to ministry. Even within denominations, we all have different ideas. But what we can all agree on is the need to reach students with the hope found in Jesus Christ. We can work together without losing our individuality and the things that make us distinctive.

Can you imagine how beautiful it would be to see a dozen or more churches in your community—of varying denominations—all come together to reach out to the school? I have seen this firsthand, and it is amazing how much we can accomplish when we come together. One church may have an ideal facility while another church may have more funds available for outreach. Still another church may have leaders with experience in reaching the schools. The Baptist church may have solid discipleship tools while the Methodist church has students who are eager to start a Bible club, but are in need of resources.

Nothing is accomplished when we argue over doctrine. It only causes further divisions and does nothing to help teachers, the school, or students. God is big enough to allow two churches to view Him in different ways. Rather than asking, "Do they believe what I believe?" ask "Do they love Jesus and want to leave this community in better condition than they found it?" That is the only common ground you need to partner with them. It is time for us to stop fighting and work together.

> *Nothing is accomplished when we argue over doctrine.*

Idea #4: Consistently Attend Bible Clubs on Campus

The precious possession of a man is diligence.
- Proverbs 12:27b

Once a student starts a Bible club on their campus, it is critical that they receive the support of their youth pastor. I serve as the co-sponsor of one of my school's four Bible clubs, *Students for Jesus*. Again, as a teacher, I am only allowed to say so much and I only have time to do so much. This is why I need youth pastors, leaders, and even parents who will come alongside me and provide leadership for these clubs. I understand that you cannot always attend *every* meeting, but make the commitment to be diligent and attend as many as you are able. Even if it doesn't seem like your presence matters, keep showing up and let God strategically position you to make a difference in the lives of students when the time is right.

There are many students who have the passion to start a club, but they are not able to pull it off on their own. They need someone to help develop them into the leader that God has called them to be. They need someone to speak into their life and encourage them when they are discouraged. As a teacher, I am committed to speaking into the lives of as many students as I can, but in a school of nearly two thousand students, there is simply not enough time to do this for every single student.

If you ask any principal what their greatest need is, I think most would tell you that they have a need for mentors who will encourage and inspire their students towards success in academics and in life. Don't go into a school with the attitude that you are going to get as many students to pray to receive Jesus as possible, because if you do, you will likely not be able to connect with any of them. Instead, help them navigate through life, help them with their studies, help them in any area where they are struggling, and point them to Jesus where appropriate.

There are many students who don't necessarily believe in Jesus who will attend a Bible club if another student that they have a relationship with invites them. High school students are at a critical age where they are questioning things and searching for answers, and we need leaders who will be there for them as they process these things. Remember that they are real people with real needs, and getting them to "pray a prayer" and then quickly moving on to the next one will likely not meet those needs.

Keep showing up. God will position you to make a difference when the time is right.

As I stated earlier, Bible clubs serve as your entry point to get into the school. If you show up and say, "I want to volunteer," but have no kids of your own in the school, you probably won't get in right away. But if you have a connection with students who are in a club, they can be your entry point. Being connected to a Bible club is the easiest means of entry into a school.

Idea #5: Promote Student Involvement in Bible Clubs During Youth Service

And let us consider how we may spur one another on toward love and good deeds, not giving up meeting together, as some are in the habit of doing, but encouraging one another – and all the more as you see the Day approaching. - Hebrews 10:24-25, NIV

While it is important for youth pastors to attend Bible clubs, it is equally important that they promote them in their youth services. If you are attending the clubs, but not promoting them, students will not show up because they do not know they exist. Whereas if you talk about them all the time, but don't actually attend them, students will not get excited enough to show up because they can see that you aren't excited enough to show up. It's one thing to *talk* about how excited you are about Bible clubs, and another to prove that you actually believe in their value by attending them. I understand that scheduling may not allow you to be at every club meeting, especially if multiple students from your youth group have started clubs at different schools. However, I would encourage you to be at every club at least once a month, and if for some reason you cannot attend a club, connect the student with another adult leader who can.

If you take the time to focus on Bible clubs and make a big deal about them, it will encourage students to get involved with existing clubs or start their own on their campus. And if you are there for them in the process of launching a club, it will help them to recapture that initial excitement in the times when they are discouraged.

While the goal of Bible clubs is to involve students who do not attend church regularly, it is important that you build a base of students who are already active and involved in church.

Students will not get excited about something if you are not excited about it.

Take a moment and picture what it would look like if the students who have the most vibrant relationships with Jesus were active "on the ground" in a Bible club on their school campus. Then, as students who don't know Jesus are brought in, they will immediately be surrounded by a circle of strong believers. They will be able to make new friends who will be able to answer any questions they have and encourage them to pursue a relationship with Jesus.

It is important to note that youth pastors should train students on how to interact with these students. They must be patient and gracious towards them, sometimes extending one-way love to those who are completely turned off to God or church. We must not be shocked when lost people sin. That is what sinners do — they sin! While we can point out and address destructive behavior, it is important that we do this in a way that does not make the person feel condemned. Jesus wasn't afraid to talk to people about their sin, but He was intentional to simply talk to them and establish a relationship first.

For years, eight youth pastors in my community have met regularly for lunch. Each Wednesday morning before school, I meet with several of the other coaches for a Bible study. On Thursday mornings, I attend the *Students for Jesus* Bible club. There is a Bible study of some sort on campus every morning before school.

After awhile, we realized that we wanted to do something bigger — some sort of outreach — on our campus. Last year, we partnered with Kyle Embry and Youth Alive to bring in a Seven Project, which was a huge success for our community. Seven Project is not the only form of outreach available for schools. In fact, it's not the only type of school assembly program available. It is simply the program that we chose to use for our community.

If you are a teacher wanting to bring in an event like Seven Project, yet have some reservations due to legal ramifications, let me reassure you—it is perfectly legal as long as it is student initiated and student led. It is essential for there to be students, youth pastors, and teachers involved in order to work with school administrators to get an event like Seven Project approved. Teachers know how to diplomatically work with fellow teachers and the administration, and they can serve as advocates to the principal on the students' behalf. If you are a youth pastor, it is important that you connect with the teacher who sponsors the on-campus Bible club, as well as the principal.

Our Seven Project was scheduled for early February. A week before school started the August before, I approached the principal and told him that several students were interested in bringing in a group to do a high-energy, in-your-face assembly. I then sent him, the lead counselor, and the principal of the junior high school an email with more information on the assembly program. I reassured them that the assemblies would contain no mention of Christ and would be catered to fit the needs of the school. They would be able to hand-pick the topics from a wide variety that included bullying, drug and alcohol abuse, sexting, and the power of positive choices.

On that Wednesday morning in February, assemblies were held in the auditorium for the entire student body. That night, a separate rally was held in the gym, with more than 1,300 students in attendance. This high return was due to students networking with other students and inviting them to come back to the openly faith-based event. This was a great opportunity for the Christian students on campus to reach out to other students, and it resulted in a huge response to the altar call with somewhere around 700 students accepting Christ.

Words cannot express how amazing it was to watch the bleachers empty as students flooded the gym floor to pray with the youth pastors and volunteer altar workers from various churches. The very same arena where I push athletes towards their potential physically was transformed into a place of eternal significance. But I think the one of the greatest things that happened that day was the fact that nearly a dozen churches, of varying denominations, all united around one common goal.

At the end of the night, countless students found me, gave me giant hugs, and sincerely thanked me for helping sponsor this outreach. Then, the stories began to roll in like a flood. One student, who had been doubting God's call on her life, committed to surrender everything to Him. An athlete who had been kicked off of his team after receiving numerous warnings genuinely apologized for his actions, without any expectation of being reinstated to the team. A student whose father had been imprisoned and whose brother had been murdered for his decision to become a Christian, made the decision to follow Christ as well.

One student in particular had previously confided in me that another student was bullying her. That night, she told me that this girl had responded to the altar call. But it didn't stop there. The girl found her and apologized to her for the way she had acted. She told her that she didn't deserve to be made fun of, that she only did it because a few onlookers thought it was funny and she liked the attention.

I heard reports of several students who considered themselves atheists, as well as students who adhere to other religions, who attended the night rally. A few of these students even came forward to accept Christ, while the others began to seek out their Christian friends and ask them questions about their faith.

"A supernatural move of God starts with a natural move from people. We have to step out." -Stovall Weems

One student told me that after the outreach, she was more willing to put herself out there and share her faith with others at school, and Seven Project gave her an angle to start conversations without being awkward.

A few months ago, an older woman approached me and said, "My granddaughter's boyfriend gave his heart to Jesus at that Seven Project. We just bought him a Bible."

The stories went on and on.

School released for the summer, and we began a fresh school year in the fall. Thanksgiving came, then Christmas, then the start of a new calendar year. February arrived. One year to date from the first Seven Project. The Youth Alive team arrived with their truck and trailer to do it all over again. That's right, the school loved Seven Project so much that they invited them back a second time!

As I was walking the halls that afternoon, I overheard a student talking to one of the team members. "I'm glad y'all are back," she said. "My friend got saved last year and it was awesome." I continued down the hall, a massive smile making its way across my face, as I knew that this was the reason why I became a teacher in the first place, more than a decade before.

It doesn't matter if you are a student, teacher, pastor, parent, or grandparent; I urge you to be proactive in reaching out to your local schools. Ask God to provide you with opportunities. Ask Him to help you recognize those opportunities. Ask Him to help you step out in faith when they arrive. Find a connection point between your church and the schools, and get involved. If necessary, be that point of connection. You don't have to bring in a Seven Project. You don't have to do anything huge. Sometimes, all it takes to make an impact is simply showing up. You never know, that insignificant pebble you toss into the water may cause a ripple effect that lasts for generations to come.

Chapter Fifteen

FAITH, FOOTBALL AND GROWING UP

Tarah Morris

These words, which I am commanding you today, shall be on your heart. You shall teach them diligently to your sons and shall talk of them when you sit in your house and when you walk by the way and when you lie down and when you rise up.
- Deuteronomy 6:6-7

"Preston Morris, over here, son," my son's football coach yelled as he firmly called him to his side during gym class.

That year, many changes came about in my son's life; he suddenly went from a normal 14-year-old to a leader, not only in school and sports, but also in church. His eighth grade coach placed him at quarterback, his band director placed him at first chair trumpet, his city league coach placed him as the prayer leader before each game, and our pastor placed him as the bass guitarist on the worship team. He was known by his peers for his kindness, hilarious demeanor, and passion to do his "very best" while encouraging others to do so as well.

Meanwhile, back on the ranch, my husband, Jason, and I would sit down each evening and discuss Preston's day, as we do with each of our four children. He would tell us about his accomplishments and/or trials of the day, and I would always say one of two things. *If you want to be on top, you need to always try to do better than yourself. Never try to compete with others, because someone will always be better than you. Or, the minute you have something "in the bag," it will be taken from you.*

He usually dismissed both of these sentiments. In his mind, life couldn't get any better. In eighth and ninth grade he felt as though he was on top of the world. But we adults know every good thing comes to an end, right? And that's why we keep a reserve of these "wise" sayings to throw into our children's heads. And it happened, of course, the chain of events that changed everything: A new head coach. A new quarterback coach. A new kid from the big city who happened to play quarterback.

"Parenting is stewardship. We don't own our kids. We are caring for them, and training them so we can return them to their real Owner." -Ken Blount

As summer progressed, the coach slowly subtracted the number of repetitions Preston threw and increased the number for the new kid. My subtle warning was suddenly coming true before our eyes.

Playing quarterback was who Preston was. Football was what he lived and breathed; what he would spend forty hours a week training for. At times, he even slept with his football. But as all of that began to be stripped away, he suddenly went from a child full of cheer and enthusiasm to a child that was full of *I can't, and it doesn't really matter, anyway, so why even try?*

It was around that time that Jason and I stopped asking how his day had been, because his interpretation of his day just kept getting worse, which in turn led our talks from family discussions into family feuds. I felt that my encouraging him to move forward became pointless and I began to feel trapped. I knew that there was nothing I could do that would make him quarterback again, but that didn't stop my mind from racing. I knew what was about to take place. I had that motherly instinct, but I just wasn't one of "those parents" who went to complain every time my child didn't get what he wanted. I also couldn't help but wonder if maybe Preston *wasn't* trying his best.

The fear of what was about to happen and the doubt of my parenting skills began to set in. I spent that summer depressed for my child and what he was going through; yet, I stayed on my knees praying for God's will to be done, even though I dreaded that first scrimmage—for him and for me.

The day of the first scrimmage, I still got that sick feeling in the pit of my stomach when Preston didn't come out on the field first, even though I knew he wasn't going to. The new kid got the field first to show off his quarterback skills, and we watched as minimal yardage was gained and a team that had once played with the utmost unity fell apart on the field. Then it was Preston's turn. We watched as touchdowns were scored and the crowd cheered. I left that night encouraged, knowing that my son was doing what he had always done, his "very best."

> "Is God sovereign only in the 'good' circumstances of our lives? Is He not also sovereign in the difficult times, the times when our hearts ache with pain?"
> -Jerry Bridges

The next scrimmage we watched as the same thing took place. On the night of the first game, I knew that Preston would not be first-string quarterback that year as the new kid took the field first. The first few non-district games were terrible to watch. Out of frustration, the team was not playing as a team anymore. They were even fighting with their own teammates on the sidelines. And it was unbearable for me to watch as a parent, because my child never got a chance on the field.

I was proud of Preston anyway, because he never lost his zeal for his teammates. I watched as he cheered the new kid on, while the new kid ignored his efforts. However, several parents approached us as we sat in the stands to compliment his integrity. The new kid or the coaches may not have noticed Preston's "very best", but it was noticed by the parents who had watched him from the stands for years.

About five games into the season, the crowd sat in despair as they watched our team lose 33-0. I will never forget this game. Five families even got up and left midway through. As they exited, one of his former coaches looked at me and said, "If Preston is not playing, we are leaving; this is absolutely ridiculous!" Another former coach also came up to me and asked why Preston was not playing, and I couldn't help but break down in tears, because I didn't have an answer for him. I had always appreciated this man, but it was at that moment that I *truly* appreciated him and what he did for my son.

"When you and I get shaken by circumstances, when our lives are turned upside down, what is truest of us will come pouring out." -Brady Boyd

Anger began to overwhelm me as we discussed the details of the game at home later that evening. Before I realized what was happening, we were laughing at how terrible the new kid had played. But Preston would have none of it. He stopped us and began quoting from the book of Proverbs: *"Do not rejoice when your enemy falls, and do not let your heart be glad when he stumbles; or the Lord will see it and be displeased, and turn His anger away from him"* (Proverbs 24:17-18).

At that moment, we all stopped short, completely speechless. Of course, I wouldn't go as far to say the new kid was my son's "enemy." And I wouldn't say that his lack of football skills was a display of God's anger towards him. Regardless, it was clear that God was doing a work in Preston's heart. As I began to collect my thoughts, I was reminded of another Proverb: *"Even children are known by the way they act, whether their conduct is pure, and whether it is right"* (Proverbs 20:11, NLT).

The following Sunday morning, I sat in the pew at church and wept through the entire service. I have no idea what my pastor was preaching about that morning; I just remember being so confused about what my son was dealing with and his attitude and the verse he had quoted in the midst of it. I'm sure my pastor thought his message that morning was stirring my heart, and while I don't remember any of his words, I remember the words God spoke to my spirit like I remember the names of my children. I felt that God was leading me to go talk to and pray with the first and second-string centers and quarterbacks.

I went home that day and wrote down what I felt God wanted me to say to them, word-for-word. I then asked my husband to lunch on Wednesday. We met for lunch, and I told him about what I had written, and that I wasn't exactly comfortable talking to a group of high school boys. So, since he is a youth pastor in our city, I asked him to share it instead. I was certain that he would; he had always done things like this for me in the past, especially since I am extremely shy.

Jason listened carefully until I finished explaining why I wanted him to be the one to talk to the boys. And then his immediate question was, "Did God tell you to do this?"

"Yes," I responded solemnly.

"Then you have to do it. Not me," he replied.

I was furious. I stood up, quickly gathered my things, and walked right out of the restaurant. I knew that God wanted the boys on the football team to hear this message, but I didn't understand why I had to be the one to do it. There were plenty of people who were qualified to minister to young people — my husband being one of them — but I did not feel that I was one of those people.

The next day was Thursday, which is game day for the junior varsity team. I always brought food to Preston and any of the other boys who needed food before the game. As I drove into the high school parking lot, I got that feeling in the pit of my stomach again. It was the same feeling I had felt at church on Sunday. I knew that I had to pray with the boys before the game. I didn't know why God was urging me to do this; I just knew that He was. I thought about Jonah and wondered if a giant fish would emerge from Lake Cherokee and swallow me whole if I tried to run.

As I put my car in park, an overwhelming peace washed over me, and in that moment I knew that God would help me speak the words that I had written down. Preston met me at the car moments later, as usual, but this time I exited the vehicle and told him to go get the other three boys I felt the words were to be spoken to. As he headed back towards the locker room, I was aware that his coach had probably told him to get his food and quickly return. I prayed that he would not insist that I speak to the boys another time when they did not have a game to prepare for.

Preston returned moments later with the other three boys. Much to my surprise, two other boys who simply wanted to tell me hello had come with him, so I welcomed them to hang out and hear what I had to say. Knowing that I only had a few minutes before the coach would wonder why six of his players were hanging out in the parking lot, I quickly gathered them around.

"I am here because, as crazy as it may seem," I paused. "God spoke to me Sunday morning during church, and I feel He wanted me to share a few things with the four of you specifically. I have called each of you out here, because I want to remind you that the rest of your team looks to you all as the leaders; the way you present yourselves to your team affects them. If you have a bad attitude, so will they. If you are kind and loving, they will be also."

I quoted 1 Peter 2:1, and told them that they cannot be successful and play together as a team if they have an issue with another boy on the team. I then turned to the new quarterback—the one who had taken my son's place—and swallowed my pride. I told him that I believed that God is the one who grants favor upon us, and I believed that God had granted him favor in the eyes of the coach.

So get rid of all evil behavior. Be done with all deceit, hypocrisy, jealousy, and all unkind speech. - 1 Peter 2:1, NLT

I went on to quote Hebrews 3:4, and told them that I believed God is the one who built their team. So it didn't really matter who was playing what position, but that everyone came together and worked as a team. To drive my point home, I turned to the centers, and I told them that I had called them along with the quarterbacks, because the quarterbacks cannot be great leaders without great centers. If the center does not get the ball to the quarterback, he cannot get it to the next guy, and the game pretty much ends there.

"Everyone plays an important role on this team," I said, knowing I was speaking to myself as much as I was to them. "Without each one of you, the team as a whole cannot be successful."

For every house is built by someone, but the builder of all things is God. - Hebrews 3:4

Before I left, the seven of us held hands as I prayed over their leadership, skills, and safety. That night, they played the best game they had played so far that season. I can remember the mixed emotions I felt as I sat in the stands. On one hand, I was amazed at how God had used me to bring the team together—and even more amazed that I had actually had the courage to obey His leading. But on the other hand I was still hurting for my son, who had to watch from the sidelines as someone else led the team that he had once led.

That night, my family and I sat in the car outside the field house discussing the game as we waited for Preston. We talked about the highlights, of course, but mainly the disappointments of Preston not playing. While we were conversing, one of the boys who had joined us in prayer earlier that day came and tapped on my car window. As I excitedly rolled the window down, I could see the seriousness on his face as he said, "That's why I love you, Mrs. Morris, because you care about us and our team, not just Preston." Tears immediately welled up in my eyes. "Will you come back next week and pray with us again?" he asked. "I think it helped." A million thoughts began to race through my head, but I quickly told him that I would be glad to. As he walked away, Preston approached the car.

"Good game," I said, forcing a smile. I could tell that he was happy and discouraged at the same time, just as I was. It's times like these when, as a parent, you have no clue what to say to your child. And it's in those moments that God enters and lifts you up.

As Preston got in the car, another boy who had joined us in prayer approached my window. Not knowing his friend had just been there, he grabbed my arm, looked me straight in the eyes, and said, "I love you, Mrs. Morris. Thanks for praying with us. If you want to come back every week, we would like that." And it almost felt as though he were issuing a command rather than asking. That was when I realized God's purpose in connecting me with Preston's teammates. I was glad that I had listened to Him (and Jason), even though I had not wanted to.

By the end of the season, what was once a small prayer group had grown to include the entire team, forcing us to re-locate to a larger part of the parking lot. I am only five feet tall, so some of the boys were jumping on their friend's backs in order to see me standing at the front of the group.

Before the final game of the season, I asked the boys to tell me what changes they had seen in the team over the last few months. They responded and told me that they had matured greatly in a short period of time, that they weren't afraid to pray together anymore, and they were the only team they knew of that prayed before leaving the field house and on the field before the game.

We were somewhat relieved when football season ended and baseball season began, but that feeling didn't last long. After a few evening baseball practices, Preston came home feeling defeated once again. One night, I decided it was time to start asking him about his days again. He told me that every time he had a great practice, the new kid—the same new kid from the football team—would cuss him out, almost as if he was reprimanding Preston for showing higher skills than he. Of course, the ostracizing was much more than just cussing him out. It began to happen on a daily basis in everything that Preston did in and out of sports. I later learned that this had happened during football season as well, even though this kid was involved in the devotions I led; Preston had just kept it to himself, because he knew it would upset me.

Preston never understood what this kid had against him; yet, he was determined to not let him know that it bothered him. As baseball season progressed, the new kid stepped into shortstop— the same position Preston had always played— almost on cue. He also drove himself to become the team's ace pitcher, which just so happened to be Preston's position as well. It seemed as though this kid could not get enough.

By the time the season ended, Preston had become a totally different child than the one I knew. The fire inside of him, the fire that used to drive him to be his "very best," had long since burned out. He became disinterested in anything that had to do with sports. Period. When I tried to talk with him about the changes I had observed, he told me that I didn't understand him anymore.

The summer before his junior year, Preston convinced himself that he did not want to play quarterback anymore and began to focus on free safety. I suppose he figured he had enough of a spark within him to try something new. When the school year started, he even quit band to focus more on football so that he could give it his "very best." The varsity quarterback, a senior, was already locked in place. So, Preston practiced the free safety position all summer, only missing one day due to a baseball game. The new kid was practicing receiver, because he knew he wasn't going to be the team's quarterback either.

By this point, I had gotten over my timidity and began going to all of the practices to watch. I wanted to make sure I knew exactly what was going on so that there would be no confusion between what really happened and Preston's perception of what happened.

It wasn't long before I discovered that the new kid always had a small herd of relatives there watching him play. The more I came to watch the team practice, the more I noticed this family give me unpleasant looks or attempt to casually edge their way within earshot when I had conversations with other parents. I recognized the politics that came into play behind the scenes; that there were certain people I apparently was not "allowed" to talk to.

At the start of the season, once again, this kid started at free safety, the position that Preston had played all summer. I asked myself how this could happen, but quickly realized it was not something that I, or anyone else for that matter, could even begin to figure out. This kid had taken every position that Preston played away from him—in football, in baseball, and now in football a second time. After this, Preston decided to remain on the junior varsity team as quarterback, just to get away from it all. I believe that this was where God wanted him all along, and I took advantage of the opportunity to continue doing devotions for him and his teammates before their games.

Before the first game, the entire team came out for prayer, as if we had picked up right where we left off. I noticed that this team began the season with a greater level of integrity than the previous year, so much so that I knew it was time for some of the boys to step up and become leaders. I began to lay out the opportunities. One of those opportunities was for one of them to lead the closing prayer, instead of me. Another was for one of them to share whatever was on their heart with the group. Each week, a different boy would volunteer to share and pray. The sincerity of their testimonies and prayers amazed me.

At the end of the season, I began to gather my thoughts from the previous two years. There were many miracles that had occurred over the season, as Preston's team won games that they should have lost. There were teams that they won against that the varsity team lost to. As I contemplated where the boys were two years prior and how far they had come, I noticed four key character traits that had been sharpened in their lives:

1. *Courage.* I watched as Christian athletes who had previously feared rejection began to step up and lead their team in prayer.
2. *Respect.* The members of a team who once fought with each other on the sidelines began to treat each other with honor and respect.
3. *Trust.* Some of the boys requested prayer for situations involving their home life, which they had previously kept secret. This instilled a deep sense of compassion among the boys for their teammates.

They began to trust one another. They even began calling me "Mom." One of the boys even told me that I was the only mom he had.

4.   *Generosity.* I watched as the boys would help their opponents to their feet after making a tackle. Other teams regularly complimented them on their kindness and generosity.

I also noticed a determination restored in Preston to lead his teammates. By this point, he was playing the entire game, including quarterback, as well as four other positions. My joy was restored during that year, after months of worry and depression.

"God gives people the exact experiences He wants them to have in order to shape the specific destiny He's designed for them."
-Steve Sammons

I do not understand why life is not fair. I do not understand why good people are sometimes mistreated. I simply do not have all the answers, and I realize I never will.

I could have gone to the school in a fit of rage when my son wasn't playing; I could have demanded answers. To be honest, the thought crossed my mind on more than once occasion. But every time I wanted to display my anger, every time I wanted to get mad at the people who had hurt me and my son, I was reminded of the words the Apostle Paul wrote to the church at Corinth: *"When I was a child, I used to speak like a child, think like a child, reason like a child; when I became a man, I did away with childish things. ... But now faith, hope, love, abide these three; but the greatest of these is love."*[1]

I knew that if I did not show love, I would not be able to show people who Christ is. And if I had not obeyed God and spoken to Preston's teammates that first time, I would have never had the opportunity to lead them in devotions for two seasons. I would have never gotten to know them personally or been able to speak into their lives. Almost every week, there would be one young man who would stop me before I would leave and ask me to pray with him about a situation in his personal life. I will never forget one young man in particular, who asked me to pray for him nearly every week, sometimes through tears.

As January rolled around, after that second season came to an end, several of the churches in town came together for a weekend youth rally. Three of the boys from Preston's football team asked if they could attend with our church, so we took them with us. Words cannot express the joy that I felt when two of the boys gave their lives to the Lord at the end of the rally. It was at that moment that I knew everything my son had gone through had contributed to what God wanted to do in my community.

"I'm thankful that I don't have to have all the answers, because my God has all the answers."
-Marielle Jackson

All three of these boys are still attending our church today. I never did find out any sort of distinct method to minister in the school system, I just followed my motherly instinct and loved Preston's teammates the way I do my own children. After all, "love covers a multitude of sins," right?2

Only give heed to yourself and keep your soul diligently, so that you do not forget the things which your eyes have seen and they do not depart from your heart all the days of your life; but make them known to your sons and your grandsons. - Deuteronomy 4:9

Endnotes

1) 1 Corinthians 13:11, 13

2) 1 Peter 4:8

Chapter Sixteen

HEALTHY THINGS GROW

Jon Catron

Go Claim Some Land: Healthy things grow. This is true regardless of whether we are talking about a beautiful plant that sits gracefully on the windowsill, an adolescent child who outgrows the jeans he received for Christmas by the time Spring Break hits, or a youth ministry in a local church.

In the context of impacting school campuses, there is even a thread of "growth" in the practical strategies and applications. If we truly believe in expanding or "growing" the Kingdom of God, we must focus on growing the influence we have in our communities and the specific regions that God has called us to—and that includes the schools.

Over the past twenty years of serving in youth ministry, I have recognized one thing that continues to be true today: Sustained healthy ministry to the public school is only birthed out of a healthy youth minister who has roots in his community and continues to grow himself and steward his influence.

A couple of years ago, my family bought a piece of land to build a house on. It was not a sprawling ranch for raising livestock or anything, just a couple of acres outside of town. The land had some heavily wooded and overgrown areas that needed quite a bit of attention. There was even a creek running along the back side, though it was not visible from the front of the property when we first purchased it.

The first time my son, Chandler, and I walked the land, we felt like settlers venturing out across the great western plains into places never before seen, even though the property was located just south of Dallas rather than in the middle of nowhere. But on that day, Chandler and I could see things a bit differently than what the present reality was. We began to dream about clearing the brush, cutting down some trees and exposing a beautiful portion of land that our family could enjoy. This has required a great deal of continued work as we clear the land little by little, but it is all driven by the vision of what that area can be.

We have lived in that house for two years now, and the landscape of our property has changed dramatically. We have cleared away the brush and some of the trees and exposed a beautiful tree-lined creek bed. We also built a really cool tree house and firepit for those spontaneous campouts with the kids. There is a quiet and serene place for my hammock. This is where I spend some of my downtime, just listening to God, and the very spot where I am working on this chapter of the book you are reading.

I firmly believe that we, as youth pastors, need to go scout out some land. Just as Chandler and I did that day, I would submit to you that it just might change your perspective of the school campus if you walked the hallways while looking through a different lens, a lens of what the school could look like if there was a godly presence there.

How would the conversations in the hallways change?

What would happen if the teachers knew that lives were being changed in the buildings they entered every morning to go about what would otherwise be a routine job?

What if the community were to support and appreciate all that the teachers did for the students on a level that far outweighed just getting a paycheck?

What if students—not just your students—actually knew who you were and when you were usually on campus?

On that day, we could see things a bit differently than what the present reality was.

What if you formed relationships with other youth pastors in your city and could surprise one of their students at lunch by mentioning, "Oh yeah, I know Pastor Ricky. We had lunch the other day"?

What if the principal was actually your friend and not just the person who provided you with a platform?

You will probably never see any of these things take place unless you commit to a long-term process that grows you and your influence in the community and in the schools.

You are the salt of the earth; but if the salt has become tasteless, how can it be made salty again? It is no longer good for anything, except to be thrown out and trampled under foot by men. You are the light of the world. A city set on a hill cannot be hidden; nor does anyone light a lamp and put it under a basket, but on the lampstand, and it gives light to all who are in the house. Let your light shine before men in such a way that they may see your good works, and glorify your Father who is in heaven. - Matthew 5:13-16

While there are many factors that can prevent you from having a powerful presence on campus, the most important thing for you to understand is that healthy fruit cannot come from an unhealthy tree. Your soul must be healthy and your relationship with God must be healthy in order for the influence that you have to be postive and healthy.

Secondly, your relationship with your family will either limit you or provide a healthy foundation for what God has called your *family* to do. You, your spouse, and your children are called to be salt and light to your community, not you alone. If your ministry to students is centered around your need to build your ego or validate yourself, your presence in the schools will not be a healthy presence, nor will it last very long.

Finally, healthy campus ministry can only be birthed out of a youth minister who has strong relationships with other youth ministers in the community. The work of reaching students is simply too great for any one person—or even one family—to tackle on their own.

Healthy Personal Relationship: You must have a thriving relationship with Christ and stay close to Him if you are going to impact the campus. This seems so simple, and yet in its simplicity rests the power to multiply the witness of Christ in the community.

The Spirit of the Lord God is upon me, because the Lord has anointed me to bring good news to the afflicted; he has sent me to bind up the brokenhearted, to proclaim liberty to captives, and freedom to prisoners; to proclaim the favorable year of the Lord and the day of vengeance of our God; to comfort all who mourn; to grant those who mourn in Zion, giving them a garland instead of ashes, the oil of gladness instead of mourning, the mantle of praise instead of a spirit of fainting. So they will be called oaks of righteousness, the planting of the Lord, that He may be glorified. - Isaiah 61:1-3

I love the way the prophet Isaiah frames our mission to reach this generation of students for Christ. What a mission we have been given! To proclaim the favorable year of the Lord, to comfort those who are hurting and grieving. To help them see their value and walk with them through their times of despair. If this takes place, they will become oaks of righteousness, that God may display His glory through them.

When my son and I were scouting out the land where we would build our house, there were some incredible huge oak trees along the creek bed. They are majestic now, but back then you could barely see them, as vines and brush had overtaken them. As we began to clear away the vines, we realized that some of the oaks had actually died due to parasitic weed-like plants, and they unfortunately had to be cut down. Every year, we have to go through and cut away some of those same vines that have grown back, in order for the towering oaks that remain to thrive.

God has called us to be those oak trees that grow strong and steady over time. In youth ministry, we must understand that if we are to be healthy, there will be times of slow growth and times of pruning. I love the imagery of the oak tree: They might not grow the fastest, but they are some of the strongest trees in the forest. They are the trees that last. I believe that youth ministers should be seen in the same way by our communities. We need to be strong and we need to last, and we will only do that if we are healthy.

Healthy fruit cannot come from an unhealthy tree.

I have seen so many individuals who were called into ministry hit the ground running with great passion and intensity. They experience a level of influence and credibility when starting out in a church and community that helps them feel validated in their call. But over time, the vines begin to grow. They may come in the form of frustration with the slow pace of growth at the church or a lack of openness at the schools, but if we are not careful, depending on God no longer becomes a priority. Either the lack of results causes us to blame God, or we blame our own lack of planning and leadership skills as the reason for our limited success, but either way, God becomes secondary to the growth of our ministries.

The only solution that I have found is to regularly get out the chainsaw, cut away the vines, and start a burn pile. There is an oak tree underneath all of the junk, an oak tree that God truly wants to use to display His splendor. But the reality is, we will never have the impact that God desires us to have unless the foundation of a healthy relationship with Him is present and growing in our lives. It's not about us looking good in the community; it's about God looking good in the community.

Healthy Family Relationship: The next area of a youth minister's life that can affect their influence is the strength of their family. This can be a positive or negative influence. I have witnessed both firsthand on countless occasions. There are so many thoughts I could share on this topic, so I will just touch the surface with a few.

First, before you get married, make sure that your spouse shares your dreams in ministry, family plans, and finances. This does not mean you have to agree on every single thing, but I have seen far too many leaders with visions for their life and ministry that are very different than the dreams of their spouse, and this only leads to trouble. When visions conflict in a marriage, one will prevail and the other will yield, or you will reach a compromise, which causes both visions to be reduced. Your marriage and family are far more important than your ministry, but I believe that if you find the right spouse and manage the balance between marriage and ministry, you can succeed in both arenas without experiencing constant conflict.

In my family, we are all in ministry. I have the privilege of leading youth ministers and students in the North Texas District of the Assemblies of God through our network of more than 500 churches. I love my job, and am continually amazed that I actually get paid to do what I do. My wife, Kim, teaches chemistry at a local high school, which gives her the opportunity to impact the lives of students in an equal — if not greater — way as I do. My three children are all in public school, which enables them each to have a ministry to their peers. Each of us touch lives in different arenas, but we are really *all* in youth ministry.

Of course, the decision to send your kids to public or private school is a decision for each individual family to make. While Kim and I have intentionally chosen to have our kids in public school so that they can make a difference there, this choice does not make us better than parents who elect to send their kids to private school. At the end of the day, you need to do what is best for your family, and you should not feel guilty about sending your kids to private school or even homeschooling them.

Is it scary sending our kids to public school? Yes. Are there things that they are exposed to too soon? Yes. Do we see the influence of pop culture having an affect on our kids? Yes. Do we believe that God is big enough to shield them and use them? Yes; one hundred percent yes.

Honestly, there are times when I hear things on the news about incidents that occur at schools and I get a little scared, as I realize that my entire family is constantly on campus at a public school. But I also realize that God will protect them wherever they are, and for us, the risk is worth the reward of shining our lights in a dark place.

My wife and I believe that God is big enough to shield and use our kids at their public schools.

In John 17, while Jesus is praying to His Father before going to the cross, He mentions that the world has hated his followers because they carry a different spirit—the spirit of the living God. I'm sure some of Jesus' followers wanted to be taken out of the world and go to Heaven, but instead Jesus prayed that they would not be taken out of the world, but protected from the evil one.[1] Just as He taught them to pray, *"Do not lead us into temptation, but deliver us from evil."*[2]

I also love the picture that is painted in Matthew 13, where Jesus is explaining the Parable of the Weeds. He talks about the reality of the wheat and the weeds growing together in the same field, and actually tells them not to remove the wheat or the weeds from the field, but to wait for the harvest. In other words, Jesus is telling us not to remove the "weeds" from among us, because in doing so, we might unintentionally remove what is spiritually healthy along with it. Rather, we should grow where we are planted, even if it is among some weeds. God will sort everything out when the time is right.[3]

As a family, we must maintain a healthy understanding that we are all in ministry together; it is not just Dad's vocation. We don't always get this right, but we do try. There are some seasons when the demands on my time are intense and I am away from home more than I am there. But after those seasons of busyness, I take time to re-insert myself into the family scene at a greater level.

Grow where you are planted, even if it is among some weeds.

As a youth minister, do your students have a greater and more instant connection with you than your spouse or your own children? Most of us would quickly answer "no" to that question. But when was the last time you were engaged in conversation with your family and were interrupted my a ministry-related call or text? Turn your phone off and be present *with* your family!

Where I live, the cell reception is terrible, and I actually love it. It has forced me to learn the art of ignoring my phone. I would encourage you to try this as well. Consider how great it would be to have dinner with your wife without having to Instagram that posed, *Yes, I'm glad all of your ministry friends are aware that you are taking me to dinner* look on her face. Wow, did I really just say that? I guess I need to go apologize to my wife now!

I think there are a lot of youth ministers out there who spend too much time on Facebook or other social networks as a means of escape from the reality of their present circumstances. This can be devastating to a marriage as it often causes their spouses to feel overlooked and neglected.

Now, I am not saying that you should ignore your students or another youth minister or whoever, but you do not *always* have to respond immediately. Consider having certain times of the day when you are unavailable, and let those close to you know when those times are so they do not feel that you are ignoring them.

My point is that you should learn to be *fully* present wherever you are. Just because you are in the same room as your family does not mean that you are spending quality time with them, and this is important in order for your family to be healthy. Your spouse and kids must know that they are more important to you than an event at church or an outreach at a school. I have yet to see a sustained impact in a community birthed out of an unhealthy home environment. Is it really worth it to have greater influence in the community at the cost of losing influence in your own home? Your ministry will only be as strong as your marriage. Fight for it.

Just because you are in the same room as your family does not mean you are spending quality time with them.

Do not be afraid of them; remember the Lord who is great and awesome, and fight for your brothers, your sons, your daughters, your wives and your houses. - Nehemiah 4:14b

Healthy Ministry Relationships: Have you ever seen a forest that only has one tree?

If there had only been one lone tree on our property that day when Chandler and I walked the land, it would not have been nearly as appealing. No matter how big or strong or healthy that tree might be, it needs other trees to provide a setting that compels us to respond in awe.

No matter how talented or anointed you may be, you need other people to minister with you! Jesus demonstrated this in Luke 10 when He sent out the seventy-two to pave the way for His ministry. What's remarkable about this is that Jesus was the Son of God; He did not need any man to prepare the way for His ministry, but He involved them anyway. If Jesus did this, how much more do we need to do it? Jesus sent them out in pairs and they returned with reports of great success and increased influence in the surrounding communities.

As iron sharpens iron, so one person sharpens another.
- Proverbs 27:17, NIV

For youth ministers, there are usually two types of ministry relationships: those inside of your church and those outside of your church. If you want to have a healthy ministry that impacts the community, you had better make sure both of these areas are healthy and growing.

As far as it relates to the relationships within the church, these are very similar to your marriage in an area we have already mentioned. They should begin before you take the job. Make sure that your vision for ministry aligns with that of your senior pastor. Will you have the freedom to be gone from the office and have a presence on the campus? Are you confined to one weekly service or can you use resources to reach out to the school after Friday night football games? All of these things should be discussed in the interview process. It is frustrating to see youth ministers accept a role at a church simply for the position, when they do not share the vision of the pastor or the church. Plus, it doesn't work.

I cannot tell you how many times I have had the following conversation with youth ministers. It always plays out slightly different, but the core message is the same.

"Jon, I have been in this spot for such a long time, almost two years!" (At this point, I try to refrain from snickering.) "It seems like my pastor is not as concerned about growing the church as I am. I have such influence with students and have seen the youth group double in size. I want to grow it more, but it seems like the rest of the church is keeping us down. I'm not sure my pastor has a vision for reaching the community."

And while they never actually say it, what I hear is that they think they could do a better job than their pastor at leading the church, and when you start thinking thoughts like this, you are in a very dangerous place.

Something I also noticed from Luke 10 is that Jesus instructed those who he sent out to remain in the same house, and further commanded them not to jump around from house to house. The modern translation of this is obvious: If you get frustrated, don't leave one church and youth ministry for another where the grass appears to be greener. Sometimes frustration is just an opportunity to trust God more, or perhaps God is trying to get your attention about something. Whatever it is, work through your frustration with God, but don't jump ship unless you feel that it is truly time to transition. Most often when you're frustrated, it's *you* that needs to change, rather than your circumstances.

My prayer for a youth minister experiencing tension with their senior pastor is that God would allow them to see the church and community through His eyes, as well as the eyes of their pastor. The pastor's role is to make sure the entire church remains healthy, and sometimes that entails pruning branches of one of the larger trees to allow another to grow.

Please do not misunderstand me. I firmly believe that you should use every amount of talent and skill that the Lord has blessed you with to grow the student ministry that you are responsible for. But of even greater importance is that you have a healthy relationship with your pastor that allows you to help him with the entire landscape of ministry that you are both called to steward. That mutually-driven relationship will help you increase your personal influence at the church and the school.

Going back to the land, I would like to point out that the fastest growing plant that produces the most visible change over the shortest period of time are the vines—the very vines that must be removed for the majestic oaks to be displayed. It's not that I am against fast growth or a dynamic youth ministry, but I am concerned that some growth in ministry is more of a short-lived vine than an "oak of righteousness" that endures from generation to generation. I want the impact that your church has in a community to last.

Most often when you're frustrated, it's you that needs to change, rather than your circumstances.

I first started out in ministry as a youth minister at a church in Paris, Texas—not France! It was a small town with a lot of potentional, but I found that there was also a lot of religion, which could stifle the growth of God's Kingdom. Fresh out of Bible college and newly married, we were longing for relationships outside of our church. I guess God knew that, because we ended up living in a duplex next door to the Church of Christ youth minister. Reagan and his family were great friends to Kim and I.

On a trip to the local Christian bookstore one day, I met Jackie. She and her husband were youth ministers at another church in town. Kim and I instantly connected with them and developed a friendship that not only helped with our ministry effectiveness in Paris, but has gone far beyond that. Mike and Jackie are two of our closest friends to this day. Our kids are very close to each other as well, and our two families usually spend Christmas Eve together, playing cards. This rich relationship only came about because Kim and I recognized that we needed friends and partners in ministry outside of our local church.

When we moved to another church in Longview, Texas, God provided more opportunities for us to build relationships with other ministers outside of our church. Over the course of the eight years we were in Longview, we formed a network of youth ministers. It began with just a few of us getting together and talking about our churches and ways to reach our city, but it wasn't long before the Longview Youth Ministers Network (LYMN) was established.

It was a diverse group, with youth ministers from Baptist, Methodist, Church of Christ, Assembly of God, and non-denominational churches. The Kingdom of God is not about the denominational name on the sign out front, but about all of us coming together through the common ground of the Cross in order to reach our city.

From LYMN, we decided to make an impact on our city through the schools. It was during that time, when *See You at the Pole* was incredibly popular and had great momentum, that *Polarity* was born. Polarity teamed up with my good friend Jeff Anderson (who at the time was directing Youth Alive North Texas), and after nearly a year of planning, we saw the birth of a movement that touched the nation, from the little-known city of Longview.

Polarity involved a kick-off rally on the Sunday before See You at the Pole and then nightly services in the high school basketball arena including a huge night with giveaways on the night of See You at the Pole.

I'll never forget inviting a little known worship leader from a Baptist church in Waco, Texas to join us for that week. When the crazy-haired David Crowder walked into the gym that day, I had never seen or heard of him. But after spending a week with him and his team reaching students in our high school, I developed a deep respect for him and the ministry that God had given him.

Polarity later became a recurring event for the next several years in Longview and included speakers such as Monty Hipp and musicians such as Jeremy Camp, Switchfoot, and Sam Perry and the Passion worship team. The second year, David Crowder returned and we knew that God was launching something bigger than we could have ever imagined.

Through that process, a dream sparked through that team, which culminated in several pastors and denominational leaders coming to Polarity to see how God was using strategic relationships between ministers and churches to change a city. It was during this time of vision casting that the ministry and heart behind the *Seven Project* was born.

This ministry is now responsible for thousands of students hearing about Jesus and accepting Him as their Savior all across the globe. What is even more incredible and ironic in a sense is that Kyle Embry, the force behind writing this book, currently leads Youth Alive in North Texas, where I get to work alongside him in the same arena that was birthed back in Longview. It is truly amazing how God can use healthy people to accomplish great things.[4]

The Kingdom of God is about all of us coming together.

Each fall, Chandler and I must return to the small forest in our backyard and do some work. It involves pruning, shaping, and burning away the old. It's a lot of work, but each spring the rain comes and those trees bloom and grow because of the ways we care for them.

My prayer for you is that you might see your influence in the schools and community in the same way. That influence is only experienced when you cultivate healthy relationships in ministry, with those inside and outside of your church. If vines are attacking any of your relationships, cut them out. If you see another ministry that needs help growing, help them grow.

It is through healthy youth ministers that we will see Isaiah's prophecy realized and be played out in our communities and in the schools.

The Spirit of the Lord God is upon me, because the Lord has anointed me to bring good news to the afflicted; he has sent me to bind up the brokenhearted, to proclaim liberty to captives, and freedom to prisoners; to proclaim the favorable year of the Lord and the day of vengeance of our God; to comfort all who mourn; to grant those who mourn in Zion, giving them a garland instead of ashes, the oil of gladness instead of mourning, the mantle of praise instead of a spirit of fainting. So they will be called oaks of righteousness, the planting of the Lord, that He may be glorified. - Isaiah 61:1-3

Endnotes

1) John 17:15
2) Matthew 6:13
3) Consider studying Matthew 13:24-30 for more insights from this remarkable parable.
4) For more information on the Seven Project, please visit www.youthalive.ag.org/seven

Chapter Seventeen

THE TEAM THAT GOES BEYOND YOU

Daniel K. Norris

I picked up my phone early one morning and noticed a missed call from an old friend from Bible college, who I had not spoken to in years. I quickly called him back. We spent a few minutes catching up before he revealed the reason for his call. He was frustrated and on the verge of leaving the youth ministry that he was leading. I could sense the fear in his voice as he filled me in on the details of the situation.

My friend had successfully rallied support from the church board to invest $150,000 towards upgrading the youth building. It was any youth pastor's dream: A cafe that featured artisan coffee and deli-style foods, a game room filled with multiple flat-screen televisions and the latest gaming consoles, and a sanctuary complete with intelligent lighting and a thumping sound system.

He had told the board that if they would allow him to build it, the students would come. And they did—at first. The youth group doubled in size during the first month post-renovations. Growth continued during the second month as well. Now, a year had passed, and the group had dwindled back down to the original 150 students that had been attending before the renovations.

"I'm down to the same students I started with and I feel like I'm under the gun because we've spent so much money, but produced so little results."

Were those tears I heard on the other end of the phone?

I paused for a moment before asking him a simple question. "How many leaders have you added to your team over the course of the past year?"

"None." His answer was telling.

The problem was not the church or city. Though he had made a great investment into creating a giant "net," he had failed to make an equal investment into establishing a leadership team. Most ministries in today's culture are pretty good at creating the net: outreach programs, special events, even facilities are all nets designed to attract an audience. Nets catch, but they don't keep.

So how do we keep the people we catch?

Leadership teams. It's a simple fact that leaders build ministry. When Jesus set out to change the course of human history, He did not do it by building a bigger and better temple complete with the latest technology; He did it by investing in people. If you want your ministry to grow, the primary focus should be on investing in people and helping them build their lives. Once your ministry begins to grow, you won't be able to do this alone. You will need a leadership team.

My wife, Jenna, and I have had the privilege of working with some amazing leaders over the past two decades. Each leader we add to our team increases our effectiveness and expands our reach. When your influence goes up, your impact goes down. This is where your leaders come in. We have built teams that now lead entire ministries within our church, without our direct oversight. These teams provide leadership for our junior high, senior high, and college ministries. There are teams that reach out to the public school campuses and college campuses. There are even teams that hit the streets each week. None of these things would be possible if I tried to do it all myself. I would be

If you want your ministry to grow, the primary focus should be on investing in people.

ineffective if I spent the majority of my time trying to do a little bit of everything, instead of doing a few things well and raising up leaders to share the rest of the workload.

If you're like me, you probably have vision for a lot of things rattling around inside of you. These is so much that you feel called to do! There is too much that you feel called to do. You realize that it is bigger than you. And that's okay. Great vision requires great teams. Far too often, we think that because we feel called to do something, we must personally do it ourselves. But that is not always the case.

Do a few things well and raise up leaders to share the rest of the workload.

No matter the size of the vision you carry, you will need to be surrounded by a great team in order to accomplish it. I love the way that songwriter Jared Anderson puts it: *"Whatever God has called you to do, He's called you to do with a team. So if you're not on a team, go find one!"*

Let's take a close look at the first chapter of the Gospel of John, in order to see how Jesus built His team.

Principle #1: He Noted Who Was Following

Again the next day John was standing with two of his disciples, and he looked at Jesus as He walked, and said, "Behold, the Lamb of God!" The two disciples heard him speak, and they followed Jesus. And Jesus turned and saw them following, and said to them, "What do you seek?" - John 1:35-38a

Leaders are supposed to lead. That may sound like a simple statement, but it can be difficult to embrace. I've watch many so-called leaders chase after people in an attempt to recruit and maintain volunteers. If you're chasing, you're not leading. The leader should be out in front encouraging and empowering a group of people to accomplish the task at hand.

Jesus' first two disciples heard about Him and started following Him. It is important to pay attention to who is following you. It does not matter if you are fresh in ministry, or if you've been around the block a few times; you must stop and look at who is following you. If you don't know who is following you, you won't know when they aren't following you, and this can be dangerous because it can create holes in your organization that you are completely oblivious to. There is an old saying that goes like this: *"He who thinks he is leading but has no one following is only taking a walk."* Enough said.

Stop and look around. Who is close by? Who is keenly observing your actions? Who is asking questions? Who is offering to help? Who is following you?

God gives people to the ministry. He has already prepared people to come alongside you and join in with what you are doing to accomplish the vision that He gave you. Good leaders will take the time to look for and identify the leaders that God has placed in their lives.

> *He who thinks he is leading but has no one following is only taking a walk.*

Principle #2: He Invited His Followers Into His Life

They said to Him, "Rabbi (which translated means Teacher), where are You staying?" He said to them, "Come, and you will see." So they came and saw where He was staying; and they stayed with Him that day. - John 1:38b-39

The disciples asked Jesus where He was going, and He responded by inviting them into His life. What a powerful leadership principle! Jesus did not simply tell them His vision directly. He did not break it down into a two minute speech. Rather, He invited them to walk with Him, so that He could unfold the vision little by little. He did this because He was more interested in the vision being caught than He was the vision being taught.

It's lonely at the top.

Leaders everywhere have exhausted this sad sentiment, in every arena, but especially in ministry. It is implied that as your level of leadership increases, the number of genuine relationships you will have in your life will decrease. That does not have to be the case. If you reach the top and find yourself alone, it is because you have failed to bring others along with you.

Some of the most fulfilling relationships in my life are with people who look to me as their leader, as well as with people who lead me. This is teamwork at its best. Relationships can develop regardless of title, rank, or positional differences.

When I first arrived in Dallas several years ago to help with a new church plant, one of the first things I did was look for leaders to join me. The first I met with was a sharp young man who expressed interest in working with our students. I shared my heart and vision with him and listened to his ideas over lunch. At the end of our meeting, I tried to buy his meal (This is an important touchpoint when meeting with potential leaders), but *If you reach the top and find yourself alone, it is because you have failed to bring others along with you.* he wrestled with me over the check. After some protest, I was able to get ahold of it, and I jokingly told him that it was a good investment on my end, and that he could work it off over the next five years. Ten years have passed since that meeting, and to this day he is a close friend. Somewhere along the journey, he married my wife's sister, and he currently pastors a large group of our students.

As you build your leadership team, take note of who is following you, but don't forget to invite people into your life as well. When you have deeper relationship with your leaders, you can ask them to take on more responsibility, and they will typically do so joyfully. When you don't have that deep relational connection, they will most often feel as though you are merely using them as stepping-stones to build your own empire. Of course, you should be careful of who you allow into your personal life; not everyone who follows you will make the cut, but the days of leaders sitting alone on the mountaintops must end. To be honest, that style of leadership never really worked in the first place.

Principle #3: His Followers Became Recruiters

One of the two who heard John speak and followed Him, was Andrew, Simon Peter's brother. He found first his own brother Simon and said to him, "We have found the Messiah" (which translated means Christ). He brought him to Jesus. - John 1:40-42a

Peter, one of Jesus' most noted disciples, was first brought to Jesus by his brother. Your greatest leaders will also be your greatest recruiters. When they truly buy in to what you are doing, they will spread the word and bring others along. When what you are doing becomes truly contagious, you won't even have to ask them to spread the word; they'll just do it naturally!

I learned this during my first three years with the church plant, as each leader who joined the team would bring a couple of other leaders on board with them. We grew to forty leaders in a relatively short period of time, and most of those leaders were brought to us. I would frequently remind leaders to be on the lookout for potential leaders within their spheres of influence. Sometimes people just need to be reminded of this, as our default tendency is to notice the flaws of others rather than their strengths and leadership potential.

When people truly buy in to what you are doing, they will spread the word and bring others along.

Principle #4: He Spoke Into the Lives of His Followers

*Jesus looked at him and said, "You are Simon the son of John;
you shall be called Cephas" (which is translated Peter). - John 1:42b*

Jesus did not just speak to the multitudes; He spoke to the disciples as well. There were distinct times in which He did both. As a staff pastor in a church, it meant the world to me to know that my senior pastor was praying for me by name each morning. When he would speak directly into my life, I knew it came from a man of God who took the time to seek God on my behalf. Therefore, I never took his words lightly.

Your leaders need this as well. You need to intercede on their behalf and get a word from God that you can speak into their life. Even though the disciples heard Jesus speak to the crowds, they still needed Him to speak certain things directly to them — things He did not speak to anyone else.

When Jesus saw Peter, the very first thing He did was speak into his life. The first part of what He spoke was corrective. He said, "You are Simon." The name Simon means, "shifting reed." Jesus was acknowledging that He saw below the surface, that He saw who he truly was on the inside — a reed easily swayed by the wind, a person in need of direction. But even though Jesus saw who he truly was, but He did not reject him because of who he was.

As leaders, we need to care enough about people to confront those that we lead if and when we see any issues in their lives. We do not love them if we simply tolerate things that need to be called out. Some of these things may even be things that the person is completely oblivious to! It is very easy to see negative patterns of behavior in others, but it can be hard to see those same patterns in ourselves. As long as we correct in love, we are actually doing them a favor.

Jesus did not stop with correction; He went on to set direction. Telling someone they need to change but failing to help them move forward is not good leadership. Jesus told Simon, "You shall be called Cephas." The name Cephas means, "rock." Jesus gave him a new identity. He was once a shifting reed, but from that point on Jesus referred to him as a rock!

I met one of our leaders on a Sunday night when I caught him attempting to skip out on our Spanish-language service, which his family attended. Instead of simply reprimanding him and sending him back into the sanctuary, I spent five minutes talking with him and getting to know him a little. After hearing a portion of his story, I looked him square in the eyes and told him that God had a great calling on his life and desired to do great things through him. He went on to become an integral part of our worship team.

Telling someone they need to change but failing to help them move forward is not good leadership.

During our leadership meetings, Jenna and I often take time to pray for our leaders. We lay hands on them and ask God to give us words to speak into their lives in order to encourage and empower them.

Principle #5: He Asked People to Follow Him

The next day He purposed to go into Galilee, and He found Philip. And Jesus said to him, "Follow Me." - John 1:43

Jesus was not afraid to ask people to follow Him. He never begged or pleaded with anyone to follow Him, but He did ask. Likewise, you should never stop asking people to be a part of your team. You should continually be on the lookout for new recruits to join your team. Don't be pushy or become "that guy," but at the same time, don't allow yourself to get to a place where you think you have "enough" leaders. The more leaders you have, the more ministry you can do!

As leaders, we are almost always moving quickly through life. I have to constantly remind myself to "walk slowly" and open my eyes to see the people who are around me every day.

When our minds are filled with everything that needs to be done, we can walk through a crowd and acknowledge a bunch of people without ever truly connecting with any of them.

When you step foot onto the campus of your church or a local school, remind yourself to walk slowly. Open your eyes. Clear your head. Your to-do list will still be there when you return to the office. Look people in the eyes, call them by name (Yes, you will need to learn their names!), and look for

The more leaders you have, the more ministry you can do!

people who can contribute to your team. But don't just think of them as people who can add value to your team; think of them as people who *you* can add value to! Giving people responsibility on your team helps to develop them into the leaders they were created to be. Often, helping someone develop their capacity for leadership is more valuable than any monetary compensation you could give them.

Principle #6: He Kept the Vision in Front of His Followers

Philip found Nathanael and said to him, "We have found Him of whom Moses in the Law and also the prophets wrote — Jesus of Nazareth, the son of Joseph."

Nathanael said to him, "Can any good thing come out of Nazareth?"

Philip said to him, "Come and see."

Jesus saw Nathanael coming to Him and said of him, "Behold, an Israelite indeed, in whom there is no deceit!"

Nathanael said to Him, "How do you know me?"

Jesus answered and said to him, "Before Philip called you, when you were under the fig tree, I saw you."

Nathanael answered Him, "Rabbi, You are the Son of God; You are the King of Israel."

Jesus answered and said to him, "Because I said to you that I saw you under the fig tree, do you believe? You will see greater things than these." And He said to him, "Truly, truly, I say to you, you will see the heavens opened and the angels of God ascending and descending on the Son of Man."

John 1:45-51

I love this passage. Jesus got Nathanael's attention by stating something that was true about him, even though He had never met him. Nathanael receives a revelation of who Jesus is from that simple comment, and worships Him as the Messiah. Jesus responds to this by essentially saying, "You haven't seen anything yet!"

As a leader, you are responsible for creating and maintaining vision for your organization. You are also responsible for keeping the vision fresh and current in the hearts and minds of the leaders who serve under you. You have to create a culture where people understand the vision, to the point where the vision is even expressed in everyday conversation.

I accomplish this by writing it on the walls, discussing it in our leadership meetings, preaching it from the pulpit, printing it on *everything*, and even writing it under my signature at the end of letters. This works! I hear my leaders nonchalantly speaking our language when they communicate with our students. This happens because they have truly caught the vision. While you cannot make someone catch your vision, you can repeat it enough to ensure that they won't be able to escape it.

Create a culture where people understand the vision and express it in everyday conversation.

What is your vision? How is it communicated? Is it concise enough to be expressed through a one-line statement? Is it catchy and alive, or boring and static? Have your leaders caught your vision? Are they reproducing it when they communicate?

Everything rises and falls on leadership. Your organization will only be as good as its leaders. Are you taking time to intentionally invest in developing the leaders around you? This is the most significant investment you will make into your ministry. It takes a lot of time and energy, but in the end the payoff is huge.

Chapter Eighteen

RE-INVENTING METHODS

Steve Pulis

"I cannot get churches to pray for schools. This prayer zone thing does not work anymore." As I listened to the words of a frustrated youth leader, I could tell that he was serious.

Prayer Zone Partners (PZP) establishes the foundation for Youth Alive's strategy to connect youth ministries with schools. The "Prayer Zone Partners" branding came from an initiative we launched that encouraged people to pray for a school every time they drove through a school zone. After a few years, the prayer opportunities needed to be expanded, so PZP evolved into encouraging people to pray for any school, anywhere, in any manner they chose.

I asked the youth leader why PZP was not working for him. He told me that each fall after a new school year began, he would stand in front of his church and challenge people to pray as they drove through school zones. The ushers would hand out sign-up cards, which included window stickers to serve as a reminder. This worked at first, but the response had dwindled over the eight years which he had been doing this.

"Only a few people committed to pray this year, and last year was the same," he lamented.

I sat there, hoping the expression on my face did not give away my reaction to his comments. I wanted to say, "You have used the same appeal for eight years, and you wonder why people quit participating?" Instead, I began to ask him questions about ways their church already encouraged prayer, and how PZP could be incorporated. During our discussion, he told me that he thought churches *had* to promote PZP in the fixed manner that he had been using for eight years. He had not considered trying new methods to encourage prayer for schools. He did not understand that by using the same method for eight years, it had created an impersonal monotony that felt more like a tired ritual than life-changing communication with God.

This is not a new problem. In fact, Charles Kraft described these symptoms long before PZP was started. "Christianity requires change ... In Christianity, there is both acceptance of what is and hope for something better. When, therefore, we seek to communicate for that something better, *we must not be captured by traditions that would render God's message impotent.*"[1]

Doing the same thing, the same way, over and over, can certainly "render God's message impotent," as this youth leader experienced in his attempts to promote PZP. Methods cease to live, breathe, and change when those developing and promoting them focus more on how the idea itself works rather than on the people who will benefit from it. Too often, leaders believe the first way they learned or communicated something remains the best way.

Just as Paul stated, *"I have become all things to all men"* (1 Corinthians 9:22), so must we enter our hearers' world. We must communicate in a way in which they will understand. God communicates with us in the same manner. He enters our world. A principle we must learn to imitate.[2]

> *We must enter our hearer's world, just as God enters our world.*

While Youth Alive is one specific program that I oversee, my job description is essentially to spur people towards youth evangelism. As the national director of Youth Alive, one of my primary jobs is to resource the 20+ regional directors that are working on the ground to reach students across the nation. But I also work with other youth leaders, churches, youth pastors, senior pastors, students, and occasionally, even the schools themselves. In my mind, anything you are doing that is student evangelism is Youth Alive, regardless of whether or not it utilizes our specific "brands" of strategies.

The four key strategies that Youth Alive utilizes in order to reach students are: Prayer, Student Empowerment, Student Networking, and Outreach. These strategies are expressed through the following specific brands:

1. Prayer Zone Partners - Prayer
2. Campus Missionaries - Student Empowerment
3. Campus Clubs - Student Networking
4. School Assemblies - Outreach

After many conversations like the one at the beginning of this chapter, we have realized that this branding can cause confusion, because it takes one of our key strategies and identifies it with a specific program or ministry. For example, many refer to the Seven Project as our "trademark" school outreach program. But it is not the only way to do school outreaches. It might be the biggest and most noticeable, but there are countless smaller outreach activities that, when put together, can make just as big of an impact on a school.

The purpose of the four concrete ideas is to help churches, leaders, and students grasp the concept that there is a great need for student outreach and evangelism in our society. But this only begins the process. Leaders must think about the ideas and adapt or change them in order to best serve their community. They may even come up with a better idea than we give them, but they wouldn't have begun thinking about school outreach much at all had we not presented them with a few concrete ideas. I have found that it is better to sow ideas than it is to transplant methods.

In some cases, the expressions of these four key strategies may require a redefinition in order to truly gain success within a community. But at the core, the same things are still happening. Prayer is taking place. Students are being empowered. Students are networking and sharing Christ with other students. Outreaches are being planned. These same results can be achieved through a variety of expressions, not just the four we have come up with and branded.

If a method works, use it. When I read through the Gospels, I see that Jesus rarely did the same thing twice. He was constantly changing the way that He did things and related to people.

Most leaders recognize the need to adapt their way of doing ministry based on their geographic regions. The way we do ministry in the South will not necessarily work in the Pacific Northwest, and vice versa. The way we do ministry in the inner city needs to be different from the way we do things in the suburbs or in a rural area. The purpose is always the same, but the methods change based on a countless number of factors that make up our unique communities.

Every church develops its own way of doing ministry. That is how we end up with a variety of models, such as traditional churches, changing churches, seeker churches, and emerging churches. They each take on different characteristics based on the people, history, location, and other factors. No two churches function in exactly the same way. Churches are not necessarily "better" or "worse" than each other because of different ministry styles, especially when we take into account that they have different audiences and settings. Instead of criticizing another church or ministry, focus that energy on making disciples.

When someone finds success with Youth Alive, they tend to encourage others to develop Youth Alive using the same methods that worked for them. Leaders usually pass on the methods that were most effective in their own lives, without regard to differences in another leader's personality, style, community, schools, or students.

This is why you must take the information you have acquired in this book and tailor it to *Instead of criticizing* fit your ministry. If you try to simply *another church or* "copy-and-paste" a ministry *ministry, focus on* strategy, you will not achieve the *making disciples.* same results as someone else. Allow yourself the freedom to experiment and be a bit messy as you figure out what is the best fit for your ministry.

Every few years, the components of your ministry need to be "re-invented." You don't have to wait for a new generation. A new class of students begin middle and high school each year. The youth culture completes a cycle and begins a new one every three to four years. Old methods lose their appeal and meaning to new groups of students. We owe it to these students to continuously evaluate what we did yesterday and make sure it still works today.

Prayer - Prayer Zone Partners: Youth Alive provides an on-going prayer plan to cover every school in prayer. Our Prayer Zone Partners commit to pray for schools, students, teachers, and administrators. They can do this from home or by prayer walking around the outside of the school, or inside the school if they are students themselves. As the movement grows, prayer groups can begin to meet on or off campus in a local church.

Here is a list of starting points, compiled by our Youth Alive directors:

1. Pray for the school while driving through a school zone

2. Encourage students to pray silently for fellow students at the start of each class
3. Encourage students to pray as they walk between classes
4. Encourage students to pray over their lunch at school
5. Dedicate a Sunday service to cast the vision of praying for the local schools
6. Distribute Prayer Zone Partners brochures and stickers in churches to raise awareness
7. Develop a "school of the week" rotating prayer list and highlight in your church bulletin
8. Pray for the "school of the week" during church services
9. Make a goal to have at least two people praying for every school in your community
10. Students can pray for their school during See You at the Pole each September [3]
11. Prayer Zone Partners can participate with students during See You at the Pole
12. Prayer Zone Partners can pray for specific students in their church
13. Coordinate a "prayer tour" in key areas of the community
14. Coordinate prayer at the city hall or county courthouse
15. Stay connected with Prayer Zone Partners through social media

Student Empowerment - Campus Missionaries: Another of Youth Alive's key strategies involves Christian students already on campus at a local school. These students should view the school as their "mission field" and become "missionaries" to their school. Campus missions equips and mobilizes students to be the hands and feet of Jesus at their schools through the "pray, live, tell, serve, and give" strategy.

•   PRAY Regularly - For friends, teachers, school administrators, and others in need of the hope that Jesus offers.

- LIVE The Word - Have a real, active, personal relationship with Jesus. Read and study God's Word and spend time with Him in personal worship.
- TELL Your Story - Share Jesus with your friends and fellow students.
- SERVE Others - Serve in an existing Campus Club at your school or start a new one. Participate in service projects with your friends around the school.
- GIVE Generously - Give time and finances to spread the message of Jesus across the globe.

Campus missionaries serve to evangelize their schools, as well as providing basic discipleship. We believe that God has placed Christian students in a unique position to share Christ at their schools.

Launching campus missions at a school begins with four steps: find, empower, send, and coach. We won't go into detail on these steps because we want you to adapt them to fit your local church. Some youth leaders have thought that because they did not have a "send" component (commissioning service), they did not have "official" Youth Alive Campus Missionaries. But following Jesus at school looks different for different students at different schools. We desire for local leaders to discover what works for their students and then help them do it.

The four steps (find, empower, send, coach) can all take place in a short period of time. They can happen through a couple of Wednesday night youth services, during a retreat, or at summer camp. The important thing to know is that if you connect with a student who desires to be a Campus Missionary at a retreat or camp, you must follow up with them through the year. Otherwise, it is unlikely that their "ministry" to the school will ever get off the ground.

Here are some additional ideas to encourage students to become Campus Missionaries to their schools:

1. Clearly communicate the "pray, live, tell, serve, give" strategy to students
2. Intentionally describe the school as a mission field when talking to students and parents
3. Discuss ways to live for God at school in student small groups
4. Preach sermons related to applying biblical teaching to everyday life during youth services
5. Do a hands-on, school-focused community service project with your youth group
6. Give students a token that will remind them of their commitment to reach their school
7. Pray over Campus Missionaries regularly, both one-on-one and during youth services
8. Allow students to share their testimonies from school during youth services
9. Hold a commissioning service for students during a Sunday church service
10. Connect every Campus Missionary with a specific mentor for one-on-one coaching
11. Encourage small group leaders or Sunday school teachers to coach Campus Missionaries
12. High School Campus Missionaries can mentor Junior High Campus Missionaries
13. Explain to Christian parents their role to coach their student as a Campus Missionary
14. Utilize free Youth Alive resources to assist with coaching Campus Missionaries[4]

The point is not *how* students share Christ at their school, but that they share Christ at their school.

Student Networking - Campus Clubs: The third principle in Youth Alive's strategy is students networking with other students. We need each other. The body of Christ accomplishes more when we come together than we do individually. One of the ways that students can link arms at school is through a Campus Club.

Campus Clubs do not belong to a specific church—not even the church their leader attends—but should function as an inter-denominational ministry, supported by leaders of local churches. They allow any student to participate, whether they are committed followers of Christ or curious seekers. Clubs exist to reinforce the local church, not replace it. They are a place where Christian students can gather and non-Christian students can discover who Jesus is in a "safe" environment that is not as intimidating as a church building on a Sunday morning.

Each club is different, and they can center around different activities. There are clubs for prayer, Bible study, fellowship, service projects, outreach, social justice, small groups, or specific interests such as athletes (FCA) or band. A club can even shift its focus, from prayer in one season to outreach or fellowship in another. The point is not what type of club students have at their school, but that they come together and share Jesus at their school.

The body of Christ accomplishes more when we come together than we do individually.

Here is a list of recruiting, mobilizing, and coaching ideas for Campus Clubs:

1. Students should continually be telling other students about their Campus Club
2. Youth leaders should continually be on the lookout for potential club leaders
3. Recruit club leaders during services, camps, youth conferences, after an outreach, etc.
4. Have students share testimonies from clubs during youth services

5. Connect existing Campus Missionaries with existing clubs, even if they aren't YA clubs
6. Leaders can speak at clubs and encourage students to reach their friends for Christ
7. Make students aware of the myriad of resources available on Youth Alive's website
8. Churches can partner with Campus Clubs for community service projects
9. Churches can "adopt a school" — help with maintenance, serve lunch, meet family needs
10. Leaders can encourage students in clubs to do service projects around the school
11. Leaders should help students develop a plan for their club at the start of each semester
12. Encourage students not to compete with existing clubs, but to work together
13. Make sure students know how effectively to present the Gospel and salvation message
14. Church leaders should intentionally and frequently communicate with club leaders
15. Exhort students in clubs to reach out to "outsiders"
16. Recruit parents to assist in coaching of club leaders

Outreach - School Assemblies: Historically, Youth Alive has provided numerous school assembly programs. School assemblies can take on two basic structural forms: bridge assemblies and process assemblies. A bridge assembly, as the name implies, builds a bridge, or strengthens an existing bridge between a youth outreach organization and a school. Youth Alive provides a multi-faceted approach to motivational school assemblies, reinforcing positive moral values while assisting students with any issues and challenges they may face. Bridge events typically do not offer an evangelistic night event since the focus is on building the bridge.

Process assemblies strategically place events within a process. The Seven Project serves as the process model for

Youth Alive. Built upon the rest of our strategy, prayer permeates the process from beginning to end. Local churches join together to bring Seven Project into the schools. Seven weeks before the school assembly, student training empowers relational evangelism and prepares students for the follow-up and discipleship process that will take place after the assembly. The day of the school assembly provides students with the opportunity to bring their friends to a night event where an evangelistic message provides further opportunities for spiritual conversations. The follow-up and discipleship process involves students discipling their friends through clubs and small groups, as well as getting them involved in local churches.

The content of the bridge assembly or Seven Project must change to fit the setting of each individual school and group of students. Schools often pick the topics of the assembly so that the messages the speakers bring will be of the most benefit to the school.

Here is a list of outreach ideas for students and churches besides school assemblies:

1. Give away donuts in the morning, pizza at lunch, or bottled water after school
2. Provide a complimentary luncheon for the principal and school administrators
3. Serve the school through projects such as cleaning a stadium or refurbishing a playground
4. Develop a relationship with the school and make yourself available for crisis counseling
5. Parents and youth leaders can make themselves available for after-school tutoring
6. Engage in one of the numerous social justice programs in your community
7. Coordinate a "30 Hour Famine" event to raise awareness of world hunger[5]

8. Coordinate a "Stuff the Bus" campaign (food drive) through your local United Way chapter
9. Coordinate an "Operation Christmas Child" event through Samaritan's Purse[6]
10. Coordinate a coat drive with the school/PTA to benefit a local charity
11. Give away candy canes and/or hot chocolate in December
12. Provide a pre-game meal for the football team
13. Host a "5th Quarter" event at your church after a Friday night football game
14. Encourage students to honor teachers through thank-you cards or gifts

It's not about doing a particular outreach at school as much as reaching out to others at the school. The methods that students utilize to reach out will vary, but the purpose remains the same. While the principles we stand behind are timeless, we must allow our methods to change constantly. If interaction and engagement with a certain method is lagging, there is probably a reason for that. You might consider stopping what you are doing and implementing another strategy. If you keep using the same old methods, you have no one to blame for your frustration.

We need to reach as many students and as many schools as we possibly can. The specific strategies that we use are not the main focus; reaching students and leading them to Jesus is the main focus.

Endnotes

1) *Communication Theory for Christian Witness*, Charles Kraft, 1991, Page 174. Italics mine.

2) Kraft, 1991, 16-17

3) Visit www.syatp.com for more information

4) Visit www.yausa.com for free resources and more information on Youth Alive's strategy

5) 30 Hour Famine is a program sponsored by World Vision to raise awareness of world hunger. For more information, visit www.30hourfamine.org

6) Visit www.samaritanspurse.org/occ for more information on Operation Christmas Child

Students

Chapter Nineteen

YOU CAN MAKE A DIFFERENCE

Kyle Embry

In my travels, I speak to groups of young people large and small, in a variety of settings, yet one thing remains the same: my message. I'm always telling young people that they can make a difference in the world right now, right where they are. They don't have to wait to grow up and be missionaries some day; they can be missionaries right now to their schools.

Most of the time there are two groups of young people I see in the crowd as I'm delivering this message. The first group is tracking and excited about what I'm saying. They're beginning to realize that God has more for them during this stage of life than just going to school and struggling to make it through life.

The second group appears disinterested and unengaged. They're the ones sitting toward the back of the room, glancing at their phones every two minutes. It's not that they don't believe what I'm saying is true; they just don't think it applies to them. They hear the stories I'm telling of students who have done great things for God and they think something like, "That's a great story, Kyle. But that's *them*. Not me. You don't know where I've been. You don't know what I've done. God could never use me like that."

But when I read through the Bible, I see God using ordinary, common people to accomplish great things, often in spite of themselves.

Now as they observed the confidence of Peter and John and understood that they were uneducated and untrained men, they were amazed, and began to recognize them as having been with Jesus.
- Acts 4:13

Peter and John were a couple of common men who turned the world upside down. They were not qualified to do what they did on their own, but they spent time with Jesus, and He equipped them with every tool they needed to make a difference in their everyday lives.

Rather than just sharing a bunch of ideas with you, I wanted to sit down with a few high school students who God has used to reach out to other students. I talked to four students: a Joe, a Sarah, a Josh, and an Allie. There is nothing special about any of these students, except that they spend time with God and share the love they receive from Him with those around them.

I love the words of the Apostle Paul in his second letter to the Church at Corinth, where he refers to God as the "Father of mercies" and "God of all comfort." He goes on to say that God comforts us in our difficulties so that we can comfort those who are going through difficulties. We comfort others because God first comforts us.[1]

Joe and I met a few years ago when he became a Youth Alive Campus Missionary during his sophomore year. Over the years, God has used him to do seemingly impossible things at his suburban high school.

When junior year began, Joe started a Bible club at his school and within six weeks of school starting, brought in a Seven Project. This outreach involved two other schools besides the one Joe attended. More than three thousand students were inspired by a message of hope during four daytime assemblies, and a separate night service resulted in seventy-four students inviting Jesus into their hearts for the first time.

One of those students was a girl named Ashley. In the wake of Seven Project, she began attending the church that Joe's dad pastors, and she brought her mother and brother with her. Her father, who had not been to church in over twenty-five years, came with them one Sunday. That morning, he was saved — and supernaturally healed of blood clots and heart problems. Today, Ashley's entire family attends church together. She is on the youth worship team and her brother helps run sound. Her parents are active and involved as well.

As Joe told me about Ashley and her family, it reminded me of the story in the book of Acts where the guard at the jail and his entire family were saved after Paul and Silas told them about Jesus.[2]

During Joe's last two years of high school, his Bible club conducted a number of outreaches. One of these outreaches involved the film *To Save a Life*. Joe purchased a copy of the film on DVD and his dad helped him acquire a license for a group showing. They rented out the school's performing arts center and fourteen people showed up. This may not seem like a large number, but six of them accepted Christ at the end of the film. When *Soul Surfer* came out, they repeated the outreach, with a few more students accepting Christ as a result.

These numbers may seem irrelevant due to the far greater numbers given a few paragraphs earlier, but they are just as important. As a Campus Missionary, you may see large amounts of people saved all at one time during an outreach. Most often, however, you will see lives changed one at a time, one after another, until an out-of-control multiplication begins. When we read through the Gospels, we see that while Jesus often spoke to large crowds, He took time to have unhurried, heart-to-heart conversations with individuals as well. Because Jesus cared about "the one," we also must care about the one.

> *Then Jesus told them this parable: "Suppose one of you has a hundred sheep and loses one of them. Does he not leave the ninety-nine in the open country and go after the lost sheep until he finds it? And when he finds it, he joyfully puts it on his shoulders and goes home. Then he calls his friends and neighbors together and says, 'Rejoice with me; I have found my lost sheep.' I tell you that in the same way there will be more rejoicing in heaven over one sinner who repents than over ninety-nine righteous persons who do not need to repent." - Luke 15:3-7, NIV*

Joe woke up early one morning, as his Bible club was scheduled to meet that day before school. Within the hour, he was driving his younger brother to school, when Jon asked if they could stop and pick up their friend Christian. Joe reluctantly agreed. They detoured to his house to find that he was still asleep. After waking him up, Joe told him to get ready in five minutes. They returned to the car and waited. That five minutes felt like an eternity. Finally, Christian came running out of the house and they drove to school.

Because Jesus cared about "the one," we also must care about the one.

Though they arrived later than planned, Christian and Jon realized that they still had time to walk around school and hang up a few posters promoting their club before it began. As they turned the corner near the second floor balcony, they saw a fellow student standing on the ledge, preparing to jump in an attempt to end his life. Christian was able to talk him down while Jon ran to find a teacher who could help.

The remarkable thing about this story is that Joe made a difference without even realizing it. Had he not had the patience to wait five minutes while Christian hurried to get dressed, Christian would not have been at the school and would not have been present to talk down the student who was contemplating suicide. The fact that Joe waited—and even the fact that Christian overslept—put them at the right place at the right time and because of this, a life was spared.

This student, who is a grade behind Joe, has since received help and support and is a senior approaching graduation.

Before graduation, Joe and his friends brought a second Seven Project to their school and held a number of smaller outreaches. They even witnessed one-on-one to students on a number of occasions and led a few to Christ. This is a perfect example of utilizing all types of outreaches, both large and small, in order to make a huge impact on a local school.

" 'I'm in.' Words which have a quiet power to change everything."
-Bob Goff

When Joe stood up and decided that he wanted to make a difference at his school, a core group of students followed. These students helped him to lead his Bible club and to plan outreaches. While he was the primary leader, it was his team that helped him to lead more than 125 students to Christ over a three-year period through a wide variety of methods. It is amazing how God used a small group of students to make a mark on the school. None of these students were great pastors or theologians, but they were willing to do whatever God wanted them to do, and He accomplished a great work through them.

Joe has now graduated and gone on to Bible college, but one of his younger brothers, Nick, and another student have stepped up to provide leadership for the Bible club, continuing the work that he started at the school.

Sarah lives across town from Joe. She is currently a senior, but I was recently told that she became a Campus Missionary during her freshman year after I spoke to the youth group at her church. On that Wednesday night, God began to stir her heart to reach out to others at her school. The passion was present immediately, but Sarah said that the action took a little while.

The culture of her school is a bit different from Joe's. It's located in a city where a lower percentage of people attend church and a lot of people don't want to associate themselves with anything that has the name "Jesus" attached to it. And those who know Jesus often seem to settle down and blend in with everyone else. They would rather not step out. They aren't very concerned with sharing what Jesus has done in their lives.

Sarah attempted to launch a Bible club during her sophomore year, but it unfortunately fizzled out rather quickly. She was, however, able to coordinate a *See You at The Pole* event one morning before school. Dozens of students showed up, and later that afternoon Sarah launched a prayer group with thirty other students.

The sky was dark and overcast as they exited the school building to begin their prayer walk around the campus. Suddenly, the sky split open and the sun began to shine down on them. The moment they were finished praying, the clouds returned and the sky was suddenly dark again. After such an amazing experience, this prayer group continued to meet weekly, as students from a variety of backgrounds came together to pray for their school.

Also during her sophomore year, Sarah began talking to a girl who most people avoided. She found out that the girl practiced witchcraft. Honestly, she wanted to avoid the girl as well, but she knew that she needed to keep talking to her. One day, the girl saw that Sarah had her Bible with her at school and began asking her questions about Jesus. Sarah went on to lead the girl to Christ, but she hasn't talked to her as much lately. She told me that if she could go back and do it over, she would have made sure she followed up with the girl, encouraging her in any way possible on her journey with Christ.

There was another girl named Courtney in Sarah's Spanish class who saw her carrying her Bible with her from class to class. One day, Courtney grabbed her Bible and began flipping through it, asking a few questions here and there. Sarah invited her to attend church with her that Sunday, and she agreed, but afterwards seemed disinterested. Sarah continued to pray for Courtney, and while she now attends a different school, they are still connected through Facebook.

One week, Sarah led a prayer during choir. Afterwards, a girl she had never met before approached her and requested prayer for her family. When Sarah saw her again later that month, the girl told her that she had re-dedicated her life to Christ.

Over the years, Sarah has met with her principal several times to discuss the possibility of doing a larger outreach at the school, such as a character-building assembly. She hasn't had any success in getting anything off the ground, but at least she keeps trying. Even with her graduation just months away, Sarah says that she still believes God wants to do something big at the school through her.

I found out from my friend Jared that throughout her sophomore and junior years, Sarah felt like a failure because her Bible club hadn't worked out as she had hoped it would. In a way, she even felt like she had let me down, as if I was counting on her alone to reach out to students at that school. But then one day, Sarah was in a worship service.

If you want to change the world, don't focus on reaching the masses — just love, encourage, and serve one person at a time.

God pulled her close, reminding her of His unconditional love for her, and after that she knew she couldn't live in regret anymore. She's learning to let go and trust God to take her small acts and turn them into something extraordinary.

Sarah now finds comfort in the words of the Apostle Paul in his letter to the Philippians, where he said that he must train himself to forget the past and look towards the future; moving forward towards the brighter days that lie ahead. He then goes on to say that we should only live up to what we have already attained.[3]

In other words, you can't compare what you're doing at your school to what Joe or anyone else is doing. It's okay if you are the one who plants the seeds rather than reap the harvest. God is not standing by with a whip to punish you if you are unsuccessful in reaching your school. He sees the effort that you are making even if you never see the results you are looking for, and He will reward you for your faithfulness in making yourself available for Him to move through you. You must remember that God is the one responsible for moving in your school. Your job is to ask Him to move and to do whatever He tells you to do. He will take care of the rest.

As I think about Sarah's comments, I realize that there is a possibility that many of our other Campus Missionaries feel this way as well. Most of the stories that make their way back to me are the great success stories; the stories of students like Joe who turned their worlds upside down. But I think it's important that we talk about the other stories as well; the stories of students who tried and tried but never obtained the success that they desired.

It's okay if you are the one who plants the seeds rather than reap the harvest.

Sarah may not be able to tell any cool stories about students falling to their knees in repentance in the school hallways, but she does have plenty of stories of how she has been able to encourage and pray for people. She has planted countless seeds on her campus over the years, one conversation at a time. Who knows what God will do in the future through the lives of those Sarah attended high school with? What if she had not been there to point those people towards Christ? I don't think we'll ever fully know.

 «« »»

Before I was the Youth Alive director for the North Texas region, I was a youth pastor in a Dallas/Fort Worth suburb. That is where I met Josh, who became a Campus Missionary in seventh grade while he was a part of my youth group.

Right out of the gate, Josh attempted to start a Bible club at his junior high school. He approached the principal, who told him that the club would have to meet after school rather than during school hours. He also told Josh that he would have to prove that there were students interested in being apart of a Bible club by getting fifty of them to sign a form. This was overwhelming to Josh at first, but he went around collecting signatures and returned to the principal with thirty-two. The principal decided that this was enough and gave Josh permission to start the club.

At its peak, Josh's club had fifteen students in attendance. They met consistently through his seventh grade year and continued on into his final year of junior high. During Josh's eighth grade year, attendance began to dwindle, and despite his efforts to grow the club, it eventually shut down.

While this discouraged Josh at first, he decided to try again a few months later as he entered his freshman year of high school. The city where he lived was experiencing tremendous growth at the time, so the incoming freshmen were sent to their own campus to begin their high school experience. It was the inaugural year of the school, with only freshmen on campus, all of who had attended junior high alongside Josh.

Knowing there were not any Christian clubs on the new campus, Josh approached the principal and expressed his desire to start a Bible club, but she politely declined his request. Josh, however, knew his rights as a student.[4] He knew that it was against the law for the principal to tell him "no," but he chose an attitude of submission and waited a week before approaching her again.

This time, the principal told him that if he collected fifteen signatures, he could use a small detention room for fifteen minutes during lunch to host his club. Josh left the meeting energized and quickly collected a notebook full of dozens of signatures — far more than the requirement set by his principal. He took these signatures to the principal who referred him to another school faculty member, so he went and met with her as well.

Another week passed, and Josh found out that the two women had brought up the Bible club he wanted to start at the recent all-faculty meeting. A few more weeks passed. There were many meetings between Josh and the principal, as well as a lot of red tape on the school's end of things. Finally, the issue was brought before the board of trustees for the entire school district, which serves nine major high schools across the city and surrounding communities.

"Faith does not deny the reality of difficulty. It declares instead the power of God in the face of the problem."
-Jack Hayford

The school board ruled in favor of Josh — but it did not stop there. They also approved Youth Alive Bible clubs for every single school within the district. From this point on, any student in the district who wished to start a Bible club affiliated with Youth Alive would be automatically green-lighted without the waiting period and red tape.

With his club approved, Josh was told that he would need to find a teacher to sponsor the club, which did not take long.

His Bible club was placed in the school club directory and he was given permission to make announcements to the entire student body over the PA system whenever he desired. The club kicked off with more than two dozen students in attendance, and it has remained steady with over a dozen students since.

One day, during their meeting, the members of the Bible club decided to put a marked box in the hallway for students to place prayer requests in. When they opened up the box at the next meeting, they were astonished to discover dozens of prayer requests. They were overwhelmed, but in a good way, as they spent the rest of their meeting praying for their classmates.

"Faith is reaching out for something that isn't yet a reality."
- Marcus Brecheen

Josh told me a story of another student who he had been friends with since first grade. This student came from a family of atheists, who preferred science and reason to the idea that a Divine Being created the world we live in. Josh would talk to him about Jesus fairly consistently, but he was never interested in listening. Finally, his curiosity got the best of him and he began attending Josh's Bible club. He came every week, always sitting in the same seat. He was the one who asked the most questions, and Josh would answer them with Scripture as best as he could.

Even though the same students attended the club most weeks, Josh always did a call for salvation before he dismissed. Most of the time, no one responded. Then one week, one person responded. Another week, two people responded. So he continued. Josh told me about a time when his call was met with the typical silence, but he felt like he needed to linger for a few minutes. The room was silent for a few minutes, and then, out of nowhere, Josh's friend slowly raised his hand.

Standing at the front of the room, Josh felt his knees begin to grow weak. He nearly collapsed right there in the classroom, unable to contain the joy that was filling his heart. He had been friends with this guy for years. He had told him about Jesus countless times, but it always seemed to fall on death ears. And then one day all of his walls were broken down.

"We forget that 'impossible' is one of God's favorite words. He dreams impossible dreams." -Max Lucado

"If this is the only person I ever lead to Christ in my entire life, it will be worth it," Josh told me. And while I know this is only the beginning, I understand exactly what he means.

Allie and I met a few years ago while she was attending my church in Dallas. While she was never an "official" Campus Missionary, she received help and resources from Youth Alive throughout her high school years. Being a Campus Missionary is not so much about signing up for a program, but more about a commitment to utilize your sphere of influence to reach people for Christ. It's about realizing that you don't have to wait until you graduate college to be in ministry, but taking advantage of your time in the public school system to minister to those around you who are in need of the hope and new life that Jesus offers.

Shortly after beginning her freshman year, Allie and her family moved from Michigan to North Fort Worth and began attending the church where my family already attended. After a youth "encounter weekend," Allie was stirred with a passion to reach her school, but wasn't sure where to start. After praying and talking with her sister, Allie decided that they should start a Bible club on their campus called *Invasion*.

The process was intimidating at first. Allie and Jocie heard from other students of a teacher who was a Christian, and they met with him to discuss their club. He eagerly agreed to be their sponsor and gave them the thumbs up to start the club. Allie and Jocie were amazed at how God had brought everything into place and opened so many doors for them in a short period of time.

One day before their club meeting, Allie and Jocie went table to table during lunch and talked to the majority of the students. They asked if there was anything going on in their lives that they could pray for and if they went to church anywhere. Somewhere within the conversation, they would casually bring up their club, telling their fellow students that if they ever needed prayer, they could come to this room at this time on this day of the week.

Allie told me that this pushed her far outside of her comfort zone, but in a good way. She would much rather have just handed out flyers promoting the club, but she knew that she needed to actually put herself out there and meet her fellow students.

Allie and Jocie received a lot of help along the way from other students in their youth group, as well as two guys named Josh and Ben, who at the time were students at their church's school of ministry.

Ben visited their school one day to help out with the Bible club. Minutes before it was set to begin, he went out into the hallway and yelled, "Hey, if you're not doing anything, come to Invasion!" Seven students entered the classroom, five girls and two guys. Allie and Jocie talked with them afterwards and found out that the two guys were homosexuals and a couple of the girls were drug addicts who would much rather attend wild house parties than Bible studies.

You don't have to wait until you graduate college to be in ministry.

Though they did not expect any of them to return, they prayed with them and invited them to come again the following week. To their surprise, this group of students not only came back the following week; they began attending the club on a regular basis. A few months later, Allie and Jocie invited these seven students to come to an outreach event at their church. The girls quickly agreed, but the guys declined. Out of the five girls, four of them accepted Christ at this outreach. Even though the guys did not want to come to the church, they continued coming to the Bible club.

Through this process, Allie and Jocie learned that you can love people and build relationships with them before they ever come to Christ. Sometimes simply telling people about Jesus is not enough; sometimes you have to love them into the Kingdom.

Jesus modeled this by engaging in conversation with people, visiting them in their homes, and even healing them before they ever decided to believe and trust in Him. Even if you never see the students you are reaching out to come to Christ, at least you planted some seeds in their life that can potentially reap a harvest somewhere down the line.

During her sophomore year, Allie met a girl named Kathleen who came from a broken home and didn't have the best relationship with her family. They became friends and spent a lot of time together. Allie felt like she needed to show her *Sometimes you have to love people into the Kingdom.* the love of Christ and take a genuine interest in her life before inviting her to Invasion.

"I want to hear about their life, their interests, the things they're passionate about before I ever invite them to my Bible club," Allie told me.

One day, after they had been friends for a while, Allie decided that it was time to invite Kathleen to Invasion. Her invitation was accepted and Kathleen showed up that week. She later told Allie that she loved it, and that she felt like she belonged. Allie realized from this experience how important it is to build genuine relationships with people, rather than just focusing on getting them to come to your club or youth group. Some students come to Bible clubs and feel like outcasts, but that was not the case this time.

Kathleen eventually began coming to church with Allie. She didn't believe in Jesus at the time, but because she considered Allie a close friend, she wanted to be involved in the things that were important to her, and church was one of those things. Kathleen came to Allie's youth group for several months before she finally met Jesus. Today, she is very focused on evangelism and is always looking for people she can reach out to in the same way Allie reached out to her.

"I don't believe that God put us on earth to be ordinary."
-Lou Holtz

As successful as Invasion was, Allie and Jocie's efforts to reach out to their fellow students was not confined to the school campus. With a combined effort from Ben, Josh, and Josh's younger brother Samuel, *Saints Established* — otherwise known as EST — was formed. It started as a Bible study on Monday nights at Starbucks, but then they began inviting so many people that they quickly outgrew this meeting location. They moved to Allie and Jocie's house, and would pack out their living room each week.

Jared actually used to attend this group long before we met and he began working with Youth Alive. That is what is great about the Body of Christ; we're all connected regardless of our backgrounds or church affiliations.

Eventually, EST grew so large that they were forced to split it off into two groups meeting at two locations. The group was strong for two years, and continues to meet today at one location, though it moves from house to house, much like the early church as described in the book of Acts.[5] This group was not a replacement for the local church, but rather a network to unite students from multiple churches and encourage them as they worked together to reach out to others at their individual schools.

At its peak, Invasion had about twenty students in attendance. Allie and Jocie led the club faithfully throughout their high school years, until Jocie (who was a year older) graduated, leaving Allie as the sole leader for her senior year. This overwhelmed her at first, until she realized that she needed to step up and become the leader she was created to be. She realized that God was calling her to move outside of her comfort zone and break out of her shell, and she responded to His call.

As she prepared to graduate from high school, Allie turned over the leadership responsibility for Invasion to another student who was a grade behind her. This student actually began attending the club during its second year, and Allie knew even then that he would be the one who she would ultimately pass the baton to. At the time, he was much like her in that he was kind of shy. He wasn't exactly an ideal candidate to lead the club, but Allie noticed that he was very humble and mature, even as a sophomore. And just as she broke out of her shell, he followed suit and began to grow in his leadership capabilities.

Shortly before Allie graduated from high school, Ben graduated from ministry school and took a position as a youth pastor in Norman, Oklahoma. Josh connected with a senior pastor from a small town in Illinois who was in Dallas for a conference, and it wasn't long before he was packing up to move across the Midwest to become the youth pastor at his church.

Today, Allie is in her first year of ministry school at Christ for the Nations in Dallas. Josh and Jocie got married and she joined him in Illinois, where he is still a youth pastor.

You can make an impact on the lives of the people around you in the same way that these four students made an impact on the people around them. You don't have to wait until you have it all together to make a difference. You can make a difference in someone's life today, even if it feels like you're just struggling to make it through life yourself.

God's grace is sufficient for you.[6] He will give you everything you need. He will equip you for every good work, just as He did Jesus.

You know of Jesus of Nazareth, how God anointed Him with the Holy Spirit and with power, and how He went about doing good and healing all who were oppressed by the devil, for God was with Him.
- Acts 10:38

Jesus went about doing good to all. He healed all who were in need of healing. And He did it all because God was with Him.

You may be thinking, "Yeah, but that was Jesus. God could never use *me* like that."

Oh, but He can! In fact, Jesus told His first disciples that they would do even greater things than He did.

Truly, truly, I say to you, he who believes in Me, the works that I do, he will do also; and greater works than these he will do; because I go to the Father. - John 14:12

Jesus said that whoever believes in Him will be able to do the same works that He did while on earth, and even greater works as well. This was more than a promise intended solely for the first disciples. Jesus widened the playing field when He said, "he who believes." Do you see that? God is ready and waiting to do the impossible, if only we will believe!

Even though Jesus said this more than two thousand years ago, His words are timeless. There has never been a point in history where God took back His offer and stopped using ordinary people to accomplish great works.

Endnotes

1) 2 Corinthians 1:3-4

2) This story is found in Acts 16:23-34

3) Paraphrase of Philippians 3:13-14, 16; NIV

4) www.everyschool.com/free-to-speak

5) One example of this is found in Acts 3:46-47

6) 2 Corinthians 12:9

Chapter Twenty

WITHOUT A MESSAGE?

Jared Stump

For the past three years, Youth Alive North Texas has been hosting an event called Together Training, which takes place at the start of each semester at different churches across the region. The purpose of this event? In short, to train students to reach their schools.

I was helping to coordinate the details of the event, along with my friends Seth, Dylan, Joe, and Geoff. My role was essentially to run all over the church taking pictures and keeping up with our social media feeds. But as I was overhearing some of what the speakers were saying to the students, I put my work aside and sat down to listen. A few years have passed since I was in high school, but the teaching was just as relevant to me as it was to the students.

One of the speakers was a guy named Al Roever. He was an older gentleman, bald with a white goatee. (The same Al Roever who contributed an earlier chapter in this book.) He spoke with an acute passion that is found in few people. You could tell that he cared deeply about this generation of students, though the age gap was staggering. But age differences don't matter as much as we think they do. He was able to connect with the students just as easily as the most "relevant" youth pastors I know.

Pastor Al painted a picture of the student who attends a Saturday event like Together Training, and gets fired up to share Jesus with a fellow student. Come Monday, they see them in the hallway, or perhaps walking home after school, and they run up to them, excited and passionate and ready to talk about Jesus. But when they get there, when they start the conversation, they realize they have nothing to say. They stumble over words, perhaps ask the other person if they want to follow Jesus, and the conversation for the other person ends up as nothing more than an interaction with a salesman trying to sell them a beat-up used car. Jesus is better than that.

One of Youth Alive's trademarks is our *Ask Me About Jesus* t-shirts. I always see a lot of these at our events or summer camp, but now and then, I'll see a student wearing one around town. I like to go up to these students and, as the shirt requests, ask them about Jesus. Most of the responses I get are pretty much the same, and not in a good way. I remember one student who told me, "Well, uh, He forgave my sins. He could forgive yours too!" While I'm sure he met well, I walked away thinking that if I was not already a follower of Jesus, that conversation would not have done anything to move me in that direction. Yes, Jesus *did* die for our sins. But the cross is not the end of the story.

Pastor Al said that if we do not have a specific message to deliver, we will just end up embarrassing ourselves. Your message needs to be deeper than "Jesus died to forgive my sins." It needs to be personal. You need to be able to put to words how Jesus has *personally* changed *your* life. When your message isn't personal, it makes Jesus out to be impersonal. When in reality, He is the most personal God who has ever existed.

Reading from 1 Corinthians 15, Pastor Al shared a four-point message with the students. He told them that Jesus died for our sins; He was buried, He rose from the dead, and then He appeared to upwards of 500 men before He ascended into Heaven.[1] The first two of these points are not uncommon. Everyone dies at some point, and then they are typically buried thereafter. It's at the point of resurrection that the supernatural comes into play.

We could travel to Saudi Arabia and see the tomb where Mohammad is buried. We could go to the tomb where Buddha's remains are buried, if anyone knew exactly where it is. And while the exact location of the tomb Jesus spent three days in is disputed, if we were to find it, we would find it to be empty!

You need to be able to put to words how Jesus has personally changed your life.

But there are many people, people you will encounter at some point in your life, who are not convinced. They have trouble believing that Jesus was a real person who lived and died and rose from the dead, but they have no problem believing that George Washington or Abraham Lincoln were real people who lived and died.

Many people would say they believe that Julius Caesar, who once ruled as a dictator over the Roman Republic, lived and died. But what they are not aware of is that Jesus actually had more historical documents written about Him than Caesar did. The first documents about Caesar's life were not recorded until around seven hundred years after his death, whereas there were already thousands of documents about Christ's life within seventy years of His death.

The evidence is overwhelming that Jesus rose from the dead. This is crucial, because the Apostle Paul tells us that if Jesus did not rise from the dead, everything we are doing in church today is completely useless and we might as well pack up and go home.[2]

It's important to note that Jesus did not rise from the dead and go straight into heaven. He appeared to countless people in order to prove to them that He was alive.[3] Most historians agree that Jesus was a real man who walked the same earth that we do. History tells us that He really did die on the cross. As

Christians, we do not have to defend our message that Jesus lived and died, because our message is historical truth. More than 500 witnesses can attest to the fact that He came back to life and got up out of the grave.

I stated earlier that the cross is not the end of the story. But if you stop and think about it, the resurrection is not the end of the story, either.

Towards the beginning of the book of Acts, the apostles were having their final conversation with Jesus. This was after His resurrection, but before His ascension into heaven. Suddenly, the conversation was cut short when Jesus, upon telling them that the Holy Spirit would empower them to spread the Gospel to the ends of the earth, began to float up into the sky.

The apostles watched intently as He ascended into the sky, until a cloud hid Him from view. He never reappeared, but I suppose they thought He might, because they kept gazing into the heavens, hoping to catch a final glimpse of Him.

You do not have to defend your message, because your message is historical truth.

Suddenly, two men dressed in white appeared on the ground next to them. "What are you doing?" they asked. "Why are you standing here staring into the sky? The same Jesus that you just watched ascended into heaven will return someday in the same way."[4]

The way I envision it, the men in white said this and then casually walked off before the apostles could even begin to process what had just taken place. I'm sure they just stood there dumbfounded for a while, unsure of what to do next.

I think the reason why the men appeared to them was because Jesus didn't want them staring aimlessly into the sky, wondering when He would return. I think He wanted them to go and be productive, spreading His Kingdom throughout the earth. I think He wanted them to go in His power and strength and turn the world upside down.

Jesus died. He was buried. He rose from the dead. He ascended into heaven. He told us He would come back someday. But between the ascension and the second coming, there is more to be done than just stand around staring into the clouds, waiting for Christ's return. Jesus said that we would do even greater works than the ones He did while on the earth.[5] Do we really believe that?

The cross is not the end of the story. The resurrection is not the end of the story. The end of the story will come when Jesus returns. On that day, heaven and earth will intersect, life will swallow up death, God will come and dwell among men, there will be no more tears or heartache or pain; everything will be made new. But in the meantime, the story is ours.

> *"The Kingdom will come; yet the Kingdom is presently among us, within us, by the Spirit." -Alan Smith*

There will come a definite point when God will make all things new. Yet He is already at work doing this, right now, through us. Every time you show someone who Jesus is, every time you let His love flow through you to the broken world around you, you are taking part in God's work of making all things new. He has called us to greater works. It is time for us to live like it.

There were two stories that Pastor Al told that grabbed ahold of my heart. They didn't just stand out to me; they moved me. They stirred up that passion inside of me to make a difference in the lives of the people around me, a passion that sometimes grows cold due to the worries, cares, and pressures of life.

The first story was about a 15-year-old boy who left a note on his desk at school. That note was found by a teacher, who later gave it to Al's brother, Dave Roever. It was a suicide note, found a moment too late.

In my life, I have felt nothing. No love, no joy, no happiness. But the worst part is I don't feel anything; I just kinda exist.

"Surely there were some Christian young people at that school who could have loved him and showed an interest in him," Pastor Al paused, his voice rich with emotion. "If you're going to make a difference, it's going to cost you. It's going to take some time. You're going to have to show some compassion. You're going to have to feel something for the people around you, even when they can't feel anything themselves."

The second story that Pastor Al told was also from his high school days. Growing up, he was not bold or outspoken. He never was able to work up the courage to witness to his classmates, but he did take his Bible to school each day. He would take it with him to class and sit it on his desk, where everyone could see it. No one ever laughed at him or told him to stop bringing his Bible to school, so he continued to do this until he graduated.

After graduation, he went off to college and got a job, and his brother became a traveling speaker. One day while Dave and Al were talking, Dave said that he had met a man in San Antonio who gave him a personal message for Al.

"What is it?" Al inquired, slightly curious.

"Well, this guy told me that he went to high school with you, and he said to tell you that he is a Christian today because of you," Dave replied, nonchalantly.

"What are you talking about?" Al questioned. "I never witnessed to anyone in my high school class."

"I know," Dave responded. "But he saw that you had your Bible on your desk every day, and he decided that if it was that important to you, he would see for himself what was in it. So he went out and bought himself a Bible, started reading it, and the rest is history." He paused, a smile spreading across his wrinkled face. "Because of you, Al. Because of you."

Standing there at the front of the church before the students, it looked as though tears were forming around his eyes. "You see, kids," Al said. "You don't have to be in-your-face all the time to make a difference." He paused. "You've got a message. You've got a story. Know it — all the details of it. And then use it."

> *"You can't live a perfect day without doing something for someone who will never be able to repay you."*
> *- John Wooden*

The room burst into applause as he took his seat.

Endnotes

1) This message is found in 1 Corinthians 15:1-8

2) 1 Corinthians 15:14

3) Acts 1:3

4) This story is found in Acts 1:8-11. Dialogue paraphrased.

5) John 14:12

Chapter Twenty-One

SPIRIT-LED AT SCHOOL

Jared Patterson

As I drive the streets of my working-class city in the middle of the Bible Belt, I see one thing that is prevalent nearly everywhere, no matter what part of the city I find myself in. Churches. There's essentially one on every corner.

This leads me to another question: How do we have so many churches in our communities, but at the same time have so many people who don't know who God is?

I don't think the problem is a lack of knowledge or even conversation about God; I think the problem is that people don't truly understand who He is. I hear a lot of people who talk like God is angry and waiting to punish them if they don't go to church and read their Bibles, but that hasn't been my experience with Him at all.

Some people talk about God like He's some sort of divine punisher, but in my eyes He is a rewarder. Apparently the author of Hebrews saw God in a similar manner, because he wrote that God is a rewarder of those who seek Him.[1]

People need to know that God is good and that He has good plans for them. They need to know that God wants to be involved in their everyday lives, right down to the smallest details.

We don't always present God this way, do we? Perhaps the reason for this is because we don't truly know in our hearts that He is good and that He has good plans for us, and that anything that matters to us matters to Him. Perhaps we're so caught up in following all the rules and doing all the right things that we've forgotten that God desires a close relationship with us. It's hard to represent someone when you don't truly know them.

I have not stopped giving thanks for you, remembering you in my prayers. I keep asking that the God of our Lord Jesus Christ, the glorious Father, may give you the Spirit of wisdom and revelation, so that you may know him better. - Ephesians 1:16-17, NIV

This isn't about obtaining more theological knowledge. That can be helpful, but growing in your knowledge of theology doesn't compare to growing in your knowledge of who God is. If you continue reading on in Ephesians, you'll see that the author wants us to know that God has an inheritance for us and His power is available in our everyday lives.

The power of God is not just something that your pastor has access to; it is available for all who are in relationship with Him. The power of God is available to us, in our everyday lives, through the Holy Spirit. We could spend all day discussing the theology of how the Holy Spirit works in our lives, but unfortunately we don't have time to go that in-depth.

For Christ's love compels us, because we are convinced that one died for all, and therefore all died. And he died for all, that those who live should no longer live for themselves but for him who died for them and was raised again. - 2 Corinthians 5:14-15, NIV

Let's pause right there for a moment. What is compelling you to reach students at your school? Is it the love of Christ, or is it something else? If not love, what is motivating you? Is it a pure motivation? Why or why not?

Therefore from now on we regard no one according to the flesh. ... Therefore if anyone is in Christ, he is a new creation; the old things passed away; behold, new things have come.
- 2 Corinthians 5:16a-17

I think it's very easy to read over this portion of Scripture and only see the part about us becoming new creations. This verse has been used time and time again in an attempt to get people to change their behavior in order to prove they are truly Christians. But, if we read the verse immediately before it, we see that we are not to regard anyone according to the flesh; that is, what we see on the outside.

It's hard to represent God when you don't truly know Him.

Even on your best day, when you've prayed and read your Bible and chosen to love others, God still loves you with the same love that He has for that person at your school—the one you brush shoulders with but never talk to—who has no relationship with Him. And you could be the one that encourages them to begin a conversation with God that could ultimately lead to a relationship. If you think about it, this really isn't much different than our earthly relationships.

This relationship that God invites us to through the sacrifice of Jesus is not about our external behavior; it is about the internal condition of our hearts. God wants to change who we are on the inside, and that will flow to the outside and change the way we think, behave, and relate to others.

Some say that, as Christians, we are to inspect one another's fruit. I disagree with that concept, and so does the verse we just read in 2 Corinthians, not to mention all the other verses throughout the Bible.

Do not judge so that you will not be judged. ... Why do you look at the speck that is in your brother's eye, but do not notice the log that is in your own eye? Or how can you say to your brother, 'Let me take the speck out of your eye,' and behold, the log is in your own eye? You hypocrite, first take the log out of your own eye, and then you will see clearly to take the speck out of your brother's eye.
- Matthew 7:1, 3-5

While it is completely acceptable to point out to another a destructive behavior, we are not to appoint ourselves as "doctrine deputies" that go around telling everyone how they are "incorrectly" living the Christian life. Someday, they will stand before God. And so will you. If you are to inspect anyone's fruit, it should be your own. We must take care of the junk in our own lives first, and then we can reach out to others and help them work through theirs.

> *Now all these things are from God, who reconciled us to Himself through Christ and gave us the ministry of reconciliation, namely, that God was in Christ reconciling the world to Himself, not counting their trespasses against them, and He has committed to us the word of reconciliation. Therefore, we are ambassadors for Christ, as though God were making an appeal through us; we beg you on behalf of Christ, be reconciled to God. He made Him who knew no sin to be sin on our behalf, so that we might become the righteousness of God in Him. - 2 Corinthians 5:18-21*

These verses can be difficult to understand at first glance, which is why most of us only put the part about being a new creation on our refrigerators. Essentially, the author of 2 Corinthians is telling us that God is the one who does the work of transformation in peoples' lives. Our job is simply to point people to Jesus. I believe that we are not called so much to "win people for Jesus" as we are to create or stir up a conversation between them and God. At the end of the day, the decision to enter into a relationship must be made between God and each unique individual. I don't want anyone to follow Jesus solely because I convinced them to; I want them to experience Him for themselves.

God is looking for people who He can reconcile to Himself, bringing them into relationship with Him by not counting their sins, mistakes, or failures against them.

We are invited to take part in this process of redemption. God has entrusted a portion of the process to us, and because

He has trusted me to represent Him, I want to be sure that I represent Him well and communicate who He truly is.

The message of reconciliation is our knowledge of who God is. This includes both our theological understanding and personal experience. Our theological understanding is what we've learned about God. Our personal experience is what He has done in our lives—our personal stories of encountering His love and grace.

The ministry of reconciliation is, in short, what we do to ignite conversation between God and those around us. We can operate in the ministry of reconciliation through our flesh by randomly telling every person around us that they need to repent and believe in Jesus, or we can operate in this ministry through the Spirit, who will point out and bring specific people into our lives that He wants us to talk to. I personally prefer this way of ministry because I know that God knows better than I do who is ready to start a conversation with Him that will ultimately lead to a relationship.

So now that we are aware that we need help from the Holy Spirit to effectively communicate who God is to those around us, how do we obtain that help? To put it simply, how do we receive the Spirit?

There are two distinct baptisms, or ways that the Spirit works in our lives. The first baptism is commonly referred to as the baptism in water. This isn't talking about literally being baptized in water at a local church, but rather the work that the Spirit does in our hearts at salvation. This is when we become a new creation. This is when we become born again.

Because God has trusted me to represent Him, I want to be sure that I represent Him well and communicate who He truly is.

The Holy Spirit comes and lives inside of us the moment we say "yes" to Jesus. When this happens, our debt is paid, our sins are washed away, and we become the righteousness of

Christ Jesus. This is the baptism in water, and it is talked about extensively throughout the Scriptures.

The second baptism, the baptism in fire, is when the Holy Spirit comes and rests upon us. The primary purpose of this work of the Spirit is to empower us to reach others for Christ.

But you will receive power when the Holy Spirit has come upon you; and you will be My witnesses both in Jerusalem, and in all Judea and Samaria, and to the remotest part of the earth. - Acts 1:8

The baptism in water is when the Spirit comes and lives inside of us. The baptism in fire is when the Spirit comes and rests upon us for a specific purpose. You could say that the Spirit is in us for us and on us for others.[2]

God knows better than I do who is ready to start a conversation with Him.

John answered and said to them all, "As for me, I baptize you with water; but One is coming who is mightier than I, and I am not fit to untie the thong of His sandals; He will baptize you with the Holy Spirit and fire." - Luke 3:16

I don't have to wake up each day and get the Spirit to come and live inside of me. That already happened when I said "yes" to Jesus. He's in me and with me and all around me one hundred percent of the time, regardless of whether I feel His presence or not. All I must do is continue to say "yes" to Jesus.

The baptism in fire is a bit different. The Holy Spirit rests upon an individual for the specific task of bringing God's Kingdom to earth. This is how we are to accomplish His directive when Jesus told us to pray, *"Your Kingdom come. Your will be done, on earth as it is in heaven"* (Matthew 6:10).

The baptism in fire is not at all like it was in the Old Testament, when the Spirit would come upon an individual and then leave shortly thereafter. The Holy Spirit is no longer interested in visitation; He longs for habitation within us. He came to abide in us and upon us! All we need to do to guarantee this lifestyle is protect our connection to Him. Life flows from Him into us through our relationship with Him. Jesus did all the wonderful things He did as a man, but as a man who was rightly connected to His Father. His connection to God created the avenue for the empowerment of the Holy Spirit.

Did you know that we can have as much of the Spirit as we desire? Jesus told us that God gives us His Spirit without measure.[3] So if we are not full of the Spirit, the problem is not with God, but with us.

Jesus jealously protected His relationship with His Father. He often left the crowds and ministry opportunities just to spend time with His Dad. Once, when asked a question about food, He said that His food was to do the will of the One of sent Him, to accomplish His work.[4] Jesus lived continuously hungry for the things of God, consumed by the zeal of God.[5]

Now, this should not seem difficult or even impossible, because the Spirit has been sent to us to make what was impossible, possible. Jesus told His disciples that it was "to their advantage" that He go away, because when He left, the Holy Spirit would come.[6] That is how important the Spirit is in the life of the believer. The Spirit was sent to release the fullness of your inheritance and to turn you into a different person, a person rightly connected to your Heavenly Father, a person who brings His Kingdom to earth by imitating Him.

It's easy to get overwhelmed when you hear the imperative *"Go reach your school,"* but it doesn't have to be complicated or difficult. Just find one person who you can share the love of Jesus with and go from there. Focus on serving them. Start with any physical needs which you can see, and before you know it, the Holy Spirit will point out spiritual needs which you can minister to as well. Spiritual needs are met when you let God's love flow through you to another, and then point back to Him.

If you want to take it one step further, pray for the Holy Spirit to place one person on your heart who you can begin serving and showing love to. The Spirit knows the needs of each individual better than we do, and He also knows where people are

"He meant us to see Him and live with Him and draw our life from His smile." - A.W. Tozer

and which student at your school is most likely to respond to Jesus if He is presented to them.

When Jesus woke up each day, He didn't have to tell Himself, "Today, I'm going to heal someone," or "I'm going to perform a great miracle today." He healed people and performed miracles as He encountered people who were in need of them because it was who He was; it was a part of His very nature.

When we become a new creation in Christ, this becomes a part of our nature as well. You don't have to try hard to do something great for God. Simply respond to the prompting of the Holy Spirit, and He will do great works through you. Pray for opportunities to speak into people's lives, and that the Spirit would help you to recognize those opportunities when they arrive. Don't let fear hold you back from being who God created and redeemed you to be.

The Spirit of the Lord God is upon me, because the Lord has anointed me to bring good news to the afflicted; he has sent me to bind up the brokenhearted, to proclaim liberty to captives, and freedom to prisoners; to proclaim the favorable year of the Lord and the day of vengeance of our God; to comfort all who mourn; to grant those who mourn in Zion, giving them a garland instead of ashes, the oil of gladness instead of mourning, the mantle of praise instead of a spirit of fainting. So they will be called oaks of righteousness, the planting of the Lord, that He may be glorified. - Isaiah 61:1-3

Do you want to live a Spirit-filled life at your school? Then find something on this list and do it. Take good news to the afflicted. Help those with broken hearts heal. Comfort those who mourn. Declare liberty to those who are held captive and bound by the chains of sin. *That* is what the Spirit-filled life looks like.

Endnotes

1) Hebrews 11:6

2) Quote attributed to Bill Johnson

3) John 3:34

4) John 4:34

5) See Psalm 69:9 and John 2:17

6) John 16:7

Chapter Twenty-Two

HOW TO LEAD A CAMPUS CLUB

Kyle Embry

As you've been reading through this book, you've probably heard us talk a lot about two things: Campus Missionaries and Campus Clubs. You know that a Campus Missionary is simply someone who realizes that they go to school every day not just to learn, but to reach out to others. You know that a Campus Club provides a place for Christian students to come together, a place where they can be built up and encouraged to live out their faith at school. You know that Campus Clubs also provide a safe place where yourself and other Christian students can bring friends who don't know Jesus. This way they can learn about who He is in an environment where they are already comfortable, their school.

It does not matter if you call them Campus Clubs or Bible clubs or small groups; regardless of what you call them, the purpose is the same: To encourage one another, to serve the school and community, and reach students for Christ.

At this point, you may be thinking something like, "That's great, Kyle. But how am I supposed to go out and start a Campus Club at my school?"

Well, I have done my best to make it very simple for you. I have laid out a step-by-step process so that you have no excuses to not start a club on your school campus.

There are four simple steps to getting a club off the ground. While these steps are simple, the process will not always be easy. It may be summer right now as you read this, and as you go back to school for a fresh year in August or September, you may be very excited about the idea of starting a club. But by the time November or December roll around, some or most of that excitement and passion may have drained. This is when you must keep going. In order for God to use you to do a great work on your campus — and really at any place in your life — you must be willing to keep moving forward even when it gets tough. This is why I recommend getting a friend to help start the club with you. You are not alone, and you do not have to do this all by yourself!

Step One - Called By God: This is the first and most important step. If God has not called you to start a Campus Club, it is all for nothing. Just because you want to start a club and are excited about it does not mean God is calling you to do it.

You may need to wait until next year to start a club, or you may be more effective in another role within a club rather than that of the leader. You have to trust that God sees the big picture better than any of us. Spend time in prayer before making the decision to start a club. Fast decisions are often not good decisions.

Step Two - Connect with your Youth Pastor: They are there to help you and encourage you throughout the process. Tell them you want to start a club and ask them to hold you accountable to it. You need adults in your life who know you are working to start a club and will check in with you as you make progress towards this goal. This role does not necessarily have to be filled solely by your youth pastor; invite your parents and/or other adults from your church into the process as well.

Step Three - Find a Teacher: Most schools will require you to have a teacher who will serve as your sponsor in order to start a club of any type. It is helpful if this teacher is a Christian who believes in what you are wanting to do in starting a club.

The teacher you select will serve as an advocate to the principal on your behalf. They will typically provide a room where your club can meet once a week, and can help you determine the best day and time to meet. They can also provide any supplies and resources you need, within reason of course. Just ask!

Step Four - Meet with the Principal: Every principal is unique. Some will want you to set up a specific time to meet and will not listen to you if you just barge in to their office. Others will be all right with you simply stopping by and asking them if they have ten minutes to talk to you. If you do not know which type of person your principal is, it is best that you assume they will want you to set up a meeting in advance. In most cases, you can approach the school secretary or another administrator to discuss setting up a meeting with the principal.

I remember when I went with Joe (who you heard about in a previous chapter) to meet with his principal. He was extremely nervous during the meeting. To be honest, it was pretty *You must be willing* rough. But he moved past his fear *to keep moving forward* and did it anyway. Had Joe decided *even when it gets tough.* not to conquer his fear of meeting with the principal, you would not have read about him in this book today.

When you meet with the principal, it is very important that you go into the meeting prepared. This does not mean that you are not nervous or afraid, but it does mean that you have done your homework. I highly recommend that you take the teacher who has already agreed to sponsor your club to the meeting with you. If you have a friend who is going to co-lead the club with you, they should also be with you when you meet with the principal.

When you meet with the principal for the first time, you should say something like, "Mr. Principal, I would like to start a Bible club that will meet at 7:30 am on Fridays. I have Mrs. Smith here with me; she is going to be the sponsor for this club and we will meet in her classroom, Room 208, every Friday before school."

If you meet with your principal without first determining what time you will meet, what day you will meet, where you will meet, and which teacher will sponsor you, your principal may not take you seriously. If all you say is, "Hey, I want to start a Bible club," your principal will most likely tell you to come back when you know what you're doing. But if you have everything together so that any questions your principal may ask are already answered in advance, they will typically say "yes" to you starting a club much more quickly.

"Missionary work is not for a select few; it is necessary for all of us who want to follow Christ." -Ross Parsley

It is also important that your principal knows that you will not be a threat to the school. They need to know that you are not going to get up on the cafeteria tables during lunch and begin preaching and screaming and causing a ruckus. Your principal needs to know that the two primary purposes of your club are to serve the school (We will provide a list of potential service opportunities later in this chapter) and to provide a place where Christian students can come together to fellowship and study God's Word. It is not necessary for you to tell your principal that you are a "Campus Missionary" seeking to evangelize the entire school. Tell the truth, but realize there are some things that are better off left unspoken.

Because you did your homework and went into the meeting prepared, your principal will most likely give you the green light to start your club. But you need to know that this will not always be the case. You have heard the story of Josh, who followed all of these steps and still did not get his club approved right away. There may be red tape. Your principal may give you the runaround. It may take several weeks or even months to get your club approved. What is important is that you do not give up at any point in the process. Decide in advance that you are going to see this thing through, no matter how difficult it may be.

If your principal's answer to you starting a club is "no," your response should be something like, "Okay, I understand that you are not giving me permission to start a club now, but what can I do to get you to say "yes" to this?"

Do not get angry. Do not flip your principal off and walk out of their office. And by all means, never post anything negative about your principal or school on Facebook or Twitter after being told that you cannot start a Campus Club. You never know who is watching, and if what you said gets back to your principal, the answer might be "no" for good.

Instead of protesting your principal's answer, pray that God will open up a door for you. Look for ways that you can serve the school while you are waiting. Get your parents involved. You would be amazed at how fast your principal may change their mind if your parents meet with them to discuss why you cannot have a Campus Club at your school.

It's important to note that the work is not over once you have gained your principal's approval. Now you actually have to lead the club each week, not to mention get people to come to it. As intimidating as this may seem, you have already done the most difficult part. Once you meet with the principal and obtain their approval, the rest should be relatively easy by comparison. It will still take a lot of work, but you can do it. God will be by your side every step of the way. He is with you and He is for you. You've got what it takes, because He has given you everything you need.

Do not give up at any point in the process.

Through many years of equipping students to lead Campus Clubs, Youth Alive has learned that if you are left on your own to do your own thing in your own way, it will not be long before you burn out. That is why we provide you with resources, ideas, and "pre-packaged" lessons for you to use in your club. You can find tons of lessons and other ideas on the Youth Alive USA website. I would encourage you to spend some time exploring this website in order to take full advantage of the countless resources it offers.

For those of you who prefer to watch a video over reading text, we have create a resource especially for you. If you visit www.YouthAliveTX.com/clubs and navigate around a bit, you will find something we like to call "Campus Club Videos." These videos are the result of my taking the Campus Club lesson notes (that you would read and then teach in your own club) from the YA USA website and putting them in video format. This way you can watch me teach the club lesson and then go out and teach it yourself in your Campus Club. You do not have to say everything I say word-for-word; the purpose of this is to give you a general idea of what a club lesson looks like.

A typical club should last anywhere from 25-45 minutes, give or take, and feature the core elements of a lesson, discussion/question time, and an opportunity for students to request prayer and pray for one another. While we recommend following the models given on the YA USA website and our website for the lessons, you can customize the discussion and prayer times to fit your group. Every club is unique.

Visit yausa.com for tons of free Campus Club resources.

Some clubs need to focus more on discussion time, while others need to be more focused on prayer for the school as well as the needs of students.

There are enough lessons on the YA USA website that you should be able to go from your first year of junior high to your last year of high school without repeating a lesson. However, if you do run out of lessons, you can check out another great ministry called I Am Second. Their website will provide you with additional resources and lesson ideas.

Most months of the year contain four weeks. You will find a weekly schedule below that you can take and use for your Campus Club. Repeat it each month and take the liberty to come up with your own agenda for those months that have a fifth week.

Visit IAmSecond.com for more resources and ideas.

Week 1 - Small Groups: Rather than a typical lesson from one person, break up into small groups of 2-3 students for this week's meeting. Scriptures and discussion questions can be found on the YA USA website.

Week 2 - Guest Speaker: This can be your youth pastor, a parent, or even a teacher. They can bring their own message or pick a lesson off the YA USA website if they prefer.

Week 3 - Student Speaker: This can be you, a friend, or anyone else involved with your club. Pick a lesson from the YA USA website and give it to your speaker to use as a model.

Week 4 - Outreach: This is the week where things get a bit different. There are two ways you can approach this. One, you can make this week a strong evangelistic focus on students who know Jesus bringing friends who don't know Jesus with them to your club. Or you can make this a week where you go out and engage in a service project on campus or in the community.

If both of these ideas sound good to you, I would recommend focusing Week 4 on evangelism and utilize the "fifth weeks" that occur a few times a year as your opportunity to go out and do a service project. Weekends are a good time for service projects to take place as well.

Here's how you make the evangelism-focused club meeting happen: Have something special to use as a "draw" for students to use in conversation when inviting their friends to attend the club. Offer free donuts or have a drawing for a $15 iTunes gift card. It doesn't have to be extravagant, just different from what you normally do. If you have donuts every week, you will want to do something special for this week.

The lesson for this week should be focused solely on presenting the Gospel. You or a guest speaker can give a ten minute presentation of the Gospel and then conclude with an opportunity for students to ask Jesus into their hearts or receive prayer. You can lead into this Gospel presentation by having one or two students share their testimonies. This will break the ice a bit and show visiting students that you are interested in sharing your story and hearing theirs, rather than just forcing Jesus on them.

If you aren't sure where to get started with service projects, talk to a parent or teacher about your school's specific needs. See below for a few ideas that our Youth Alive leaders suggest. Keep in mind that if there is already something going on at your school, it is often better to get involved with it than it is to do your own thing. Many schools already hold food drives, coat drives, and toy drives for families in need during the Christmas season.

- **School Supply Drive** - Talk to your school counselor to see if there are any students in need of school supplies. Have the students in your club pool their money together in order to purchase school supplies to give to these students.
- **Shopping Cart Food Drive** - Borrow shopping carts (one for each classroom) from a local grocery store. Each class can decorate their cart and fill it up with non-perishable food items. Conclude the event with a shopping cart parade during lunch. The class with the most food in their cart and the class with the best decorated cart are the winners.

- **Make a Change Week** - Begin discussing how much loose change students carry in their pockets. Take buckets into classrooms to collect this money to "make a change." Then, donate the money to a local charity. Make sure you have at least one parent or teacher involved for accountability purposes.
- **Adopt an Elementary Classroom** - This is accomplished by visiting an elementary class once a month to serve them by reading books, playing math games, and/or offering one-on-one tutoring. Students can also practice their correspondence skills by writing letters back and forth with the elementary students. This is a great opportunity to refine your leadership skills and truly understand, through purposeful activity, the importance of modeling positive behavior.
- **Custodian for a Day** - Recruit a group of students to clean up a specific portion of the school. It can be an interior hallway after school or the football field bleachers on Saturday morning after a game. Coordinate the details with your school custodian. Provide gloves, trash bags, and cleaning supplies as needed. Get adults and/or older students to help supervise. Break up into small groups and fan out throughout the campus, with one supervisor in each group. Optional: Purchase a blank card. Write the name of your club, as well as what you did specifically to help clean up the school on the inside of this card. Have every student who participated sign it and deliver it in the school office for your principal and other school administrators to see. This will show them that you care about the school and are committed to making it a better place. Actions speak louder than words. It's one thing to say you care about your school, and another to do something that demonstrates it.

Each leader should, through their Campus Club, serve as a bridge, a friend, and a force at their school. Let me take a minute to explain what I mean by that as we conclude this chapter.

Be a Bridge: There are a lot of students out there who aren't interested in going to a church. But chances are, if you build a relationship with them and invite them, they will go to a Campus Club. For these students, your club is not the end, but the beginning. Ultimately, students who meet Jesus through a club need to be in a local church, but the club serves as a bridge to get them there.

There are a lot of students who won't go to church, but will go to a Campus Club.

Be a Friend: Every time you step foot on your campus, be a friend to whoever crosses your path. When students come to your club, be nice. Have fun. Don't make it boring. Learning about God and growing in our faith should be fun and exciting.

Be a Force: Get involved in serving your school and community. Engage in service projects such as the ones mentioned previously, or choose your own. But don't let it end there—begin to intentionally live a life of serving others. As Jesus said, the greatest in the Kingdom of Heaven will be the one who serves others.[1]

I remember one time when I was talking with a pastor, and he began to tell me about a girl at his church named Zoe, who felt that God was calling her to start a Campus Club—in elementary school. So in fourth grade, she started a club, and by the end of the year, there were more than eighty students in attendance. If Zoe can do it, so can you!

If there is already an active club at your school, whether it be FCA or Young Life or whatever, get involved with it and help them grow stronger. Most clubs are in need of help and it is unlikely that they will decline your offer to partner with them to further their vision, which is ultimately connecting students to Jesus Christ.

Most people would much rather go out and start their own club than serve in an existing club. But the true test of leadership is whether or not you can serve someone else. Maybe God is calling you to serve another before He entrusts you with your own ministry. Every school and situation is different. Do whatever God calls you to do; just don't settle for doing nothing!

Endnotes

1) Mark 9:35, 10:43-45

Chapter Twenty-Three

SIX THINGS

Kyle Embry

As pastors, we're used to sharing information with people that will influence and shape their lives. If someone attends your church for one year, they'll hear more than four dozen sermons on a variety of topics. But what if you didn't have an entire year to influence them? What if you had to be more concise and only share the things that matter the most, the things that make the most impact?

I was thinking through these things the other day when an idea hit me. If I could get all of our Campus Missionaries together and tell them six things—and only six things—what would those six things be?

It doesn't matter if you carry the title of "Campus Missionary" or not. These six things are extremely important if you have any interest at all in reaching your school for Christ. And personally, I believe that if Jesus has truly made a difference in your life, you will want to share Him with someone else.

Someone Is Always Watching: As you go about your life, people are watching. Who's watching? Everyone. But more specifically, there are two groups of people watching you each and every day of your life: Those who know Jesus and those who don't.

Those are the two groups of people that are always watching. Even when you think they aren't. Especially when you think they aren't. They're watching as you walk out your front door, when you're waiting for the bus, when you're at school, when you're at the grocery store, when you're at the dentist, when you're at

If Jesus has made a difference in your life, you will want to share Him with someone else.

the movies, when you're at Starbucks, when you're on a date, when you update your Facebook status, and when you're in the church parking lot. Every waking moment of your life has one thing in common: Someone is always watching.

Those who don't know Jesus, the majority of the people you encounter, are watching to see how you respond when life doesn't go your way, when someone wrongs you, when you're treated unfairly. They're watching to see how you respond when someone makes fun of you at the lunch table. They're watching to see how you respond when you have to wait in line for five minutes at Starbucks. They notice when you're talking with one friend about the church service you attended last Sunday and another about how much you hate your math teacher. They notice when you cuss up a fit while wearing a cool, relevant shirt that says *Pick Jesus*. They notice when you put someone down to build yourself up. They notice how you treat those who can do nothing for you.

St. Francis of Assisi said it this way: *"Preach the Gospel every day; if necessary, use words."*

Of course, there will be times when we will have to use our words to tell people about Jesus, but sometimes our words get in the way. Listen for the still, small voice of the Holy Spirit, and don't be afraid to speak up when He prompts you. There will come a time to tell people about Jesus with your words, but it's equally important that they can see Him through your actions. Your actions have to back up your words, otherwise what you say loses its meaning.

The people around you who already know Jesus are watching too. If you're positive and encouraging and life giving, it will rub off on them. However, if you're living a double life, it will only show them that it's okay to do the same.

We aren't talking about perfection, because none of us are perfect. What makes us different, as Christians, is our willingness to humbly admit when we've messed up and seek to make things right. Perfection is not required, as long as you are heading in the right direction. If Jesus has truly changed your heart, you should want to be loving, kind, patient, gracious, and compassionate. It should be your default response rather than an afterthought. It's not always easy, but it's important that you aim to be like Jesus in everything you say and do.

Let all that you do be done in love. - 1 Corinthians 16:14

When you make the choice to build someone up—especially when it's much easier to tear them down—people notice. You don't have to walk around quoting John 3:16 all the time; all you have to do is simply be nice. I'm amazed at how many *How do you treat those who can do nothing for you?* people I meet who are not nice people. Sometimes being nice is all it takes to stand out. It really can be as easy as smiling at someone or saying hello to that person at your school who you never talk to.

I met a guy once who told me he tries to encourage as many people as possible every day. One of the ways he does this is by complimenting people. But he doesn't just tell them they have nice hair or cool clothes or the latest iPhone; all those things are honestly quite vain when you stop and think about it. Instead, he looks to compliment people on their character. He's always watching for someone who goes out of their way to do something nice for someone, even if it's as simple as holding a door or letting someone go ahead of them in line. He looks for random acts of kindness or positive attitudes and when he sees them, he always tries to let the person know that he noticed.

The secret is to always seek to be genuine. You're better off to say nothing than to say something that sounds fake or forced. It's important that you love people the way Jesus has loved you.

We love, because He first loved us. - 1 John 4:19

Loving others in the same way that Jesus loves you can be difficult if you don't understand how deeply Jesus loves and cares for you. It is critical that we receive a revelation of the depths of our Heavenly Father's love, and this does not come by merely telling yourself "Jesus loves me" repeatedly. Rather, it is something that you receive as you encounter and behold more of who Jesus is, and there is always more out there waiting to be discovered. That's why we draw near to Him through prayer, worship, devotions, reading the Bible, or simply talking to Him as we go about our day. We don't do any of that stuff to make Him love us; we do it so that we will remember just how much He loves us!

Love people the way Jesus has loved you.

Most people are familiar with John 3:16 — even people who don't know Jesus. Unfortunately, many people have heard this verse so many times that it loses its meaning. It becomes so familiar that they just glaze over it without really giving it much thought. The other day I heard a pastor say that he loves this verse because it doesn't just say that God loved the world; it says that He "so" loved the world. He didn't just love us a little; He loved us a lot. He loved us enough to give us the extravagant gift of relationship with Him, a gift that cost Him the life of His son. And He loves the worst sinners we can imagine in the same way that He loves us.

What marvelous love the Father has extended to us! Just look at it — we're called children of God! That's who we really are. But that's also why the world doesn't recognize us or take us seriously, because it has no idea who he is or what he's up to. - 1 John 3:1, The Message

I keep asking that the God of our Lord Jesus Christ, the glorious Father, may give you the Spirit of wisdom and revelation, so that you may know him better. I pray that the eyes of your heart may be enlightened in order that you may know the hope to which he has called you, the riches of his glorious inheritance in his holy people, and his incomparably great power for us who believe.
- Ephesians 1:17-19a, NIV

He brought me out into a spacious place; he rescued me because he delighted in me. - Psalm 18:19, NIV

Jesus doesn't just love you; He likes you! Take a moment and let that sink in.

May you be graced with a spirit of wisdom and revelation, that you may know Him better. May you know the hope that He has called you to. May you know the greatness of His power. May you know that He is for you, not against you. May His love catch you totally and completely off guard.

I pray that out of his glorious riches he may strengthen you with power through his Spirit in your inner being, so that Christ may dwell in your hearts through faith. And I pray that you, being rooted and established in love, may have power, together with all the Lord's holy people, to grasp how wide and long and high and deep is the love of Christ, and to know this love that surpasses knowledge – that you may be filled to the measure of all the fullness of God.
- Ephesians 3:16-19, NIV

At this point, you're probably thinking that we've gotten way off track from "Someone is always watching." However, I am convinced that it is impossible for us to express the love of Jesus through our words and actions until we first experience His love for ourselves.

The people who are watching you aren't looking for you to arrogantly tell them that they are going to Hell. They aren't looking to see how well you can argue about theology or apologetics. What they are looking for is whether or not you've learned how to love. In fact, Jesus even said that the most convincing proof that you belong to Him is your love for others.

A new commandment I give to you, that you love one another, even as I have loved you, that you also love one another. By this all men will know that you are My disciples, if you have love for one another. - John 13:34-35

You Are Not Alone: With our culture growing increasingly godless, it's easy to feel like you are all alone, as if you are the only one left who still desires to live for God. I think a lot of students, and even a lot of adults, can't help but feel this way from time to time.

I'm reminded of Elijah, one of the great heroes of our faith, who challenged followers of a false god to a showdown on Mount Carmel.[1] In short, Elijah won the showdown, made those who opposed the one true God look foolish, and then killed all 450 of them. He was on top of the mountain after that experience. For a moment, at least.

Elijah had experienced a pinnacle in his life, but there was one problem: an evil woman named Jezebel. She caught wind of what had happened and sent Elijah a message: "By this time tomorrow, I'm going to kill you."

How did Elijah respond to this threat? He freaked out and ran for his life. It's interesting to think that the fearless man who had just killed 450 people was afraid of one person who threatened to take his life.

And so Elijah ended up in the desert. He had a guy who was fleeing with him, but he left him behind and went off on his own. Finally, he spotted a tree and sat down beneath it, desperate for shade. And then he prayed. But he didn't ask God to protect him or strengthen him or give him courage or any of those things you would think he would have prayed for. Instead, he asked God to kill him. And then he fell asleep.

What an odd story.

So here we have Elijah sleeping in the desert. He's fresh off the greatest victory of his career, and interestingly enough, he's also on suicide watch. And then an angel appears and shakes him awake and tells him to get up and eat before he starves himself to death. Elijah sat up to see that a loaf of bread and pitcher of water had appeared out of thin air. While he was sleeping. In the middle of the desert.

The angel walked away, but it wasn't long before he returned to the tree that Elijah was sitting under. Our hero had decided to take another nap, apparently. The angel shook him awake a second time. I'm sure at that point Elijah was getting a bit of an attitude, wondering why this angelic being kept bothering him.

"Hey, Elijah," the angel said to him. "You're going to need to get up. You're going to need to eat. You're going to need to stop being depressed. Your situation is not going to be like this forever. The journey ahead is far greater than you know."

I'm sure Elijah grumbled a bit, but he got up and did as he was told. He ate and drank and began walking again. He walked for forty days, until finally he came to the mountain of God, where he spent the night in a cave.

And then God came and asked a question that He loves to ask His disillusioned children. "What are you doing, Elijah?"

"Well, God, I have been serving you very passionately and wholeheartedly, I think. But those *The journey ahead is far greater than you know.* other people that used to go to my church; they've rejected you. And the people at my school; they've rejected you. Everyone is off doing all kinds of crazy things and I am the only one left who is still living for you."

"Okay," God replied. "Get out of this cave and go climb the mountain. I want to meet with you personally."

Elijah was a bit frustrated at this, I'm sure. God had failed to answer his question. Instead, He responded with what was a seemingly unrelated command. In his frustration, Elijah disobeyed. He stayed in the cave.

And then a mighty wind came. Like a hurricane, you know. This wind was strong enough to shatter rocks on contact. But God was not in the wind.

Then there was an earthquake. But God wasn't in that, either.

Next, there was a fire. A big fire. A fire that made the burning bush look insignificant. Elijah looked, but God was nowhere to be found. He wasn't in the wind. He wasn't in the earthquake. He wasn't in the fire.

"We often look for the next big thing, when God is just looking for us to be fully in the moment."
– Matthew Barnett

"Uh ..." Elijah hesitated. "God, I thought you said you wanted to meet with me?"

And then, it came. A gentle whisper. So soft that Elijah nearly missed it. But he didn't. He got up and walked to the mouth of the cave. He stood in the opening and covered his face with his shirt.

"What are you doing, Elijah?"

What was Elijah's response? The exact same thing as before. He repeated the same monologue, word for word, about how he was the only one left living for God.

I think at that point, God couldn't help but chuckle.

"Go home."

"You've got to be kidding me. Don't you know that that woman is waiting to kill me?"

"Elijah. I have seven thousand men waiting for you. They will defend you. You are not alone. Now go home. Get back to work. I am going to use you to do something greater than anything you could ever imagine."

That's the way we are sometimes, isn't it? We think we're the only ones serving God, so when trouble comes, we run and hide.

You are surrounded by people every day that share your desire to see heaven invade earth. You are not the only one who wants to see greater things take place in your community. In fact, the only time you're actually alone is when you run and hide because you believe the lie that tells you that you are on your own.

I am going to use you to do something greater than anything you could ever imagine.

Therefore go and make disciples of all nations, baptizing them in the name of the Father and of the Son and of the Holy Spirit, and teaching them to obey everything I have commanded you. And surely I am with you always, to the very end of the age.
- Matthew 28:19-20, NIV

You Will Regret Not Doing Anything: As I travel across Texas, I ask some of the older people I meet this question: *If you could go back and do it all over again, what would you do differently?*

The responses I receive vary, but they all have one thing in common. Each and every person I talk to lives with regrets. They regret spending too much time on things that don't matter and not enough time on things that do matter.

I've talked to parents who regret not getting involved and helping their kids reach their school. I've talked to grandmas and grandpas who regret that they didn't do more to reach their classmates during their school days. I've even talked to former teachers who regret not using their influence to make a real and lasting impact in the lives of the students who surrounded them each and every day.

Let's be clear, we don't do things for God in an attempt to finally win His approval or make Him happy with us. If you've given your life to Jesus, that is enough. God is already pleased, and you will spend eternity with Him. But we're not just saved so that we get to go to heaven someday; we're saved so that we can bring heaven to earth. God has chosen us to enter in to His story and play a role in the work that He is doing on the earth today. May we no longer view being apart of God's story of redemption as something we have to go, but something we *get* to do.

You Will Have More Help Than You Think: Not only are you not alone, but there is more help waiting for you than you think there is. There are countless books, sermons, blog posts, tweets, and other resources that talk about evangelism. But beyond that, you are surrounded by people who can help you as you work up the courage to begin those conversations with other students at your school who are in need of the life-changing love that Jesus offers.

I recently read a book that talks about how we can use our personal stories to tell others about Jesus, rather than just quoting Bible verses at them and walking away. You will probably have more success if you get to know people, listen to their stories, and share your own than if you just spew a bunch of Bible verses at them and walk away when they shake their heads. The verses are true, but if you don't show people that you love them and truly care about them, they won't want to listen to you.

I don't think you necessarily need books to help you, though they can be a great resource. You can always talk to a pastor or mature believer at your church who can give you advice. If you ask them, I'm sure they'd be happy to tell you about their own struggles and victories. It's not all about the success stories; sometimes you can learn just as much from failure.

If you don't show people that you truly care about them, they won't want to listen to you.

One great resource that we have utilized is called the *Life Book*. It is basically the Gospel of John presented in a conversational format. It is one of the best practical tools I have found. Giving someone a Life Book is better than giving them a tract or a puppy or a slap in the face or even a plate of cookies.

I heard a story about a girl in Kentucky named Natalie who found a Life Book on the floor at her high school. She put it in her purse and took it home with her. That night, she got it out and began reading. She didn't know much about Jesus or the Bible, but that didn't matter so much. God met her right where she was. As she read through the little white book, it slowly began to change her life. It answered some of the questions she had been asking herself about the meaning of life and put her on the path toward an encounter the Author of life.

Your youth pastor can to go online and sign up to receive a bunch of free Life Books for you and the other students in your youth group to hand out at school—or anywhere else, for that matter.

Let me tell you a secret about youth pastors: they are human, just like the rest of us. They tend to get busy and forget about things. Sometimes they're lazy. You've been there too, I'm sure. So if you really want your youth group to get ahold of a case of Life Books, you'll need to follow up with them. Keep reminding them until they go online and place the order.

Tell them that it can make a huge difference in your school. Tell them that it's what Jesus would do. Tell them that it won't cost them a dime. (Youth pastors love free.) Keep reminding them, even if you feel like you're just being annoying. Call them, text them, send them a tweet, write on their wall, send them an email, show up at their house at 6:00 in the morning. Okay, maybe not that last one, but do whatever it takes to get them to order you some Life Books! Seriously, you can't lose with this.

Life Books can be ordered at TheLifeBook.com

Another great resource is a little book called *Fresh Start with God* by John Siebeling. It gives very practical advice on how to get started in your walk with God, covering topics like: transformation, prayer, church attendance, the Holy Spirit, building godly friendships, and establishing a consistent time to read the Bible and hear God talk to you. It's seven chapters and is designed so that you can spend about fifteen minutes reading one chapter a day and get through the book in a week.

The books are printed by a church in Memphis, Tennessee and are available to order online. The cost is $6.00 per book, but you can order a case of 100 for $300, which is a 50% discount. Talk to your parents or maybe a businessperson at your church if you're interested in purchasing some of these books. They may be willing to help cover a portion of the cost for you.

Fresh Start books are a little different than Life Books. Life Books can be handed out to anyone, from people who believe God exists but don't have a relationship with Him to hard-core atheists. However, Fresh Start books are for those who have already made the decision to follow Christ. They are not something you want to hand out randomly to every student who will take one, but they are a great resource if you lead a Bible club at your school, because you can put something

Fresh Start with God books can be ordered at JohnSiebeling.com

concrete in the hands of a student who has just made the decision to ask Jesus into their heart.

There are also plenty of resources available on the Internet. As we've mentioned a few times before, our parent

Check out yausa.com for tons of free resources.

organization, Youth Alive USA, has tons of free resources on their website.

The bottom line is this: you can't reach your school alone, and why would you want to? Don't be afraid or arrogant; ask for help. It could be the deciding factor of whether or not you succeed or fail in your desire to make a difference within your sphere of influence.

You Are Not All That: As a pastor, it is my job to comfort the afflicted while at the same time afflicting the comfortable. I love to encourage students who want to make a difference at their schools, but are afraid to step out. And I also love to shoot down those students who are doing something at their school, but have become cocky about it.

Hey, guess what? You aren't all that. Oh, wait. You lead a Bible club at your school? Congratulations. That means you've been chosen by God for this great work—this great work that *He* is doing. This isn't about you. It's never been about you. It never will be about you.

As one pastor put it, *"We spend our days trying to hijack the story of God, turning it into the story of us."*[2]

When you share what God is doing at your school or in your life with others, the focus should always be on Him rather than you. This doesn't mean you walk around hanging your head or reject every compliment that comes your way. Simply smile, say "thank you," and quietly thank God that He was the one that gave you the strength to do what you did in the first place.

What, after all, is Apollos? And what is Paul? Only servants, through whom you came to believe — as the Lord has assigned to each his task. I planted the seed, Apollos watered it, but God has been making it grow. So neither the one who plants nor the one who waters is anything, but only God, who makes things grow.
- 1 Corinthians 3:5-7, NIV

As you read these verses, notice that it's really God who does it all. But He allows us to play a role in the story. He chose Paul to plant the seed and Apollos to water it, but He was the one who made it grow. Neither of these men would have been effective if God hadn't made the seed grow.

You may be thinking something like, *If God's the one who does it all, does He really need me? Why should I do anything?* That's an excellent question; one I think many of us ask ourselves on a regular basis.

The truth is, God doesn't *need* you. But He does *want* you. He wants you to play a role in His story, and there are benefits to doing so.

The one who plants and the one who waters have one purpose, and they will each be rewarded according to their own labor.
- 1 Corinthians 3:8, NIV

When you play a role in God's story, you receive a deep satisfaction and sense of purpose in this life, along with eternal rewards in the life that is to come. However, we shouldn't be motivated solely by rewards. We should desire to play a role in God's story because we love God and want to see His Kingdom come on earth, just as it has already come in heaven. The earthly and eternal rewards are merely a perk. Don't chase the rewards; chase God. When you chase rewards over God, you'll always end up disappointed.

It's really God who does it all. But He allows us to play a role in the story.

You don't always get to be the one who reaps the harvest of bringing someone into the Kingdom. Sometimes you're the one who plants the seed. Other times you're the one who waters the seed. But no matter which part you play, you're working with other followers of Christ towards the same goal. Everyone who is pointing people to Christ is on the same team. It's not a competition to see who can become the greatest and most well-known evangelist, or who can get the most people in their church or youth group; it's about people coming into relationship with the God who loves them and calls them each by name.

The greatest Christians who ever live at best only receive the accolade of *Best Supporting Actor*, because the role of the Star is already filled for all of eternity, and it's not you or me. We are not all that, but we are loved and cherished by the One who is.

Your Impact is Greater Than You Know: I was speaking at a church once in a small town in East Texas when I met Daniel, who was a freshmen at the high school in a neighboring town. It wasn't long before I found out that he had attended one of our events a few weeks before. That event was Together Training, where we give students practical instruction on how to be successful Campus Missionaries and reach their schools for Christ.

Daniel is only fourteen years old, but he took the information we gave him and ran with it. The next week, he met with his principal to inquire about starting a Bible club on campus. At first, the principal was hesitant. Daniel had to go back for a second meeting and deal with a lot of red tape. The principal told him he needed to get a classroom to hold the club in, but Daniel couldn't find a teacher who was willing to help him out. So, with four other students, Daniel decided they would go ahead and begin their Bible club outside until a classroom could be secured.

On the day they were scheduled to hold their first meeting, the principal came back and told Daniel that they wouldn't be allowed to meet outside, but a teacher had stepped up who was willing to allow the group to use their classroom.

I was so excited to hear Daniel's story. I was amazed at the work of God that was taking place on his high school campus. I told him several times that I was so proud of him for getting out there and doing something, no matter what obstacles he encountered. He politely nodded and said "thank you," but I don't think he fully understood how much of an impact he had already made and will make over the next four years.

I drove home that afternoon in awe of what God was doing across the region. I knew that there would be Bible clubs started after Together Training, but everything changes when you see the faces and hear the stories behind the statistics. I didn't realize how much of an impact the event had until I met Daniel.

Everything changes when you see the faces and hear the stories behind the statistics.

As I tried to connect the dots in my head, I began asking myself a few questions. *What if Daniel had not attended our training that day? What if his pastor had not been willing to get up at the crack of dawn and sacrifice an entire Saturday to drive a small group to Dallas? What if we had decided to have the training in another city that was too far away for Daniel to attend? What if myself and the other leaders had not been willing to spend a day pouring into students?*

You see, there were many factors that played into Daniel starting a Bible club at his school. If one little thing had happened differently, there might not be a Youth Alive club at this particular high school in East Texas today.

It wasn't our event or me by myself that caused Daniel to go do something at his school. Rather, it was multiple factors happening all at once, intertwining with one other, all directed by the hand of God. There was one point in the day, in one session, with one speaker, where a particular word or phrase of what was spoken stood out to Daniel. That was the moment when God put it on his heart to go home and start a Bible club. And he did.

We can never fully understand or comprehend the impact that the choices we make every single day have on our lives and the lives of those around us. God can take the small, seemingly insignificant things in our lives and do something extraordinary with them. That is the way He works, because He is so much bigger than us.

The Apostle Paul tells us that God calls into existence things that do not exist.[3] God was the one who, from the beginning, from before Together Training, called the Bible club that Daniel leads into existence. I simply had a small role to play in the story.

Endnotes

1) You can read more about Elijah in 1 Kings 18 and 19

2) Quote attributed to Louie Giglio

3) Romans 4:17

Chapter Twenty-Four

THE POWER OF SOCIAL MEDIA

Jared Stump

Communication.

We're immersed in it every day. Sometimes it gets the best of us, because most of us assume we're good at it, and assumption is in many cases the first step towards destruction.

I was hanging out with some friends late one Tuesday night, and this guy Tony who was sitting across the table from me began talking about this very topic. He told me that he has this problem where he can't go much longer than ten or fifteen minutes without checking his phone. And it's not just to see whether or not he missed that important phone call, either. He has this addiction stronger than a drug even, where he can't stop checking his text messages and Facebook and Twitter and Instagram and whatever the next big social network will be.

Tony told me that he hates how everything in our world is beginning to center around social media, but he loves it at the same time. He loves staying connected to people he doesn't see very often. And he loves being able to influence people and have others influence him.

That's the thing with social media; it can take away from our life and physical relationships, but it can also connect us to never-ending resource pools that build and shape and define our lives in positive ways. But that's not exactly what we're going to dive into right now.

Whether you realize it or not, you have a platform. Even if you don't have a smartphone or Twitter account. However, I'm here to talk to you about the platform of social media. Because if you're on any social networks, you have a platform, regardless of whether or not you want it.

You are free to use your platform for a positive or negative purpose. Some even choose to use it for both. But you must choose. Will your platform be positive, adding to your life and the lives of others? Or will it be negative, taking away from your life and the lives of others? The choice is yours. And it is a choice you have to make and then run with.

The Negative Platform

I've seen so many people on Facebook and Twitter, Christians in particular, who apparently think it is there job to criticize and beat up everyone and everybody. As if God is somehow helped when we're angry and attacking and policing every speck of doctrine we find on the Internet.

I see so many brothers and sisters in Christ arguing and attacking over things that honestly don't even matter. I used to go to a church where several people acted this way, and I made the observation that they didn't have very many friends. Except those who agree with them, of course. I've got to be honest: I don't care if it's John Calvin or Jacobus Arminius who is correct in their doctrinal views; I just want people to love Jesus more.

"The world is watching ... When Christians get mad at other Christians, somehow I don't think God is pleased."
-Perry Noble

I was in Oklahoma once with Youth Alive for a school assembly. As the students were entering the gymnasium, I would stand outside the entrance and greet them. But I didn't just say, "Hey, what's up?!" Instead, I was random and awkward about it. And there was this one guy who apparently didn't like it. I walked up to him and his friend and asked them if they were excited about the worst school assembly of their lives. Reverse psychology, you know. He just looked at me, and then began cussing me out. He told me I was a nobody, and had no right to even begin a conversation with him. Talk about arrogant!

As the assembly was about to begin, I entered the gym and sat down center stage next to our DJ to run ProPresenter. As I sat there, I couldn't help but wish I could see the look on that kid's face. He cussed me out because he thought I was just another awkward high school reject, but as it turned out, I was part of the team in charge of putting on this event at his school. If he had known who I was, perhaps he would have treated me differently.

Don't forget to show hospitality to strangers, for some who have done this have entertained angels without realizing it!
- Hebrews 13:2, NLT

This was the verse that popped into my head in the aftermath of this encounter. I wonder if I've ever blown anyone off who was in fact an angel sent from God Himself? The thought that at some point in my life I probably have is sobering.

The Positive Platform

When I was still in high school, I got a Twitter account because a couple of pastors I knew had them, and I wanted to be cool like them. So I began tweeting about any and everything—from what movie I had just watched, to what music I was listening to, to what I was eating and whether or not I was going to church on Wednesday night. It was all a bunch of nonsense, really.

After awhile, I began to realize that I could use social media to do more than just share random information. I was intrigued by the idea that I could actually influence people and help them along their journey of life. So I began to post cute, encouraging

Scriptures and quotes from books I had read. After several months of doing this on a regular basis, I began to think long and hard about different spiritual matters and aspects of life, and it was then that original material would make its way into my mind. It wasn't great at first, but it improved over the years to where, by the time I had graduated, people were beginning to ask me if I was going to become a pastor.

I began to realize that I could use social media to do more than just share information.

I'm a bit of a people person, so I have several contacts on social media outlets that I don't necessarily have much relationship with in my day-to-day life. But when I see those people— there are a dozen or so of them—they almost always comment on how much they enjoy the things I post on Facebook or Twitter. They tell me how encouraging I am, or how something I said helped them on their spiritual journey, and I smile and say, "Thank you." It feels good to know that what I say makes a positive difference.

Therefore encourage one another and build up one another, just as you also are doing. - 1 Thessalonians 5:11

I used to be one of those people; I used to be one of the angry Christians. But one day I decided I didn't want to be like that anymore. I didn't want to attack and tear down others on social media or in person. Over time, God began to soften and shape my heart. Now instead of hate and judgment, my default reaction is love and grace. I don't always get it right (trust me, sometimes I completely screw up and have to go back and fix it) but I'm in a completely different place than where I was a few years ago.

God is Watching

For the eyes of the Lord move to and fro throughout the earth that He may strongly support those whose heart is completely His. - 2 Chronicles 16:9

God is watching. He sees when we argue and get angry and attack others. Even when it's on social media. But He also sees when we are loving and kind and gracious and patient, especially to those we don't like or think we need in our lives. A wise man once said that you can judge the true character of a man by observing how he treats those who can do nothing for him.

Discuss the issues, debate the issues, but be careful to protect the relationships that God has given you. People matter more than theology. Even the ones you don't like.

Everyone

Chapter Twenty-Five

FACES IN THE CROWD: BEGINNING

Jared Stump

Midland is like any West Texas town, except bigger. One of those places that has everything yet nothing at the same time. In Midland, oil is a way of life, football is king, and churches are conveniently located on every corner.

Amy Parker poured herself a cup of coffee and slowly made her way from the kitchen to the other end of her single story ranch home, which was basically a carbon copy of every other house in town. Her husband had left for work hours ago, long before the sun graced the West Texas horizon. She still had not adjusted to waking up without him at her side. Things were different when they lived in Tulsa, before the oil company transferred her husband to the Permian Basin. They had thought it would just be temporary, but eight years had come and gone, leaving Rick and Amy with more questions than answers.

She paused outside her son's door, which was cracked slightly. The silence? Deafening. Stephen had passed away in a car accident the year before. Amy had not yet found the strength to enter her son's room without Rick by her side, let alone begin to clean it out.

She blinked forcefully, shoving the tears back into her eyes; ignoring the one that had escaped and was making its way down her cheek. She continued down the hallway to her daughter's open door. Elizabeth turned over in her sleep to face her mom as she stood in the doorway, almost as if she could

263

sense her presence. Amy entered her daughter's room. Noticing a small pile of clothes on the floor, she walked across the room and bent over to pick them up. It was then that she noticed a small plastic bag poking out of Elizabeth's backpack, filled with what appeared to be processed Astroturf. She frowned. *"When did my little girl start smoking?"* Of course, she wasn't so little anymore. But still. Marijuana? It just didn't seem like her. This wasn't the Elizabeth she knew.

Meanwhile, a few blocks away, Nancy Coleman watched from the window as her husband's truck disappeared down the driveway. Darrell was approaching his fortieth year of teaching math at the high school. Somewhere along the line, he had gotten in the habit of arriving an hour early each morning to pray. He would pace up and down the darkened hallways, calling out the names of the students as he passed their lockers. He knew each one by name. And they knew him. Darrell Coleman wasn't just the math teacher; he was a part of the very fabric of the school. Teachers, coaches, principals; they had all come and gone, but he was always there. He was committed. Loyal. Few could remember a time when he *wasn't* around.

On this Monday morning, Mr. Coleman found himself drawn to one cluster of lockers in particular. He knew exactly who they belonged to before he had even turned the corner. A makeshift memorial still surrounded the locker that had at one time belonged to Stephen Parker. I guess one could say it still did. No one else wanted it; that was for sure. It was like a moment frozen in time. He still got chills every time he passed by, as he was taken back to that October night.

He vaguely remembered the phone ringing shortly after midnight. His wife had answered, only to hear sobbing on the other end. Amy Parker. Rick had been out on the rig when it happened. Nancy had hung up the phone and shook him from his sleep. He responded without even thinking, like a dad. Bolting upright, he quickly dressed and ran to the Parker's house as fast as his aging legs could carry him. He cut through a few backyards and moments later saw Elizabeth slumped over, her back against the garage door. He picked her up and embraced her as golden strands of hair stuck to her tear-stained face. He held her for what seemed like forever, unable to let go. She wouldn't let him.

It all seemed so vivid as he pressed his wrinkled hand against her locker. "Jesus, I pray you would make yourself real to Elizabeth. Let her experience Your love like she never has before."

He lingered for a moment before continuing to the next locker. "Jeff." He heard himself say the name aloud. He didn't know him very well, even though the two families had attended church together at Antioch Fellowship for as long as either party could remember. Jeff was a junior at Midland. Not shy, but not outgoing either, he was the type of person who fit in without standing out.

Mr. Coleman hovered around the locker for a moment, waiting as thoughts stirred in his mind. "Jesus, give Jeff a boldness to share Your love with others."

"Elizabeth!"

"Catch you later, mom!"

Amy grabbed her shoulder before she could make it out of the kitchen. Elizabeth spun around to face her, almost defiantly. "What? I'm going to be late for school."

Amy was holding a plastic bag. She knew exactly what it was.

"Where did you find that?" Elizabeth demanded, silently hoping she had masked the fear in her voice.

Amy was silent.

"Have you been going through my stuff?!"

Silence once again. Elizabeth tapped her foot impatiently. Hands on her hips. She meant business.

"Well?!"

"Listen, I was in your room, and just happened to—"

"Do me a favor. Stay out of my life." She shot her mom a withering look as she turned and walked briskly out of the room.

"Elizabeth Ann!"

The front door slammed. She was gone. Amy leaned against the counter and sank to the floor, not holding back the tears this time.

Ryan entered the high school through the side door an hour before school started, carrying a worn faux leather Bible and several boxes of donuts. He had started the Bible club on his campus a few months before, when school started. There were already more than three dozen students in attendance, a third of them, new Christians. So much had happened in a short period of time, but there was still much to be done. The vision was huge: reach every student in the high school. The task was enormous, but he was up for the challenge. It didn't help that nearly everyone in Midland already believed that there was a God out there somewhere, and that was all they needed to get their foot in the door.

He smiled at Mr. Coleman as their paths crossed outside the auditorium, remembering that not long ago he thought the old man was out of his mind. I mean, it was cool that he would come early and pray, but it didn't seem to make much difference. Ryan had been one of those kids, like most in his youth group, who went to church every Sunday and

Wednesday, but didn't really give God the time of day the remainder of the week. But that was all before the accident happened.

Everyone had loved Stephen, and Ryan was no exception. He was one of those people who you could have a five-minute conversation with and feel like you'd known him all your life. He didn't see people through the typical high school filters as most did. In his eyes, you weren't a jock or a prep or a punk or a band geek or any of those things; just a person, and that was why everyone loved him so much. When his life was suddenly cut short a semester before graduation, it was as if the pause button had been pressed on the lives of those around him as well.

Ryan, however, did not stay in pause for long. Stephen's death triggered all of those questions relating to mortality inside his mind, and it wasn't long before he found himself looking for an outlet where he could process everything he thought he knew.

Mr. Coleman ended up being that outlet. It was two Saturdays after the accident when he and Ryan ran into each other at the supermarket. It couldn't have been mere chance, as Ryan rarely set foot in the place. But on that particular morning he had decided to run a few errands for his mom, and just happened to arrive in the produce section at the same time as his math teacher.

The two struck up a conversation that lasted half an hour, and ended with the off-duty teacher leading one of his students to an encounter with Jesus, right there between the watermelons and carrots.

From that point on, everything in Ryan's life was different. He no longer viewed church as a ritual, and his mundane life became a mission field. He wasn't interested in getting people to come to church or intellectually agree with his beliefs; he just wanted them to experience Jesus the way he had that day in the supermarket.

Ryan crossed paths with Jeff just outside the entrance to Room 107. "What's up man?? How are you?" He grabbed Jeff's shoulder and squeezed.

"Hey," Jeff replied, awkwardly wiggling out of his friend's grip.

"You alright?"

"Yeah." He paused. "I've just got a lot on my mind."

"Alright. Let me know if you want to talk."

Jeff was typically quiet, but not this quiet. Something was up. Ryan was sure of it. He pushed his suspicions to the back burner and arranged the donut boxes on one of the tables. He was always nervous about speaking to the group, but today he was more nervous than usual. His youth pastor had called him a few weeks before and asked him to speak to the youth group on a Wednesday night. Today, Ryan's youth pastor, Jacob Murray, would be attending the Bible club to hear him give a run-through of the message he would be bringing to the youth group in two days.

Jacob arrived a few minutes before the club was scheduled to begin, as the students were beginning to stream in. Forty in all. One more than the day before. They pulled their chairs in close, stuffed their mouths full of sugar, and opened their Bibles to the first chapter of Acts.

Ryan began reading aloud. *"But you will receive power when the Holy Spirit has come upon you; and you shall be My witnesses both in Jerusalem, and in all Judea and Samaria, and even to the remotest part of the earth. And after He had said these things, He was lifted up while they were looking on, and a cloud received Him out of their sight."*[1] He finished reading and closed his Bible. "Now, we've all heard that passage a hundred times, haven't we?"

"Yes." The response was the same throughout the room.

"Yeah, of course you have. Jesus is about to leave the earth, but before He goes, He tells His followers that the Holy Spirit is going to come and give them power, and they will become His witnesses everywhere they go. He said Jerusalem, Judea and Samaria; but He might as well have said Midland, the state of Texas and the entire United States. The point is this: start where you are, and eventually, you'll touch the world."

In the front row, Sarah ran her fingers through her hair as she listened to Ryan burst into his full-on preacher mode. There was something attractive about a guy her age who loved Jesus just as much as the heroes in the faith. She loved his boldness. He wasn't afraid to stand up and talk about what he believed in, but at the same time he was compassionate enough to listen to and engage in conversation with those who disagreed. *"I could totally marry him,"* she caught herself thinking. *"I guess I could get used to being a pastor's wife."*

He caught her eye as he paused, interrupting her daydream. He smiled at her, slightly. She winked back as he continued his monologue. Jacob, standing off to the side, witnessed this exchange. He smiled to himself, doing his best to ignore it.

"Everybody wants to change the world. But few want to change *their* world. There are close to two thousand students in this school, and most of them would probably say they believe in God. If they were given the chance to do something great for Him, they would in a heartbeat. But how many of them are actually here early, connecting with other students who want to make a difference on their campus? I see twenty ... thirty ... it looks like forty of y'all. And that's okay. More will come. But right now, we've got to get down in the dirt and change our world. We've got to stop being so focused on the next big party or if our clothes are still in style, and start looking for the opportunities that have been right under our noses all along.

We're going to have to go out of our way to talk to those kids that no one else talks to. We're going to have to listen when we would rather yell why we're right and then run away. We've got to show God's love to the football players, the cheerleaders, the weird kids ... everyone."

Jeff felt Ryan's eyes on him as he was speaking. He put his head down and stared at his shoes, thinking back to the day before when his pastor had preached a similar message. Jeff had felt something stirring inside of him as he listened. It started out deep, a faint inkling, but grew with every word. It terrified him. He swallowed hard and forced it down. *"I'm just barely making it through life ... how am I supposed to make a difference in someone else's?"* He didn't really have a problem talking to people; he just didn't want to become *that* guy. He didn't want to stand out; he just wanted to fit in and get along with everyone. And if someone steered the conversation in the direction of spiritual things—sure, he would jump in. Only problem was, no one ever did. At least not when he was around.

Moments later, Jeff looked back up and caught Ryan's eye as he continued his monologue. *"It's as if he can see right through me,"* he thought to himself.

"Now, let's go back to that passage in Acts and read the two verses right before it." Reaching down, Ryan picked up his Bible from the table and began reading. *"So when they had come together, they asked Him, saying, "Lord, is it at this time You are restoring the kingdom to Israel?" He said to them, "It is not for you to know times or epochs which the Father has fixed by His own authority."*[2] Ryan closed his Bible and began to scan the room, locking eyes with Sarah again for a few seconds.

A girl towards the front of the room raised her hand.

Ryan pointed in her direction. "Lauren?"

"Isn't that referring to the end times or something? How exactly does that tie in with what you were talking about?"

"Great question," he replied with a smile, "I'm glad you asked." Ryan paused, taking a moment to think through his answer. "You see, Jesus and the apostles are hanging out, and they're basically asking Him to restore their political power and influence. And that's when Jesus calls a time-out, and tells them it's not about that. But they will receive the Holy Spirit. They will be witnesses." He paused again, this time for effect. "And that's how they'll influence and ultimately win over the world. Jesus looked at His followers and told them He wasn't going to instantly fix everything, but He was going to give them power to go out and restore broken humanity. And that's what we're called to do. We are called to rebuild and restore the broken, and when we start with those around us, when we help them piece their lives back together; the effects will reach far beyond us; and that is how you start a revolution that will change the world."

The room burst into applause. Sarah was the loudest, of course, with Lauren coming in at a close second. Even Jeff was won over.

Jacob stood at the back of the room, a broad smile stretched across his face. *"Wow. This kid can preach. He's going to tear it up Wednesday night."*

Five minutes later, Ryan stood at the door greeting students as they exited into the hallway. Jeff was the last to leave, and Ryan grabbed his arm as he passed. Jeff turned to face him, awaiting an explanation. Ryan hesitated for a moment before giving in to his unspoken request. "You know, you *can* do this."

"Do what?"

"You can make a difference in someone's life."

Jeff hung his head, mostly so Ryan would miss him rolling his eyes. He looked up and realized that Ryan had seen him. He sighed. "I know. I just … I don't know."

"It's okay. It's not like we're in the second grade; I don't need an excuse." Silence filled the space between them. "Don't think of it as something you *have* to do; think of it as something you *get* to do. Something you *want* to do."

"Listen, it's not that I don't want to—" Jeff trailed off, still unable to find the right words.

"You just don't know how," Ryan replied, finding his thought for him.

"Exactly," Jeff replied, as silence filled the air again.

"It's not really something that can be taught." He paused. "People are already talking about God, whether they realize it or not. You just have to get out there and listen."

"What do you mean?"

"Listen to their conversations. They're full of insecurities. Worries. Fears. *Am I going to make it to graduation? Will I ever truly be good at anything? Am I beautiful? Who am I, really?* People are longing to know their Father; they just don't all realize it. Don't be afraid to join the conversation. That is how we change our world. One conversation at a time."

"I don't think it's that simple," Jeff said quietly.

"Of course it is. You just have to listen and know when to speak up."

Jeff exited Room 107 and saw a well-dressed girl with blonde hair sitting on the floor with her back against the wall. Elizabeth Parker, of course. They had grown up alongside each other, but she had no clue he existed. Jeff shuffled past her at first, but then stopped. Turning around, he doubled back to where she was sitting and knelt down beside her. The first thing he noticed was the mascara streaked around her eyes. She had been crying.

"You alright?"

"Yeah, I'm fine."

"Okay. I just wanted to make sure." He paused. "I'm Jeff, by the way."

"Elizabeth."

"I know."

She looked at him in a way he couldn't quite discern. Either she thought he was being nice or a total creep; he couldn't tell the difference.

"Everyone knows you. You're Elizabeth Parker—Stephen Parker's sister."

"Yeah, not anymore."

He joined her against the wall.

"How does it feel?" he asked quietly, shattering the uncomfortable silence.

"Like hell," she replied without hesitation.

"Do you ever get tired of people asking you that?"

"Asking me what?"

"How it feels?"

"Actually, no one's ever asked me that. Most people just ask how I'm doing, which is basically the dumbest question you could ask. How do you think I'm doing?" She paused momentarily. "Of course, they don't really care. I try to be nice; I smile and offer some cliché answer, but by that point they aren't even listening. They've either moved on to something else, or literally moved on to talk to someone else." She looked up, surprised to find him looking at her intently. It was an odd feeling, having a complete stranger — well, sort of a stranger — listen to her for this long.

"People are just so fake, you know?

"Tell me about it," he replied, without missing a beat. He really was listening.

Ryan exited the classroom and saw Jeff and Elizabeth in the hallway. *"What is he doing? Chris will kill him if he sees him talking to his girlfriend."* Ryan checked his watch. Fifteen minutes until the first bell. Chris probably wasn't even out of bed yet.

"How long have you been sitting here?" Jeff asked.

"I don't know. At least half an hour." Elizabeth replied.

"Why are you here so early?"

"My mom found some weed in my room and threw a fit, so I left."

He nodded. "I tried smoking once, a couple years ago behind my church."

"Behind your church?" Elizabeth interjected, a smile making its way across her face.

"Yeah, one of my friends stole some weed from his uncle, so a couple of us smoked it out behind the church."

"How was it?" she asked inquisitively.

"Not that great."

"Yeah, well, I've never smoked in my life. Not even cigarettes."

"You haven't?"

"No. That's disgusting," she said plainly. He noticed her words were without an ounce of self-righteousness.

"Then why did you ...?"

"It's my boyfriend's. But did my mother give me time to explain that?"

"Did she yell at you?"

"No, actually, I yelled at her," she paused, for a moment. "I guess she did give me time to explain; I just didn't want to."

The two sat in silence for what felt like hours.

"Well, if you ever happen to be here this early again, some friends and I have a Bible study right over there in Room 107." He had succeeded at replacing the silence with a much more awkward feeling.

"That sounds really boring."

"Yeah, that's what I thought at first. But then I went and found out they had donuts."

"Except too bad I can't eat donuts," she said with a smile.

"You can't eat donuts?" Jeff asked, slightly surprised by her comment. "Why not?"

"Uh, because I'm on the cheerleading team."

"So?"

"So ... I have to look good."

"Really? They told you that?"

"Yeah, it's more of an implied thing ... it doesn't really matter that much."

"Well," he hesitated, but only for a moment. "We meet every Monday, forty-five minutes before the first bell. But if you'd rather sit here in the hallway by yourself, I understand.

She smiled. "Okay. I'll think about it."

"Pray about it."

She looked at him, more confused than ever. She clearly missed the point of his cheesy spiritual joke, as most do unless they've been in church for much of their lives.

"Never mind," he said, laughing nervously as he stood up. Extending his hand, he pulled her to her feet. "I'll see you later."

"See you later."

She watched as he walked down the hallway. There was something different about the way he talked to her. It seemed most people only wanted to talk to her to advance their social status, but Jeff wasn't like that. He was genuinely interested in her life, and actually seemed to care about how she was feeling. He hadn't sat down next to her because he wanted anything from her. He just saw that she needed someone to talk to and stepped in to meet the need. She wasn't used to that. It was almost a bit unsettling. When you've gotten used to people using you, it's shocking when you encounter something different; so shocking that you convince yourself it isn't real.

Chris slowly opened his eyes and rolled over in his bed. Glancing over at his alarm clock, he bolted upright and quickly jumped out of bed. He hurriedly dressed and rushed out the back door. Scaling the fence in one leap, he landed on the neighbor's trampoline. Rolling off the edge, he picked himself up and began to run.

Ryan began jogging to catch up to Jeff when he turned the corner and saw him at the other end of the hall.

"What's up?" Jeff turned as Ryan grabbed him by the shoulder.

"Hey, I saw you talking to Elizabeth earlier. What was that about?"

"Nothing. We were just talking."

"Sure. You and Elizabeth freaking Parker were just talking."

"Yeah," Jeff said slowly, slightly annoyed. "You know she's dating Chris, right?"

Ryan just stared at him, a smile on his face.

"What? You said I should talk to people about their lives."

"Yeah, I did. But I meant everyone—the weird kids, the losers ... Not just the attractive ones."

"You said we needed to show God's love to the cheerleaders and football players! She's a cheerleader, and Chris is the quarterback of the football team."

"So you really were listening, eh?" Ryan said with a smile.

"Of course. I always listen." Jeff turned and continued down the hall as the warning bell rang. The first classes of the morning would begin in less than a minute.

"Hey!" Ryan called after him.

"What?!" Jeff asked as he turned around to face his friend.

"I'm proud of you. You're finally doing it." He paused. "I knew you had it in you."

Jeff just turned and continued down the hallway.

Chris kicked it in to high gear as his feet hit the asphalt of the school parking lot. He had run the entire way there, three blocks, in under five minutes. If he kept this up, the coach might have to move him to starting running back.

Chris tumbled through the front door of the school as the final bell rang, nearly falling to the ground. *"Man, I'm good,"* he thought to himself. He imagined the main hallway of the school lined with spectators. Reporters. Photographers. Adoring fans. They were all there for him. Flashbulbs popped as he made his way through the sea of reporters. He saw Elizabeth, waiting for him in the middle of the crowd. He walked briskly towards her, stopping along the way to pose for a picture. *"That'll make the front page of the Reporter-Telegram for sure."* Walking the remainder of the distance to Elizabeth, he linked his arm in hers, and the two of them, Midland's power couple, walked arm-in-arm down the hall towards their first period math class.

"Good morning, Chris. Thank you for joining us." Mr. Coleman's voice interrupted his daydream.

"Huh?"

A hushed laughter filled the classroom as Chris stood in the doorway.

"Well, Chris, this is first period math, and while I can see that you're here, I can't help but wonder if you're here."

"I'm here, Mr. Coleman," Chris replied as he stepped into the classroom. "I'm here."

"Great. There's a seat open next to your Ms. Parker, so you can have a seat and continue your daydream. Just try to pay attention to math at some point today, okay?" the teacher said with a smile.

The class laughed again, more openly this time. Chris sat down at the only open desk, conveniently located next to Elizabeth, and reached for his backpack. It wasn't there. *"Darn! I knew I was forgetting something!"*

"Is there a problem, Chris?" Mr. Coleman asked. The teacher seemed to be reading his mind today.

"Yeah, I guess I forgot my math book."

"That's okay. I have an extra one you can borrow." Mr. Coleman walked over to his desk and opened the bottom drawer. Reaching in, he took out the book and held it out towards Chris, who came forward eager to receive it.

"I've got your back." Mr. Coleman looked him squarely in the eyes as he held onto the top half of the textbook, Chris gripping the bottom half. "Don't forget that."

"Thanks," he replied, as his teacher let go of the textbook. He turned and walked back to his seat.

"Hey, I'm mad at you," a voice whispered from his right. He turned the corner of his eye towards Elizabeth.

"Why?" he said in more than a whisper. Mr. Coleman heard him at the front of the room, but decided to dismiss it.

"Because my mom found your you-know-what and blamed it on me."

His heart sank. "Listen, I'm sorry ... We'll talk later," he whispered.

"You are correct," Elizabeth said confidentially, with a tone in her voice that he rarely heard.

Mr. Coleman began the lesson, and for once Chris actually focused on what he was saying, if for no other reason than to push what Elizabeth had said out of his head for the moment. There was something different about the way this teacher talked to him. He seemed to actually care about him, as if he were more than a name on a role sheet or another mediocre grade point average. It was almost as though Mr. Coleman believed in him, not just in his ability to turn in his homework on time, but in him personally. That gave him the courage to sit down and face algebra head on when he would much rather tune the whole thing out and rely on his athletic skills to carry him on a free ride to a passing grade.

Endnotes

1) Acts 1:8-9

2) Acts 1:6-7

Chapter Twenty-Six

FACES IN THE CROWD: MIDDLE

Jared Stump

Mr. Coleman picked up a stack of papers off his desk and placed them in his open briefcase. School had been over for two hours, but he had stayed late to help Jackson, one of his students who was having trouble understanding the algebra problems. They had spent the first hour talking through the lesson, but somewhere, the conversation shifted. The second hour was spent talking about a wide range of topics, from problems at home to faith and the mystery of existence.

Closing his briefcase, he picked it up and exited his classroom into the hallway. It was still and quiet, just as it had been that morning while he was praying.

This was a typical day for him—the first one in, the last one to leave. He didn't mind it though, not at all. In fact, it was the whole reason he had become a teacher in the first place. He wanted to do more than just make sure the kids behaved and learned a few things; he wanted to make a difference in their lives. He knew there were certain things he could and could not say, but he also knew that if a student approached him after school hours, as Jackson had, it wasn't his fault if the conversation shifted towards spiritual matters.

He exited the building and looked across the faculty parking lot towards the football field, where a lone silhouette was running laps in full uniform. He knew exactly who it was. Walking past his truck, he continued to the edge of the field and waited for Chris to pass him.

281

Chris slowed down when he saw his math teacher standing on the sidelines. He took off his helmet and jogged briskly towards him.

"What are you still doing here?"

Mr. Coleman chuckled.

"Us teachers don't always get to leave when you leave."

Chris nodded.

"What are you doing here?" Mr. Coleman asked, flipping the question. "Didn't practice end twenty minutes ago?"

"Yeah, it did."

"You only answered one of my questions."

Mr. Coleman didn't miss a beat. He had a way of holding people accountable, but managed to do it in a way that was loving and gentle. The last thing the students need is another harsh, mean teacher who couldn't seem to relate to them. There were plenty of those out there, and he was determined to be different.

"I mean, there's no point in going home," Chris said hesitantly.

"Why is that?" Mr. Coleman implored.

"It hasn't been the best environment ever since my dad left. My mom works nights, so she's usually completely wasted by the time I get home from school. It takes her most of the evening to sober up, and then she has to get ready for work."

"So you just hang out until then, huh?"

"Yeah. Not just here though, I usually go to a friend's house. She doesn't leave for work until midnight, so most of the time I don't go home until after that."

"So that's why you're always late for my class."

"Yeah, pretty much. It's not that I want to stay out late; it's just better than the alternative."

"Have you tried talking to her?"

"When she's sober. Which is hardly ever. I don't think she even realizes that I'm never around."

"I saw her at your last game."

"Yeah, she always comes to the games. She's proud of me when I'm winning."

"That's why you work so hard; you've got to win so she'll be proud of you."

"Pretty much."

"Well, you're doing a great job. Just remember that there's more to life than football."

"What do you mean?"

"Go out forty yards and throw me a pass."

"Huh?" Chris just stared him.

"You heard me." Mr. Coleman set his briefcase down and took off his jacket.

"Uh ... all right," Chris replied hesitantly before turning and jogging thirty yards.

"I said forty!" Mr. Coleman yelled after him.

Chris rolled his eyes, but moved back the remaining ten yards.

"Alright, show me what you've got!"

Chris lobbed a pass through the air. The wind caught it, veering the ball several yards off target. But that didn't seem to faze Mr. Coleman. The aging teacher ran after it at full speed, reaching out to pick the ball out of the air seconds before it hit the ground. Chris's jaw dropped as his teacher turned and began jogging towards him.

"Dang, Mr. Coleman! Where did you learn to catch like that?"

"Partly in high school, mostly in college."

"You played?" Chris asked, still in shock.

"Yeah, I played," he said with a grin.

"Why didn't you go pro?"

"I had an offer, but I turned it down."

"What?! Why did you do that?"

"Because I had another offer, and it was my dream job."

"What was that?" Chris asked eagerly.

His teacher grinned again.

"No way!"

Mr. Coleman nodded. "Yep. And I've been right here ever since."

Amy was in the living room folding laundry when she heard the back door open. She continued about her work, not wanting to face her daughter. She heard Elizabeth throw her backpack onto the kitchen table and open the fridge.

"Hey mom!"

Silence.

"Mom!"

Amy stood up and walked into the kitchen. "I thought you didn't want me in your life," she said with a smirk.

"Yeah ... about that."

"What about it?"

"Listen, mom," Elizabeth paused. "I'm sorry."

"Okay," Amy replied coldly.

"Mom! That stuff isn't even mine, okay?"

"I know," she replied after a long pause.

"Really?"

Amy laughed under her breath, the enmity between them quickly fading. "I've seen you two out on the front porch late at night. I've seen Chris smoke that crap. I've seen him offer you some." She paused long enough for Amy to feel the love in her eyes. "And I've seen you turn him down."

"I would've told you that if you'd just given me a chance." Elizabeth paused. "If you knew it wasn't mine, why did you make such a big deal about it?"

"I'm not the one who made a big deal about it."

"I guess that's true," Elizabeth said quietly, after another long pause.

"I love you," Amy said with a smile.

"I love you too," Elizabeth replied as the two embraced.

The next day after school, Jeff exited the building through the side door, into the faculty parking lot. The first thing he saw was the cheerleading squad practicing on the football field in front of him. He began to walk toward the field as Ryan exited the building behind him.

"Going to talk to Elizabeth again?"

Jeff turned to see Ryan behind him. "You're hilarious," he replied flatly.

"What are you doing, man?"

"Well, if you must know, I was going to invite her to church tomorrow night."

"Alright," Ryan said with a shrug. "I guess that's admirable."

Jeff turned and walked toward the field without a word.

Elizabeth saw him out of the corner of her eye as he walked across the parking lot. "Crap!" she said aloud. Chris was running laps around the field, as he did nearly every afternoon after school. Fortunately, he was at the opposite end of the field, though it wouldn't be long before he passed within ten yards of where she and the other girls were rehearsing their cheers.

Jeff stopped at the chain-link fence, which bordered the field. Elizabeth left the group and headed toward him.

"Hey," Jeff said as she reached the other side of the fence.

"What are you doing here?"

"I just wanted to ask you —"

"Ask me what?" Elizabeth interjected, a sense of urgency in her voice as she looked over her shoulder. Chris was rounding the end zone and heading back up the field toward them. Meanwhile, the cheerleaders had stopped their routine when they noticed someone was missing.

"Hey Ashley, where did Liz go?" one of the cheerleaders asked.

"She's over there," Ashley pointed. "Talking to some guy."

"Oh my gosh. Is that Jeff?"

"I think so," Ashley replied.

"Why is she hanging out with that loser?" another girl named Brittany added.

Chris saw Elizabeth as he neared the fifty-yard line. "Who is she talking to?" he said to himself. Cutting across the field, he walked right through the group of cheerleaders.

"Hey Chris!" Brittany yelled. "Your girlfriend is over there talking to that loser, Jeff."

"Not for long," Chris replied.

"So, my friend Ryan who leads our Bible club is speaking at my church tomorrow night." Ryan stopped short as he saw Chris approaching over Elizabeth's shoulder.

"And?" Elizabeth asked.

"And I was wondering if you'd like to come."

"She's busy," Chris interjected, pushing Elizabeth behind him as he pressed against the chain-link fence just inches from Jeff's face.

"Hey, she came over here," Jeff replied, knowingly instantly he had chosen the wrong words.

Chris leaned closer until his nose was almost touching Jeff's. Then, without a word, he turned, linked arms with Elizabeth, and walked away, leaving Jeff alone on the other side of the fence.

The following night, Ryan preached the same message he had preached in the Bible club two days before, about the Holy Spirit and changing the world and all the other things that that entails. Jacob looked on from the back of the room, a smile on his face. A year and a half ago, Ryan had little idea that Jesus desired a relationship with him. Now, he was standing at the front of the church on a Wednesday night, talking about Him like he knew Him intimately. It's amazing what can happen when Jesus gets ahold of someone. Ryan was no exception. He had received the fullness of God's love, and now he couldn't wait to share Him with others.

The next morning, Elizabeth's alarm went off an hour earlier than usual. Yawning, she climbed out of bed. The house was dark as she quietly opened her bedroom door and slipped into the hallway. Her dad was long gone, but she could hear her mom breathing gently through the open door a few feet away. She tiptoed to the other end of the house and slipped into the kitchen.

Ten minutes later, Amy awoke to the sounds and smells of coffee brewing. *"What in the world? Is the coffee making itself this morning?"*

Elizabeth was sitting at the kitchen table with a bowl of cereal and a mug of java when Amy entered the room.

"What are you doing up?" she said with a yawn.

"Have a seat. There's coffee on the counter."

"So I see," Amy said as she moved toward the fresh-brewed smell which enveloped the far end of the kitchen. "Are you feeling alright?" she asked as she made her way to the table, coffee in hand.

"Yeah. Why wouldn't I be?"

"Just wondering."

Elizabeth downed her last bite of cereal and stood up. "I've got to go get ready."

"This early?"

"Yeah, mom," Elizabeth replied, already in the doorway.

"What about your coffee?" Amy called after her.

"You can have it," came a voice from the living room.

Amy shrugged as she reached for her daughter's mug, dumping it into hers. Something was going on, that was for sure, she just wasn't able to put her finger on it.

The weekend came and went. Monday morning, Jeff stood at the back of Room 107 as Ryan conversed with two students, who were new to the Bible club, at the front of the room. Nearly a week had passed since the run-in with Chris on the football field, and Jeff had not talked to Elizabeth since.

They had seen each other in passing on Thursday and Friday, and of course he had seen her on the sidelines during the game, cheering her boyfriend—and all of the other jocks—on. He secretly wished he could be like them—big and strong and not so afraid all the time, but what he didn't realize is that those guys wrestled with the same insecurities as him; they were just a lot better at covering them up with their trophies and achievements on the football field.

He had sent Elizabeth a tweet before falling asleep Sunday night. It wasn't much, just a simple reminder of the Bible club the next morning. She hadn't replied, and he didn't really expect her to come, but he was holding tightly to the small part of him that remained optimistic.

Within ten minutes, the room was full of students, forty-three to be exact. Ryan wrapped up his conversation and summoned the group's attention.

"Hey, how is everyone doing this morning?"

"Good!" the group resounded.

"Wow, there's so many of you here today. I'm going to need a microphone if y'all keep brining your friends like this."

"We may just have to move into the auditorium," Sarah offered with a slight wink from her typical spot on the front row; off center, of course, in a weak attempt to not be totally straightforward with her affections.

"Maybe so," Ryan replied with a smile. "We've got a couple of new students today." He moved up the aisle toward the back of the room as he spoke. "Say hello to Scott and Hannah."

The rest of the group turned and offered their greetings as Ryan moved back toward the front of the room.

"I got to talk with them a few minutes ago and found out they're pretty new to the faith. They gave me permission to single them out, so I'd like for us to discuss a question that Scott asked me, because I think it's a question that a lot of us have." He paused. "Scott asked me how to share Christ with his friends without appearing to have a hidden agenda. And actually, Jeff has had a lot of experience with this lately."

"What are you doing?" Jeff said under his breath from the back of the room.

"Jeff, do you mind coming up and sharing for a few minutes?"

"Share what?"

"You know."

"No. I don't," he said flatly.

Ryan walked across the room and put his arm around him, leading him against his will to the front of the group.

"I don't want to do this," Jeff said, looking him right between the eyes.

"You'll be fine," Ryan reassured him. "Just be yourself."

"Hello everyone. I'm Jeff."

"Hi, Jeff," came the response. He hadn't even begun to share his story, and it was already like an *A.A.* meeting gone bad.

Elizabeth made her way down the hall toward Room 107. She was late, and she knew it. Hidden beneath her tardiness was her desire to sit alone in the back of the room without having to talk to anyone beforehand. She would slip in late, and leave immediately after it was over. She hesitated as she reached the door of the classroom. She could hear Jeff's voice, muffled through the heavy oak door. This was it. She was really doing it.

"Here goes nothing," she said aloud as she pushed open the door.

"I saw her sitting alone in the hallway and I sat down next to her. I asked her how she was doing, how she was feeling. I didn't say, 'Hey, do you know Jesus?' though that was my secret intention, if you will." Jeff stopped abruptly when he saw Elizabeth standing in the doorway. She stood there, frozen.

"He's talking about me." A sinking feeling intruded into her stomach. She was terrified, absolutely terrified. She wasn't sure if her legs were still under her, but soon discovered that they were, as she turned and ran out of the room.

"Elizabeth!" He ran after her, forgetting about everyone else in the room.

"Elizabeth, wait!"

She turned to see him jogging down the hallway after her. "What do you want?"

"I'm sorry ... Ryan wanted me to talk about ... it's not what you think!"

"Oh, so now you know how I think?! What are you, some sort of machine?"

Elizabeth didn't wait for Jeff to respond. Turning her back on him, she continued down the hallway, not wanting him to see her cry this time.

Meanwhile, back in Room 107, Ryan was trying to divert attention away from what had just happened. He wanted to shut down the rumors before they began—before Chris got wind of anything that had happened.

"I think if there's anything we can take away from this, it's that we should get permission before telling someone else's story in a setting such as this. Sarah, if you want to finish things up ..."

Sarah stood nervously and made her way to Ryan's side. "What do you want me to talk about?" she whispered.

"I don't care," he whispered back. "Anything but this." To the group, he said, "Let's keep this situation in this room. The last thing we need is rumors spreading throughout the school. Especially to the football team." And with that, Ryan made a beeline for the door, leaving Sarah standing alone in front of the group.

Chapter Twenty-Seven

FACES IN THE CROWD: ENDING

Jared Stump

The week that began with Elizabeth walking out of the Bible club had come and gone. Like most Friday nights, Jeff had nothing better to do than go to the game. If there was one occasion when he *didn't* want to be there, this was it, but he reasoned that if he sat toward the top of the bleachers, he could remain out of her line of sight.

Elizabeth looked stunning as she took the field, as usual. She was one of the few girls in Midland who had perfected the "natural" look, spending hours in front of the mirror in an attempt to make it look as if she hadn't given her appearance a second thought. Elizabeth went to great lengths to make herself look as "real" as possible, while most of the other girls got up each morning and simply existed. Being the best-dressed girl in town was not a difficult title to obtain, but she got up each morning and earned it all over again.

She had been ignoring him all week, which didn't surprise him too much. He didn't blame her, really, because he realized that he had been describing her as more of an object than a person at the moment she entered the classroom a few days before.

His head shook back and forth slightly as he thought about the irony that always seemed to follow girls like Elizabeth. The bulk of their free time revolved around buying the coolest clothes and doing their hair and makeup past the point where normal people stop, north of "good enough" but still shy of perfection. Because perfection is never within grasp, no matter how badly you crave it. And the irony came in to play by how often they complained about guys treating them like objects, when much of their time was spent packing and marketing themselves like common merchandise, trying to prove themselves to people who already stayed up at night thinking about them.

Jeff's mind wandered around this topic for much of the game, which was as exciting as seeing a truck with New Mexico license plates. The rivalry between Midland and San Angelo typically made for an exciting contest, but things had grown stagnant in recent years. Now it was just the bridge between the presumed loss against Odessa Permian and the toss-up against Midland Lee.

It wasn't the biggest game of the year; that had already taken place two weeks prior when they lost to Permian. But if you're new in town, the first thing you'll learn about Texas high school football is that every team is treated as an arch rival and every game is played like it's the biggest game of the year. They would play their crosstown rivals the following week to close out the season, but for now they just needed to beat San Angelo, a task they presumed to be accomplished from the moment they took the field.

Three grueling hours later, it was all over. Both teams had remained scoreless for much of the night, until Midland came alive in the fourth quarter, crushing San Angelo into the ground with a mediocre score of 10-3. It was games like this that made even the most loyal of fans wish they had stayed home to eat frozen pizza and watch re-runs of *Duck Dynasty*.

Jeff tried to slip out quietly after the game ended, until he inadvertently locked eyes with Elizabeth at field level. It was a moment when most people would quickly look away, but she didn't. Exhaustion covered her face like a mask as she nodded slightly, her eyes failing to miss a beat.

She swiveled forty-five degrees as Chris approached. He caught her in a full embrace as he dropped the helmet he had been carrying onto the perfectly manicured grass. Jeff turned away quickly.

"It's okay. Let her go." The voice came from behind him. He didn't have to turn around to know who it was.

"You don't know what you're talking about."

"Oh, really?" Ryan replied, this time grabbing Jeff by the shoulder. Their eyes met for a moment, as both searched for the right words to fill the silence.

"Do you even realize what I did?" Jeff spoke first.

"The whole school knows what you did," Ryan replied flatly. "You tried to break up Chris and Elizabeth; it didn't work. It's okay. Move on."

"That is not what happened."

"Alright. Tell me your side of the story," Ryan replied as his face tightened.

"I've already told you everything," Jeff said, with more sorrow than anger. "But I don't need you to believe me." With that, he turned and walked away, leaving Ryan alone in the crowd.

Elizabeth slowly made her way across the parking lot, her body weighed down by the pink backpack that held her uniform and all sorts of other items. She looked across the nearly empty parking lot to see the interior lights of the Baptist church were illuminated, as they typically were every Friday night after a game.

"Who goes to church at 11:00 on a Friday night?" she wondered as she began walking parallel to the massive mission-style building. Living halfway between the high school and Memorial Stadium had its advantages, especially since she had spent the past year walking nearly everywhere.

It was a typical muggy fall night, dust and oil circulating through the air, but that was the least of her concerns. She was six blocks from home, and she wanted to make it there before the jocks began their drunken escapades, lighting up the otherwise quiet neighborhood nestled between downtown and Andrews Highway.

Win or lose, the majority of the football team and the rest of Midland's high school elite would meet up at the Taylor's house after the game for the sole purpose of getting completely wasted before midnight. After a big win — or any win, really — they would hit the streets like they owned the town, often drag racing their trucks down Texas Avenue, starting at the Catholic church and continuing until they reached the concrete towers, miniature versions of those one would find in Dallas or Austin. They would make their way home around two or three, sleep most of Saturday away, and then wake up Sunday morning in time to attend church with their families.

Drag racing on city streets after the lights go out is an inevitable past time in Midland, where nearly every street runs in a perfectly straight line for miles. The cops always look the other way on Friday nights after a victory, none of them wanting to be the one to arrest a star player for driving while intoxicated, potentially ending up costing the team a win.

Brad Taylor was the star center of the football team, not to mention one of the wealthiest kids in town. Oil money had been good to Midland, and the Taylor's had certainly received their share. His dad managed a bank that occupied much of the space in one of the concrete towers downtown, and had built his family a sprawling estate amongst the modest ranch houses surrounding the stadium. In a time when the majority of Midland's upper-class families were moving to subdivisions on the outskirts of town—if for no other reason than to get their kids in the district for the high school with the better football team—the Taylor's had planted their roots in the heart of the city.

Jeff exited the side door of the church in time to see a blonde girl lose her balance as her foot entered a small pothole along the side of the street. He quickly made his way toward her, realizing the girl was Elizabeth as he jogged across the street.

"Are you alright?" he asked, helping her to her feet.

"Yeah," she replied quietly as their eyes met. "Thanks."

"What are you doing?" Jeff asked.

"Are you asking why I'm not with Chris?" she said with a slight smirk.

"I guess," he replied, nonchalantly.

"Well you see," she began, slinging her backpack over her shoulder once again as she continued on down the street. "Chris is at the Taylor's house right now, and you know what happens there every Friday night after the games."

"No, I don't," he said, shaking his head.

"Seriously?"

"Do you really think I'm cool enough to go hang out at the Taylor's every Friday night?" he asked, before answering his own question. "No, that's why I'm here."

"That's a good point," she paused. "So what is going on here?"

"They're having this thing called a Fifth Quarter. I help out with the games and stuff sometimes."

"That's cool," she said, in a tone that told him she could care less. Realizing that he sensed her disinterest, she followed up with a question. "So do you go to church here?"

"No, I go to Antioch Fellowship, out on the loop near the mall."

She nodded. "I think I've seen that place. The one with the big, white steeple?"

"Well, you just described more than three dozen churches in Midland, but yes," he replied with a slight chuckle.

"You're probably right," she said. "Although it's been awhile since I've been anywhere near one." She trailed off, realizing that she needed to switch gears before he attempted to convert and baptize her in the backyard of the closest house with a swimming pool, as any other body of water is hard to come by in West Texas. "So what exactly is a Fifth Quarter?"

"Just this thing where they open up the church for anyone who wants to hang out with their friends after the game without getting completely wasted."

"So you do know what goes on at the Taylor's house," she said with a smile.

"I guess," he replied, almost as more of a question than a statement.

"There's alcohol," she said bluntly, in case he still didn't get it. "A lot of alcohol. And sex, drugs ... you know. But more alcohol than anything else."

"Does Mr. Taylor know about all of this?" he asked, almost as if he didn't believe her.

"He could care less. Ever since the cancer took his wife, he just works all day, and at night he goes out and hits the bars until he doesn't know which way is up ..." she paused. "Brad says he hardly ever sees him anymore. And when he does, he's just not the same, you know. He aches inside. Deeply. I saw him in the checkout line at the supermarket the other day ... I said hello, but he just stood there, staring at me."

A long pause ensued. The kind where you let the emotion hang thick in the air, neither person wanting to say a word, mainly for fear of saying the wrong thing and killing the moment.

"Wow," he said, struggling for words. "So you never did answer my question ..."

"And what was that?" she asked, before he could finish.

"Why aren't you with Chris?" he asked, knowing the moment the words left his mouth that he had said the wrong thing.

Another long pause. This one, however, was much more uncomfortable. Little more than the sound of shoes hitting the pavement was heard as Jeff and Elizabeth walked down the darkened street, houses on one side, a nearly empty hospital parking lot on the other.

"I used to go out with Chris all the time after the games. We would drink and fool around, or whatever," she paused to catch her breath. "Until last year," she paused again, longer this time, giving him a hint of where she was going with this.

"Oh. Stephen," he said, filling the silence with nothing more than what was needed. This time he had said the right thing. He was still learning that in moments like these, a few carefully chosen words carry more weight and do less damage than many words.

"Yeah," her voice barely rose above a whisper. He turned and saw a tear making its way down her cheek. "He was out with his girlfriend that night. They weren't drinking or anything like that; they were just hanging out," she paused, breathing in as much of the autumn air as her lungs could hold before quickly releasing it in the form of a long sigh. "I was at the Taylor's house that night. Andrew and Bobby had been throwing back so many beers that it was practically seeping out of their pores. Then they started talking about their trucks, which one was faster and what not, and then this other guy dared them to race each other."

They crossed the street and turned onto Tennessee Avenue. Now less than four blocks from the Parker's house, Jeff realized that he had forgotten his responsibilities back at the church. *"Oh well,"* he thought to himself. *"I might as well walk her the rest of the way home."*

"The guys were racing down Texas Avenue like they owned the town. Stephen and Hannah were driving down Main Street. Bobby hit his breaks when the light turned red, but Andrew barreled on through the intersection. You know the rest of the story," she said quietly.

They walked in silence for a block. Jeff knew better than to speak.

"You know what the worst part is?" Elizabeth asked, abruptly breaking the silence. He turned to look at her, knowing she was about to answer her rhetorical question. "I should have been in that car. Andrew tried to get Chris and I to go with him. I wanted to, but Chris wouldn't let me. I think he saved my life."

Jeff was recalling the story in his mind as she spoke, vividly remembering the things he had read in the *Reporter-Telegram*. Now that Elizabeth was filling him in on the story behind the story, it was all beginning to make sense. He now understood why Andrew's family had abruptly packed up and moved to Odessa, while Bobby's remained.

"So that's why you don't go to the Taylor's anymore," he stated aloud, all the while wondering why Chris left her alone each week after the games.

Elizabeth must have been able to read his mind, because she quickly answered the question he was asking himself. "Chris still goes every week, but it's more of a political thing.

Everyone on the football team goes, and he's the quarterback, you know."

"So because he's the leader, he feels that it's necessary to lead his teammates into destroying their lives and futures, while his girlfriend walks home alone every Friday night?" This time, he realized he was saying the wrong thing as the words were leaving his mouth, rather than after.

Elizabeth didn't even blink. "I should slap you in the face," she stated flatly. "But I won't. Because you're right."

The two walked in silence for another block.

"That's my house up there," she said, pointing toward one of the ranch houses that, under cover of darkness, looked no different than the others.

"That's Midland for you," he thought to himself, still trying to figure out how he had ended up in this town in the first place.

"Thanks for walking me home," Elizabeth said, managing a tight-lipped smile as they came to a stop in front of her house. "You're a good friend."

"So we're friends?" he inquired, raising his eyebrows.

"Of course. Why wouldn't we be?"

"Well, I didn't know that you ever considered us friends to begin with ... and that was back before you heard me talking about you like you're some sort of project."

"I *am* a project," She responded, looking him right between the eyes. "And so are you."

"I guess you're right," he replied. "I guess I better get back to the church before they call in a search team."

"Oh! I am so sorry; I didn't mean to keep you."

"It was worth it," he replied.

Another pause ensued. This one, the most awkward. He contemplated if it was time to turn and walk away. She contemplated if it was time to turn and make her way up the front walk. They stared at each other, neither party wanting to be the first to break eye contact.

"I haven't been to church in forever," she stated in a matter-of-fact tone, breaking eye contact as her gaze sank to the asphalt.

"How long has it been?"

"Well, we had Stephen's funeral at the Presbyterian church across the street from school. If you count that, I guess it's been a year."

"That doesn't count," he said as he shook his head.

"Hmm," she said, trying to recall the memories. "We used to go to church a lot when I was younger, like in elementary school. Then we stopped going so much, and it kind of slowed down to just Easter and Christmas. But even that stopped a few years later," she paused, still trying to count the years. "I guess it's been, I don't know … seven years?"

"So you haven't been since you were —"

"Nine," she said, completing his thought.

A smooth silence hung in the air.

"Well," he began. "If you ever want to come to Antioch, you know where it's at."

"Big white steeple," she said with a smile.

"Big white steeple," he echoed quietly.

"Thanks again for walking me home," she said, her eyes filled with genuine gratitude.

"Anytime."

Turning away, she stepped over the curb and made her way up the front walk toward the door of the house that looked like all the others. He remained motionless in the street, taking in the moment, before turning and making his way back down Tennessee Avenue, a bit of a spring in his step as he effortlessly covered the six blocks back to the church.

In most cities across America, people wake up slowly as Sunday morning progresses. Not in Midland. Most of the town wakes up at 8:30, almost on cue, to begin the hustle and bustle of the morning that centers around church and culminates with dinner around the dining room table.

The Parker house was one of a few exceptions. Stephen's room was cold and dark, Elizabeth had gone to bed the night before without setting an alarm, and in the master bedroom, Rick was sleeping like a rock after a long week on the oil rig, Amy buried into his side. She had been awake for hours now, unable to sleep past six most mornings, but she closed her eyes and pulled him close whenever he stirred. These moments of closeness were few and far between, as they grew older and less in love, and something inside of her wanted to take hold of as many of these moments as she could and save them for the times when he wasn't around.

It wasn't that they tried to drift apart over the years, it just sort of happened. Like with any relationship, maintenance is the hardest part. It's easy to just live with one another and go through the motions, faking the whole thing until you wake up one day and realize that you simply cannot do it anymore. This dynamic played out in Rick and Amy's marriage, in their relationship with their kids, and in their church attendance. So far, they'd managed to keep two of the three alive, but time was not on their side.

Elizabeth herself was still on the fence about the idea of returning to the building with the big white steeple. When she went to bed Saturday night, she told herself that she would go if she woke up in time, and if she didn't, she wouldn't give it another thought.

Rick began to stir as the digital clock rolled over 8:54. Amy turned into him as he let out a hushed groan.

"Is it raining?" his voice was groggy, as half of his body came alive while the other half remained in a dead slumber.

"I think it's the shower," Amy murmured, pretending she had just awoke. "Elizabeth must be up."

"Does she realize it's Sunday?" he questioned through the morning fog.

No further words were exchanged as Rick and Amy lay in bed, staring at the ceiling through their eyelids. The muffled sound of water stopped. The bathroom door opened. Wrapping her hair in a towel, Elizabeth made her way down the cold hallway, stopping outside Stephen's door in typical fashion. She stood there for a solid minute and a half, fidgeting with a loose string on her bathrobe, before continuing down the hallway. Amy heard the footsteps and the silence from the other end of the hall, and she too remembered.

Finally making her way to her bedroom, Elizabeth opened the closet and parted everything to one side, digging towards the back in search of the two dresses she owned. Finding them, she held one in each hand. To the left was the somber black dress she had worn once, about a year ago. To the right, a white sundress she had purchased in Dallas the summer before the accident. This one she had never worn, aside from trying it on in the store. She had yet to find a moment that felt right.

Looking over her options, Elizabeth threw the dress her left hand held onto the bed.

Mr. Coleman slipped into the front row as worship began. The math teacher would turn preacher in less than half an hour. Robert Ector, who had pastored Antioch for more than thirty years, was spending the autumn weekend on a beach somewhere in the Caribbean, celebrating a union with his wife that had lasted even longer than his tenure at the church.

The worship team played around with a few fast songs before a rendition of the British anthem began, the one about the road marked with suffering, pain in the offering, and praising God anyway in the midst of it all.[1]

Ryan saw Jeff standing towards the back of the room during the song. Slipping quietly out of the row, he made his way back to Jeff and placed his hand on his shoulder. Turning to face Ryan, Jeff smiled politely in response.

The two stood side-by-side for the duration of the song. As it came to a close, they watched as Mr. Coleman appeared at stage right, mic in hand. He quickly made his way to center stage and stood confidently in front of the worship leader, who had taken a few steps back as he approached.

"As we were singing that song," he began, addressing the congregation. "I was reminded of a passage from the book of Revelation. John, one of the original twelve disciples was in exile on the island of Patmos. Jesus appeared to him, and instructed him to write letters to seven communities of believers," he paused momentarily, opening the Bible he held in his free hand. "In the last letter, to the church in Laodicea, he wrote, *"Because you say, 'I am rich, and have become wealthy, and have need of nothing,' and you do not know that you are wretched and miserable and poor and blind and naked – "*[2] he stopped abruptly, his gaze fixed straight ahead. "I often wonder, if Jesus were to physically attend one of our services—would He say the same thing to us? I wonder, if He were to slip into the back of the room and see us happy and comfortable with the lives we've built, totally self-sufficient and in need of nothing—would He tell us that we are wretched, poor, and blind?" he looked out across the faces in the crowd, seeing a few eyes fixed on him while others darted to the shadows. "And it's not about what we have or don't have—that isn't what Jesus is talking about at all. Jesus is looking at the church and saying, "You have everything you've ever wanted, but you've forgotten about Me—and when you forget about Me, you really don't have anything at all."

Hushed groans began to fill the room, as the congregation breathed in the weight of his words and exhaled the things that had been getting in the way of them and the Father.

"The letter goes on to say," Mr. Coleman squinted under the dim lights, "'I advise you to buy from Me gold refined by fire so that you may be rich, and white garments so that you may clothe yourself, and that the shame of your nakedness will not be revealed; and eye salve to anoint your eyes so that you may see.'[3] Have you ever read that and thought to yourself, 'What on earth is Jesus saying here?' I know I have," he said with a chuckle, knowing that he had lost several people with the reading of the second verse, also knowing that he was about to bring them back. "You know, Job was a man who lost everything he had in life—not just the trivial things, but the things that meant the world to him."

"Where is he going with this?" Ryan thought to himself, momentarily missing Pastor Ector. Both men were aging rapidly, but at least one of them could stay on topic.

"Job grieved and mourned and worked through the mess … but he never accused God of mistreating him, even though he had many reasons to do so. And then he fell to his knees in worship and he said, *'Blessed be the name of the Lord.'"*[4]

Mr. Coleman paused again, leaving Ryan to wonder if he was finished. *"Is he done? He never tied in any of that stuff about gold refined by fire. Why didn't he just tell us about Job and be done with it?"*

"Once everything was stripped away, Job began to look at his life and his relationship with God. This went on for some time. And then, in the middle of the mess, we see Job saying, 'I look in all directions, and I can't seem to find God anywhere. But He knows exactly where I am, and when I come out on the other side of this, I will come out as gold.'"[5] Mr. Coleman paused, a broad smile spanning his cheeks. "Do you see it?"

Ryan just stood there, shaken to the core. *"Why is he not a pastor?"* he asked himself. It was then that he realized, he was. Though Darrell Coleman lacked the title of "pastor" in front of his name, he was a pastor to hundreds of students at Midland High School.

"At the end of the story, Job made this statement: *'My ears had heard of you but now my eyes have seen you.'*[6] He had to lose everything that meant anything to him—even his closest family members—before he could see the One who was more important than everything else. That is what it means to *buy from Me gold refined by fire so that you may become rich.*"

The congregation burst into applause, as the level of faith in the room surged to a point where it was nearly tangible.

"That would be a really good story if we stopped there," he paused, gazing out into space. "But it doesn't end there," he said, as he shook his head, which at this point could barely contain his smile. "God restored everything that Job lost. He had seven more sons, three more daughters, and twice as much of everything else than he had before."[7]

Reaching into his pocket, he produced a handkerchief and wiped away the beads of sweat that had appeared on his forehead. "You know, God isn't looking to take away the things we enjoy in life. He just wants us to care about Him more than any of that other stuff. What I love about this song that we just sang, is that Job did not say 'Blessed be Your name' at the end of the story, after everything had worked out for him. He said it at the beginning of the story, when nothing was working out for him!"

The band members began to play the same tune as before in the background as Mr. Coleman's speech reached its culmination.

"As we go back into worship today, let's bless the name of the Lord. Even if you feel as though you are searching in every direction and He is nowhere to be found, can you rest in the fact that He knows exactly where you are? Will that be enough for you today?"

The worship leader stepped forward and launched into a power chorus of *Blessed Be Your Name* as Mr. Coleman calmly exited the stage.

"Hey," Ryan turned to Jeff, speaking just loud enough to be heard above the music. "I just wanted to say I'm sorry for all that stuff I said the other night."

"It's alright, man. Don't worry about it," Jeff replied, as the two friends moved closer to one another. Through their embrace, Jeff saw a blonde girl in a white dress standing less than two feet inside the door that led from the foyer into the sanctuary. A smile made its way across his face, as he wondered how much of Mr. Coleman's speech she had heard. Then, as he noticed the tears flowing freely from her eyes, he realized that she had heard all that she needed to hear.

Endnotes

1) Blessed Be Your Name, Matt Redman

2) Revelation 3:17

3) Revelation 3:18

4) Job 1:20-22, Paraphrased

5) Job 23:8-10, Paraphrased

6) Job 42:5, NIV

7) See Job 42:10-13

Chapter Twenty-Eight

THE STORY IS YOURS

Kyle Embry

Do you identify with any of the characters in *Faces in the Crowd?* While Jeff, Ryan, Elizabeth, Chris, Mr. Coleman, and all the others do not technically exist, they represent real people with real stories. These are the types of people I meet in my travels—ordinary people who have turned their worlds upside down. I believe that you too came become an "ordinary hero" in your community. Every time you set out to make a difference in someone's life—no matter how insignificant it may seem—you bring the characters in this story to life.

One Tuesday morning, as we were bringing this project to completion, I pulled my truck into the parking lot of a junior high school in a suburban Dallas community. We were scheduled to do an assembly at the school that morning, to have an honest discussion with the students about the importance of good morals and the dangers of bullying.

As I approached the main entrance of the school, I noticed two brightly colored posters taking center stage on the glass wall, both advertising a Bible club called *The Jesus Movement*, which met each Tuesday after school in the library. I couldn't help but smile, knowing that this was one of our Youth Alive clubs, started by a Campus Missionary named Anna.

Anna started her club a few years ago, after being inspired to make a difference on her junior high campus. She graduated last year, and has recently started a club across the street at the high school. But before leaving, Anna made plans for the future

310

of The Jesus Movement, turning over leadership of the club to her younger brother, Jared, who still has a year and a half of junior high remaining before joining his sister at the high school.

Anna's second club did not come as easily as her first. There was a much longer process involved in getting it started. It required more meetings with the principal and help from her parents. Though she is a talented athlete, Anna chose to give up playing basketball in order to start her club. This was a big sacrifice for her, but she knows it is worth it to reach her school.

Anna's club currently has around a dozen students in attendance. It is not as big as the club at her former junior high school — the one that her brother currently leads — but I have heard the stories of some of the students in her club, and I know that God is at work in their lives.

We often only want to minister when we can reach large groups of people; it can drive us crazy when we are only reaching a handful. It is good to want to reach as many people as possible, but we should never be dissatisfied with the influence God has given us. When we steward what we have well, God will bring the increase. He sees your heart and your sacrifice, and that is enough. Do what He calls you to do, and let everything else work itself out.

"He is no fool who gives what he cannot keep to gain what he cannot lose." -Jim Elliot

Anna and Jared don't have a bunch of cool stories like some of those you have heard in this book. They are a couple of ordinary kids, from an ordinary family — but we all know that Scripture is full of stories where God used ordinary people to change the world.

I don't think most of those people realized they were writing history at the time. They just followed God and messed up a lot along the way, but in spite of their humanity God used them to do great things that continue to inspire us today.

You have the rest of your life ahead of you. What kind of story will you write? Will you be like Jared or Anna or Jeff or Mr. Coleman? Will you go out of your way to do the little things that touch people's lives even when you feel like what you're doing doesn't matter?

You may never get the chance to change the entire world, but God has put you where you are for a reason, and each one of us get the opportunity to change our corners of the world every single day of our lives.

The story is yours. Start writing, my friend.

Acknowledgements

God — You who gave us this idea in the first place and helped us complete it.

Janelle — My amazing wife and best friend. You are beautiful, crafty, smart and spiritual. I would not be who I am today without you. Thank you for modeling Christ to our family.

Mallory & Tyson — You are the pride and joy of my life. Remember that nothing in life happens by accident, but only through hard work and endurance. If dad can do it, you can do it. I love you both.

Jared Stump — Thanks for all your hard work on this project. It wouldn't have happened without you. You were involved from start to finish, from the first phone call to the first printed copy in hand.

David Thomas — Thanks for helping us travel down a road we'd never been on before. Your advice and wisdom was invaluable.

Thanks to all the pastors and leaders who contributed chapters to this book. We would not have wanted to do it without you.

Thanks to all the coaches, leaders and mentors who have poured into my life over the years. You know who you are.

— Kyle Embry

Jesus — You were with me every step of the way, especially on the days I wanted to give up. I saw Deuteronomy 1:31 come to life during the year that was spent working on this book.

Mom & Dad — I couldn't do what I do without your love and support. I'm grateful to be your son.

Kyle — Thanks for taking the risk involved in selecting me to help manage this project. It has been the opportunity of a lifetime.

Michell Conner — You believed that I was a writer before I believed it myself. Thank you.

Christy McFerren — I've known you for years, but I never thought your design work would end up on a BOOK with my name on it. Thanks for all your hard work. You created a product that stands out on a crowded shelf.

Nancy Smith — You are one of the best communicators I have ever worked with. Thanks for all your help with this project, especially answering all of my questions about proper grammar.

David Thomas — Thanks for all your wisdom, insight and constructive criticism. It made a huge difference and influenced several of our key decisions.

— Jared Stump

About the Authors

Kyle Embry is the director for Youth Alive North Texas. He grew up in the Dallas/Forth Worth Metroplex, and is a graduate of Irving High School and Southwestern A/G University in Waxahachie, Texas, where he holds a B.A. in Church Ministries. Kyle has been in ministry for over a decade, first serving for two years as the youth pastor at Aurora First Assembly near Denver, Colorado, before returning to North Texas, where he was the youth pastor at Grace Community Church in Flower Mound for five and a half years. In September 2008, Kyle transitioned to his current role as Youth Alive director for the North Texas region, where he works to equip leaders, students, and parents to reach out to their local schools.

Kyle met his wife, Janelle, over the summer before sixth grade when his family began attending the church where her dad was pastor. They were friends through junior high and high school, and were married in 1999. Kyle and Janelle have two children: Mallory and Tyson, ages eight and five, respectively. Mallory is a star soccer player and has already developed a passion to share Jesus with the students at her elementary school. Tyson is about to begin kindergarten and is on his way to becoming a professional golfer—just ask Kyle about his shot with a nine iron from forty yards off the green! The Embry family resides in Flower Mound, Texas. You can connect with Kyle online at www.kyleembry.com or on Twitter (@kyleembry).

Jared Stump is a freelance writer currently working as an intern for Youth Alive North Texas. He was born in Springfield, Missouri and grew up in the suburbs of Austin and Dallas, Texas. Jared is passionate about reaching and connecting with people through various forms of media. He has been with Youth Alive for two and a half years, and has served in a variety of roles, including: photography, social media, marketing, editing, communication, and administrative support. Jared is based in Frisco, Texas, where he works extensively with his church in the youth and communications departments. You can connect with him on Twitter (@jaredstump).

Dave Roever was born in McAllen, Texas, not far from the border of Mexico. He grew up in Fort Worth, Texas, where he graduated from Lake Worth High School. At the height of the Vietnam War, Dave received his draft notice. Eight months into his tour of duty, he was burned beyond recognition when a phosphorous grenade he was poised to throw exploded in his hand. Dave was brought back to the U.S. and underwent numerous surgeries during a 14-month period of hospitalization. Today, he is an internationally recognized public speaker who takes his message of hope, courage, commitment and survival to a variety of settings, including churches, schools, youth conventions and military functions. Because of his unique experience, he is often called upon to bring encouragement to troops at domestic and international military bases.

Dave is the founder and president of two non-profit organizations: Roever Evangelistic Association and Roever Educational Assistance Programs, both of which are based in Fort Worth. He has received a Purple Heart from the U.S. Navy, as well as several other medals in honor of his service. In 2005, Dave received an Honorary Doctorate of Theology in recognition of his life and contributions to the Body of Christ.

Dave has been married to Brenda since 1967 and they have two grown children and four grandchildren. They are co-founders of Eagles Summit Ranch, with locations near

Westcliffe, Colorado and Junction, Texas, where they train young leaders, wounded warriors, and other military personnel in the areas of public speaking and emotional/marital recovery in the wake of devastating injuries. Dave and Brenda reside in Fort Worth, Texas. You can connect with Dave online at www.roeverfoundation.org or on Twitter (@daveroever).

Garland Owensby is an evangelist, stand-up comedian and professor at Southwestern Assemblies of God University in Waxahachie, Texas. Originally from a small Pennsylvania town nestled between Philadelphia and Delaware, Garland is a graduate of Kennett High School. He holds a B.A. in Pastoral Ministries and an M.S. in Practical Theology from Southeastern College in Lakeland, Florida and Southwestern A/G University in Waxahachie, respectively, as well as a Doctor of Educational Ministry from Southwestern Baptist Theological Seminary in Fort Worth. With 23 years of ministry experience, Garland first served as a missionary to El Salvador, then as a youth pastor in Elizabeth City, North Carolina and Ocala, Florida before joining the staff at Southwestern. Garland married Tiffani in 1992 after returning to the states. Together, they have three sons: Austin, and identical twins Bryson and Logan. The Owensby family resides in Midlothian, Texas. You can connect with Garland online at www.garlandowensby.com or on Twitter (@gowensby).

Andrew Burr is the youth pastor at Longview First Assembly, located in East Texas between Dallas and Shreveport, Louisiana. Born and raised in Austin, Andrew is a graduate of Crockett High School and Southwestern A/G University in Waxahachie, Texas. He began serving in ministry in 1999 as the interim youth pastor at Harbor Light Church in Wrangell, Alaska. After a summer in Alaska, Andrew returned to Texas, where he served on the staff of Seven Student Ministries at

The Oaks Fellowship in Red Oak. He was then the youth pastor at Wichita Falls First Assembly from 2005-2007, before moving into his current position at Longview, where he continues to minister today. Andrew has been happily married to Angela since 1:00 in the afternoon on May 21, 2005. The joy of his life are his two young children: Eliana and Ethan. The Burr family resides in Longview, Texas. You can connect with Andrew on Twitter (@andrewburr) to learn more about his ministry and sense of humor.

Steven Reed is the youth pastor at Restoration Family Church in Benbrook, Texas. Born and raised in Fort Worth, Steven is a graduate of Southwest High School and holds a bachelor's degree in Church Ministries from Southwestern A/G University in Waxahachie, Texas. Steven began working in ministry while in college, and currently possesses ten years of experience. He previously served as the associate director for Youth Alive North Texas before joining the staff at Restoration Family Church. Steven married Elizabeth in 2007, and they welcomed their first child, Fiona Elise, on October 31, 2012. The Reed family resides in Fort Worth, Texas. You can connect with Steven on Twitter (@stevenareed).

Adam Herod is the executive pastor at First at Firewheel Church in Garland, Texas, as well as the principal of Firewheel Christian Academy. Born in Fort Worth, Adam grew up just outside the city in the town of Joshua. A graduate of Joshua High School and the University of Texas at Arlington, he holds a B.A. in Kinesiology. Adam began serving in ministry in 2003 at Crossroads Church in Belton, Texas. In 2010, he partnered with Kyle Embry and Youth Alive North Texas to host the Seven Project outreach, which resulted in more than 125 students coming to Christ. Shortly after this outreach, Adam transitioned to his current church, First at Firewheel, near Dallas. He served as the youth pastor for nearly three years before recently moving into his current role. Adam has been married to Susan since 1997 and they have three children: Katelynn, Adam Cade, and Alex, ranging in age from eleven to six. The Herod family resides in Garland, Texas. You can connect with Adam on Twitter (@adam2749).

Jim Coursey is the youth pastor at Marble Falls First Assembly in the Hill Country of Central Texas. A native Texan, Jim was born in Dallas and grew up in a small town just outside of the city. After graduating from Kaufman High School, Jim spent four years in the United States Marine Corps. Since then, he has worked as an engineer and business consultant, helping entrepreneurs launch successful small businesses. Jim entered the ministry world in 2009, serving as an associate pastor at Marble Falls First Assembly before transitioning to youth pastor a year later. He has been married to Joy since 1996 and they have three children: Rachel, Raegan, and Reese, ranging in age from fourteen to five. Jim and his family reside in Marble Falls, Texas.

Ricky Franklin is the senior pastor of New Day Church at Southlake in the Dallas/Fort Worth Metroplex. Born and raised in Fort Worth, Ricky graduated from R.L. Paschal High School and went on to attend Southwestern A/G University in Waxahachie, Texas, where he earned a B.A. in Cross Cultural Communications. With 24 years of ministry experience, Ricky first served as youth pastor at two churches in the Metroplex from 1989-1994. He then served as the youth and associate pastor at Abundant Life Church in Bozeman, Montana until 1998, before transitioning to Victorious Life Church in Wesley Chapel, Florida, where he served from 1998 through 2005. In 2006, Ricky and his family successfully planted New Day Church in Roanoke, Texas. In their seventh year of ministry, New Day merged with First Assembly in the neighboring city of Southlake—retaining their name while assuming a new facility—in the fall of 2012. Ricky has been married to Joni since 1992 and they have nine children: Joseph, Jonathon, Nickolas, Emily, Nathan, Nathaniel, Anna, Armando, and a two-month year old baby girl who they are in the process of adopting. Several of Ricky and Joni's chldren are involved with Youth Alive Bible clubs at their schools and their oldest is finishing up his first year at Southwestern. The Franklin family resides in Roanoke, Texas. You can connect with Ricky online at www.newdaydfw.com or on Twitter (@rickyfranklin).

Al Roever is an associate pastor at Heartland World Ministries Church in Irving, Texas, and an instructor at Heartland School of Ministry. A native Texan, Al was born in Fort Worth and grew up in numerous places across the state. After graduating from Cuero High School in South Texas, Al attended Rice University, where he graduated with a B.A. in Romance Languages. He went on to study Philosophy at the University of Texas at Arlington before beginning his long-tenured career in ministry in 1967 at a church for the hearing impaired in Fort Worth. He then served at Church of the Rock in Odessa, Texas for 11 years before transitioning to work with his brother, Dave, at the Roever Evangelistic Association for eight years. In 1995, Al moved to Hurley, Mississippi to serve at Magnolia Springs Assembly of God for another decade. During this time, he also taught for three years at the Brownsville Revival School of Ministry. Al returned to Texas in 2006 to serve at Heartland, where he continues to minister today. He has been married to Arneta since 1968, and they have three grown children and three grandchildren. Al and Arneta reside in Keller, Texas.

Jaroy Carpenter is a highly experienced youth evangelist who currently "moonlights" as the Director of Sports Medicine at Southwestern Assemblies of God University in Waxahachie, Texas. Born on the Texas-Oklahoma line in the town of Denison, Jaroy grew up two hours west in a small town surrounded by oil rigs and wind turbines. He is a graduate of Jacksboro High School and East Texas State University, now Texas A&M University — Commerce. Jaroy began his career as a high school athletic trainer in 1983, working at two North Texas schools over an eight-year period. During this time, he also served as a Fellowship of Christian Athletes (FCA) huddle leader and volunteer youth pastor. Jaroy left the academic world for vocational ministry in 1990, working as a youth pastor at Calvary Church in Irving, Texas and adjunct professor at Christ for the Nations Institute in Dallas. In 2000, he founded Solid Rock Resources, which provides training and consulting to youth ministries through a myriad of methods and programs. Jaroy is also the developer of the popular interactive school assembly, Game Day Challenge. In addition, he has been leading an annual summer camp, Camp Padre, which has been meeting on a South Texas island for the past 24 years. He has been married to Kim since 1991 and they have three children: Carli, Cade, and Corbin, ranging in age from sixteen to eleven. The Carpenter family resides in Midlothian, Texas, and are active members of The Oaks Fellowship in Red Oak. You can connect with Jaroy online at www.solidrockresources.com or on Twitter (@jaroycarpenter).

Landon Huie is the founding pastor of The Wave young adults ministry in Rockwall, Texas. Born in Little Rock, Arkansas, Landon grew up in Memphis, Tennessee. A graduate of Bartlett High School, Landon attended Christ for the Nations Institute in Dallas, Texas, where he graduated with a degree in Biblical Theology. Landon served as the youth pastor at Oasis Church in Caddo Mills, Texas from 2004-2009, and Family Worship Center in McKinney, Texas from 2010-2012. While at FWC, he also oversaw the creative department and young adults ministry. Landon is currently a traveling evangelist and is also working to launch The Wave young adults ministry, affiliated with Harbor Church in Rockwall, Texas. Landon has been married to Kristin since

2007 and they have one two-year-old daughter, Avery, with a second (Allie) on the way. The Huie family resides in Rockwall, Texas. You can connect with Landon online at www.landonhuie.com or on Twitter (@landonhuie).

Steven McKnight is the youth pastor at Terrell First Assembly, located in a diverse community not far from Dallas. A native Texan, Steven was born in Dallas and grew up in the neighboring city of Garland. He attended North Garland High School and Southwestern A/G University in Waxahachie, Texas, where he received a bachelor's degree in Church Ministries. He began serving in ministry as an associate/youth pastor at Royse City First Assembly in 1999. During this time, he also operated the Main Street Grill, a local restaurant that the church utilized for outreach events. In 2004, Steven moved 30 miles south to Terrell, where he continues to serve in a similar role as an associate/youth pastor today. He has been married to Racheal since 1996 and they have three sons: Tristan, Ethan, and Elijah, ranging in age from fifteen to five. Steven and his family reside in Terrell, Texas.

Josh Poage is the senior pastor of Onalaska First Assembly, located in a town just north of the Houston metro area. A native of East Texas, Josh was born in Livingston and grew up in Lufkin. He graduated from Hudson High School, attended Angelina College, and is ordained through Berean School of the Bible in Springfield, Missouri. Josh served as the youth pastor at Clawson Assembly, located just outside of Lufkin in the rural community of Pollok from 2006-2010. After that, he served as youth pastor at a church in Texarkana, Texas, before transitioning to senior pastor of Onalaska First—not far from his hometown—in February 2012. Josh has been married to Kristina since 2004 and they have three sons: Rylin, Kaynin, and Aydin, ranging in age from seven to four. Josh and his family reside in Onalaska, Texas.

Stacey Hendrix is a teacher and coach at a 4A high school in East Texas. A native Texan, Stacey was born and raised in the Houston area. A graduate of Hawkins High School and Southwestern A/G University, she holds a B.S. in Secondary Education. Stacey has been a public school teacher and basketball/volleyball coach for more than 12 years. She has been married to Kevin since 1999, and they have three children: Kyle, Brayden, and their firstborn daughter, Kinsley, who is expected to arrive by the summer of 2013. Stacey and Kevin recently began leading a church where Kevin serves as senior pastor. The Hendrix family resides in Whitehouse, Texas.

Tarah Morris is a wife and mother, as well as a youth leader and worship team member at Trinity Assembly in East Texas. Born in Longview, Tarah grew up in the neighboring city of Kilgore through elementary school. She spent her junior high and high school years in the nearby city of Henderson, where she graduated from Henderson High School. Tarah attended Kilgore College and the University of Texas at Tyler, where she graduated with a degree in Junior High Education. She then returned to her hometown of Kilgore, where she continues to live today. Tarah has been an active member of Trinity Assembly her entire life, where she taught the Missionettes club for young girls for ten years, as well as serving with the youth and worship team. Tarah has been married to Jason since 1997, and they have four children: Preston, Eli, Alec, and Addi, ranging in age from seventeen to ten. Jason currently serves as the youth pastor at Trinity Assembly. The Morris family resides in Kilgore, Texas.

Jon Catron is the district youth director for the North Texas District of the Assemblies of God. Born in Independence, Missouri, Jon grew up in Aggie country: College Station, Texas. A graduate of A&M Consolidated High School and

Southwestern A/G University in Waxahachie, Texas, he also attended Texas A&M University. Jon holds a bachelor's degree in Youth Ministries and is currently working on his master's in Bible and Theology. Jon began serving in ministry in 1992 as a youth intern at Victorious Life Church in Waco, Texas. He then served as youth pastor at two churches in Paris, Texas and Arlington, Texas, before transitioning to First Assembly in Longview, Texas, in 1996. After nine years in Longview, Jon moved into his current position as district youth director. His primary responsibilities include empowering and coaching youth pastors and serving more than 500 churches across the district, as well as coordinating summer camps, missions trips, and an annual youth convention. Jon has been married to Kimberly since 1994, and they have two teenagers: Chelsea and Chandler, as well as one adopted ten-year-old daughter from China: Chloe. The Catron family resides in Midlothian, Texas. You can connect with Jon online at www.joncatron.com or on Twitter (@joncatron).

Daniel K. Norris is an evangelist and executive producer for Frontlines.tv, a division of Steve Hill Ministries. Born and raised in South Carolina in the foothills of the Blue Ridge Mountains, Daniel graduated from Walhalla High School and Clemson University, where he studied business and management. Daniel served as the youth pastor in his home town of Seneca, South Carolina for five years before becoming a youth intern at Brownsville Assembly in Pensacola, Florida. Most recently, he served for ten years as the student ministries director at Heartland World Ministries Church in Irving, Texas, before transitioning to Steve Hill Ministries. Daniel has been married to Jenna since 2003 and they have two young children: Reijah Joy and Caden Taylor. The Norris family resides in Grapevine, Texas. You can connect with Daniel online at www.danielknorris.com or on Twitter (@danielknorris).

Steve Pulis is the student outreach director for the General Council of the Assemblies of God in Springfield, Missouri. Born and raised in Springfield, Steve moved to Olathe, Kansas midway through high school, where he graduated from Olathe South High School. He attended Central Bible College and the A/G Theological Seminary, and holds four degrees: A.A. in Music, B.A. in Bible, B.A. in Missions, and M.A. in Christian Ministries. Steve has been in ministry for 24 years, having served as youth pastor at Central Assembly and Park Crest Assembly in Springfield, as well as Abundant Life Church in Grapevine, Texas. He has also worked with the Northeast Urban Church Planting Network to assist in planting two churches in New Jersey, focused primarily on the youth departments. Steve directed the Youth Alive regional office in Southern Missouri from 1998-2002 and began working with Youth Alive on a national level in 2002, becoming the national director in 2008. He has also served as an adjunct professor for Central Bible College since 1999. Steve has been married to Melissa since 1994 and they have two sons: Nathan and Colin, who are thirteen and nine, respectively. The Pulis family resides in Springfield, Missouri, where they are active members at Central Assembly. You can connect with Steve online at www.yausa.com or on Twitter (@spulis).

Jared Patterson is the senior pastor at The Bridge Church in Arlington, Texas. Born and raised in Irving, Texas, Jared is a graduate of Irving High School and attended some college at Southwestern A/G University in Waxahachie, Texas. A lifelong resident of the Dallas/Fort Worth Metroplex, Jared has been in ministry for nearly two decades, much of which was spent at Family Worship Center in Irving, now More 2 Life Church. He was the youth pastor from 1994-2006 and executive pastor from 2006-2008, before transitioning to his current position at The Bridge. Jared has been married to Mandy since 2002 and they have two sons: Josiah Ray and

Mathias Hunter. In addition, Jared has been Kyle Embry's brother-in-law since 1999. The Patterson family resides in Arlington, Texas. You can connect with Jared online at www.bridgechurcharlington.org or on Twitter (@patterson_jared).

Youth Alive North Texas

P.O. Box 838

Waxahachie, Texas 75168

Web: www.youthalivetx.com

Facebook: www.facebook.com/youthalivetx

Twitter: www.twitter.com/youthalivetx